THE ENGLISH NOVEL IN HISTORY 1950–1995

Bringing theoretical and historical approaches together, this book describes and analyses the most striking features and developments in postwar prose fiction. It shows the dynamic interrelations between the novel and the social, economic and political conditions in Britain during the latter half of the twentieth century. It also provides stimulating discussion of the relationship between the novel and other cultural media in the postmodern era.

Steven Connor incorporates an extensive and varied range of writers in his analysis, including both the well-established, such as George Orwell, William Golding, Angela Carter and Doris Lessing, and the less widely discussed, such as Timothy Mo, Hanif Kureishi, Marina Warner and Maggie Gee.

The English Novel in History: 1950–1995 will be not only valuable reading for any student of English literature or popular culture but also highly accessible to the non-academic reader of contemporary fiction.

Steven Connor is Professor of Modern Literature and Theory at Birkbeck College, London.

THE NOVEL IN HISTORY
Edited by Gillian Beer
Girton College, Cambridge

Informed by recent narrative theory, each volume in this series will provide an authoritative yet lively and energetic account of the English novel in context. Looking at the whole spectrum of fiction, at elite, popular and mass-market genres, the series will consider the ways in which fiction not only reflects, but also helps shape contemporary opinion. Incisive and interdisciplinary, the series as a whole will radically challenge the development model of English literature, and enable each period – from the eighteenth century to the present day – to be assessed on its own terms.

Other titles in the series

*The English Novel in History
1895–1920*
David Trotter

THE ENGLISH NOVEL IN HISTORY 1950–1995

Steven Connor

London and New York

First published 1996
by Routledge
11 New Fetter Lane, London EC4P 4EE

Simultaneously published in the USA and Canada
by Routledge
29 West 35th Street, New York, NY 10001

© 1996 Steven Connor

Typeset in Baskerville by
Ponting–Green Publishing Services, Chesham, Bucks
Printed and bound in Great Britain by
Clays Ltd, St Ives plc

All rights reserved. No part of this book may be reprinted
or reproduced or utilized in any form or by any electronic,
mechanical, or other means, now known or hereafter
invented, including photocopying and recording, or in any
information storage or retrieval system, without
permission in writing from the publishers.

British Library Cataloguing in Publication Data
A catalogue record for this book is available from
the British Library

Library of Congress Cataloguing in Publication Data
Connor, Steven
English Novel in History, 1950–1995 / Steven Connor.
p.   cm. – (The novel in history)
1. English fiction–20th century–History and criticism.
2. Literature and history–Great Britain–History–20th century.
3. Historical fiction, English–History and criticism.
4. Postmodernism (Literature)–Great Britain.
I. Title   II. Series.
PR888.H5C66   1995
823'.0810914–dc20   95-4304

ISBN 0–415–07230–1 (hbk)
ISBN 0–415–07231–X (pbk)

CONTENTS

Acknowledgement		vii
1	THE NOVEL IN CONTEMPORARY HISTORY	1
2	CONDITIONS OF ENGLAND	44
3	OUTSIDE IN	83
4	HISTORIES	128
5	ORIGINS AND REVERSIONS	166
6	ENDINGS AND LIVING ON	199
	References	246
	Index	255

ACKNOWLEDGEMENT

Some of my discussion of *Nineteen Eighty-Four* in chapter 6 previously appeared in the *English Review*. I am grateful to the editors for permission to reprint these passages here.

1
THE NOVEL IN CONTEMPORARY HISTORY

HISTORY AND NARRATIVE

The novel has always been a useful resource for history and historians. Typically, the novel promises a view of that fine grain of events and experiences which otherwise tend to shrink to invisibility in the long perspectives of historical explanation. Novels seem to have some of the authority of the eye-witness account, in providing the historian with enactment, particularity and individual testimony. There are good reasons why this should be so, of course; it is hard to think of another kind of evidence which so abundantly and yet so economically concentrates together representations of how the world is, or seems to be, with the shaping force of fantasy or imagination; which balances, in other words, reality and desire. Novels also represent a meeting point between the individual and the general, bridging the isolated subjectivity and the peopled world, and giving an individual dimension to the otherwise abstract or disembodied nature of shared norms and values.

Nevertheless, and despite every delicacy and precaution, it is very hard for social and cultural histories not to reduce novels to a kind of second-order phenomenon, to a reflection of a given or already existing set of historical facts and conditions, whether these be political, economic and social. This book proposes that a different account of the postwar novel is possible; one that sees the novel not just as passively marked with the imprint of history, but also as one of the ways in which history is made, and remade. This is not to reduce history to textuality; though it certainly is to suggest that the processes of writing and reading novels are not fully distinct or finally distinguishable from the forms and processes of conflict, deliberation and evaluation that belong to the social, economic or political realms. Once again, this is not to say, as some have incautiously said, that such social forms and processes are nothing but fiction; it is rather to say that the processes we associate with the making and substantiation of fictional worlds are to be seen at work within the making of the real, historical world.

What of that real, historical world? A sketch of the principal historical developments in British life since the Second World War suggests a complex interrelationship of decline and transformation. In domestic political terms, the development of the Welfare State was followed by its dramatic erosion from the mid-1970s onwards. These were also the years of the definitive stripping away of Empire, and, as effect and cause of this from the 1950s onwards, the loss of British power and influence in the world in political, military and economic terms. Externally, this was accompanied by the growth of a globalised world economy and balance of power, in which Britain has come to play a smaller and smaller role (though it remains one of the richest industrialised nations). Internally, it has had as its direct effect the arrival of considerable numbers of immigrants from different regions of the Empire and the challenge to an undisturbed sense of Englishness and Britishness produced by the resulting plurality of impinging and co-operating cultures and histories. In cultural terms, the years since the Second World War have seen in Britain, as elsewhere in Europe and the USA, a prodigious explosion of cultural forms and technologies, which have fundamentally readjusted the relations between art, culture and society. In the age of information and of the society of the spectacle, dispositions of power have fundamentally shifted. In an economy that has shifted from a dependence upon industrial production to the provision of services and consumer products, a politics once organised largely around bilateral antagonisms, most dramatically that between capital and labour, has given way to much more shifting and complex forms of competition and affiliation. Of greatly increased importance in this period are the relations and distributions of power between different through often overlapping interest groups centred on gender, race, sexuality, age, and so on. Most importantly, the assumption that cultural representations primarily reflected or expressed these relations of power has given way to an intimation of the power of culture itself to construct and transform such relations of power.

These changes both produce and are expressed in a redefinition of attitudes towards history as such in postwar Britain and the Western world. Over the course of the twentieth century, but with accelerating force in the years since 1945, the assurance of the special relationship between the history of Britain and global history has steadily been eroded. Where the history of Britain and the English-speaking peoples had at one time seemed to be identical with the history and development of culture in general, the final splintering of Empire and the redefinitions of world power after the Second World War made that association less than credible. The long, continuous narrative of Britain and the West began to seem narrow, arbitrary, even a bit ramshackle, in the light of all the omissions, glosings and distortions necessary to maintain its coherence. After the Second World War, Britain seemed progressively to lose possession of its own history. Michel Foucault has suggested that the history of man over the last two centuries has had as its aim the creation of a 'subject of history' (1972: 3–17). Rather than assuming first of all that there is a homogeneous entity known as 'man', to whom certain events happen, Foucault's work suggests that the narration of history is actually designed to establish such a being. Borrowing Foucault's terms, we may say that, in the postwar period, Britain came progressively to lose its confident belief that it was the subject of its own history. This eviction from historical self-possession came about in two ways. An increasingly hostile 'outside' pressed in upon Englishness, in the ever more aggressive relations of military superpowers and the ever more rampant and uncontrollable dynamisms of a capitalism organised in multinational forms not subject to the control of sovereign states. And then, with the multiplication of alternative forms of belonging and self-definition, the very idea of what Englishness meant also began to come apart on the inside.

To say that postwar Britain has undergone a disturbance of its sense of historical belonging and coherence is to imply also that a certain pressure has been put upon the powers of historical narrative to organise the world. Narrative may be defined in an elementary way as an articulation of temporality with transitivity; all narratives involve the passage of time and the ordering of events with relation to sequence, duration and temporal connection, and all narratives, even the most seemingly impersonal, involve the shifting dispositions of subjects and objects, or entities who do things to others. The creation of Foucault's 'subject of history' depends upon narrative because narrative secures the idea of history as a series of actions performed by and upon agents. The novel contributes significantly to this process because it is one of the most important ways in which the world is made accessible and comprehensible by narrative.

Much energy has been expended over the last twenty years or so in trying to define what narrative is, what its elementary forms of organisation and rules of combination are, and so on. But there are many advantages in also asking what narrative (or the particular form of it we recognise as the novel) *does*. Such a question is less likely to compel a singular or all-inclusive answer than questions about the nature of narrative. It is also likely to open up a range of uses, effects and values of narrative which may be relegated as accessory or irrelevant by the enquiry into the nature of narrative in itself. Most importantly, it may help to restore narrative to history in a way that does not make it merely the mirror or register of historical events. It may suggest that narrative is historical because it is one of the most important forms of symbolic action, or communicative behaviour, in which human beings indulge. The history of human acts cannot afford to ignore the far-reaching and variegated effects of the act of narrating.

To define narrative not as a special kind of object but as a distinctive form of action does not lead straight to simple answers. Depending on the context, it may plausibly be said that a given narrative might act to persuade, explain, reassure, combine, transform, instruct, liberate, enslave, uplift, excite – in fact, to bring about all of the effects that human beings commonly seek to bring about via other linguistic or communicative means.

Despite this, we can distinguish two contrasting forms of action or effect typically associated with narrative. Firstly, narrative can bring about psychological and cultural *enlargement*. Narrative can lengthen memory or extend forethought, in the elaboration of the past and extrapolation into possible futures. Narrative can effect an imaginative colonisation of unknown or alien spaces, allowing a fuller sense of habitation and belonging. Connected with these broadly enlarging functions of narrative is its function of *consolidation*. To extend the self, whether individual or collective, into different sorts of unfamiliar or otherwise unavailable experience may also allow the self to become more apprehensible to itself. The effect of much travel writing, for example, may be to give dimension and definition to national identity precisely by pulling it inside out. Jon Stratton (1990), arguing for the close relationship in the West between travel and writing as such, suggests that writing is a form of consolidating travel, just as travel is a form of writing. In spatial as well as temporal terms, to go to the edge of oneself or one's habitual contexts may be to solidify as well as to stretch the sense of identity. In the case of historical narrative, this effect of binding consolidation works in a collective as well as an individual way. To narrate a history is often both to imagine collectively and to imagine a collectivity.

Any yet, despite its cohering and consolidating functions, the novel is characteristically produced and consumed under conditions of privacy, and, in most cases, of isolation. In the extreme contemporary conditions that Jean Baudrillard has described as 'obscenity', in which 'all becomes transparence and immediate visibility, when everything is exposed to the harsh and inexorable light of information and communication' (1988: 21–2), the reading of novels stands as an almost impossible ideal of utopian retreat and privacy. At the same time, however, the novel, as form and commodity, is bound in inextricably to mass culture and communications; arguably, it is with the novel that mass communication begins. As D. A. Miller has suggested, the novel mediates structurally between these two dimensions of the domestic and the economic, the molecular and the molar, the private and the public.

> What the form secures is a close *imbrication* of the individual and social, domestic and institutional, private and public, leisure and work ... In reading the novel, one is made to rehearse how to live a problematic – always surrendered, but then again always recovered – privacy.
>
> (Miller 1988: 83)

There is a close relationship between this imbrication of the public and private in the material conditions of the circulation and consumption of novels, and the forms of thematic and ideological binding that have often been claimed for the form. I will suggest in chapter 4 that historical narrative contributes significantly to this mediation of individual and collectivity, of private and public experience. Even where it does not actually fill out, reinforce or draw upon actual shared memories, the novel of history always holds the promise of some possible collective memory.

However, set against those functions of narrative I have been describing as broadly enlarging or consolidatory are a range of functions that are better described as *transformative*. Included here would be the effects of diversifying, exploring, experimenting, undoing, disorientating, and dehabituating to be found in narrative. As well as enlarging and extending, narrative can also transform, criticise, displace, limit, interrupt. Such effects have not gone unobserved in critical writing on the novel; indeed, discussions of realism have tended to split along a contrast between the habilitating and transformative effects of narrative in the claim that, where realism too comfortably confirms the mutual accommodation of self and society, modernist and postmodernist interruptions of realism productively thwart this reciprocity. Such accounts tend to be insufficiently attentive to the complex and differential effects of narrative, which almost always combines the allegedly narcissistic or regressive consolations of habituation with the allegedly enlarging or subversive effects of transformation. Transformation can work in conservative ways, to bind and create communities of interest; just as the consolidation of certain kinds of community or collective belonging can be, or can lead to, a disruption of forms of power.

It has often been claimed that the novel has a distinctive and significant relation to the forms of modern society. According to Ian Watt, the rise of the novel in the eighteenth century is linked to the secularisation and individualisation of the mercantile middle class; as the 'new' story, which follows the unprecedented, unpredictable shape of the individual life, the novel embodies the new philosophical preference for the strenuously self-creating individual subject over inherited systems of value and belief (Watt 1957). More recently, it has been claimed that the principal function of the realist novel in the nineteenth century and beyond has been to effect various kinds of mutual accommodation between atomised individuals and the larger groups and communities in which they participate. For Franco Moretti, for example, the representative form of the novel is the *Bildungsroman*, the novel of education and development. Such a novel offers the promise of a reciprocal mirroring between the individual and society; in the *Bildungsroman*, society becomes visible as the enabling field of operations for the individual, and the individual as the actualisation of social possibility. The *Bildungsroman* is for Moretti nothing less than 'the "symbolic form" of modernity' (1987: 5), in its focus upon mobility, change and development, combined with its capacity symbolically to frame and channel the boundless dynamism of the modern.

It may be said, therefore, that the novel is central to modern societies, in that it dramatises the process of integrating self-formation that is important to them. The centrality of the novel principally concerns the powerfully cohering function of narrative. Although in theory and in actual historical fact, there can be forms of social imaginary that are predominantly poetic, modern societies have tended to give a certain privilege to the organising powers of narrative. In one sense, it might be said that the new technologies of reproduction and simulation which have grown up since the Second World War have begun to discourage or discredit the claims of narrative to make sense of the social world. Influentially, Jean-François Lyotard (1984) has suggested that the postmodern condition is one in which the organising power of large or inclusive narratives is greatly diminished. On the other hand, there is clear evidence of something like a return of the explanatory privilege of narrative among social and cultural theorists, for whom the processes of cultural and political life seem to come to life most convincingly as struggles in, over and between narratives. Here is Alan Sinfield, for example:

> The stories that require most attention – most assiduous and continuous reworking – are the awkward, unresolved ones. They are what people want to write and read about. When a part of our world view threatens disruption by manifestly failing to cohere with the rest, then we must reorganize and retell its story again and again, trying to get it into shape – back into the old shape if we are conservative-minded, or into a new shape that we can develop and apply if we are more adventurous.
>
> (Sinfield 1989: 37)

The centrality of the novel to the period following the Second World War is due to the dramatic swings in the fortune of narrative itself in this period. Certainly the authoritative narratives of this period – narratives of progress towards a universal humanity, of shared peace and prosperity – have compelled less and less assent. In some writers in Britain and in Europe, this has produced an austere impulse to do without the comforting illusion of narrative progression towards discernible goals, even to dispense with the notion of a feasible or available subject of such a narrative. This may be seen in the abandonment of logical or causal sequence in some of B. S. Johnson's work, and in the radical assault upon the idea of character to be found in the work of Beckett and others. The growing dissatisfaction with the forms of explanation offered in particular historical narratives produced in some quarters a suspicion of narrative explanation as such. Increasingly, as we will see in chapter 6, the prospect of an imminent and actual end to history, as represented firstly by the horrors of the holocaust and secondly by the threat of nuclear extermination, has produced a suspicion of the narrative of history itself. Nevertheless, narrative has not completely lost its authority, even in a culture that allegedly has come to depend much more upon immediacy and transient intensity than on the articulation of meaning in complex sequence. In fact, if the meanings and values of narrative have diversified in this period, the demand for narrative explanation has by no means diminished and appears in fact to have intensified. The novel participates in this process to the degree that it is a form of imaginary laboratory which can produce not only new narratives but also new readers, forms of reading and reading purposes. The novel in this period has not only turned to different kinds of subject but has also turned inwards to reflect on its own nature; this being both an expression and exemplification of a more widespread concern with the powers and possibilities of narrative.

ADDRESSIVITY

In recent years the structures and forms of organisation of the novel have been the subject of intense and illuminating enquiry. Narratology has advanced some interesting suggestions about the elementary structures of narrative and the grammar of their combinations, and philosophers have begun to turn their attention to the nature of fictional or narrated worlds (Pavel 1986; Rimmon-Kenan 1989; Riffaterre 1990). Psychoanalytic criticism has explored the role of narrative in building and sustaining identity, and the sexual and affective dynamics of narrative (Brooks 1984); and Marxist and postmodernist theories of narrative have, with differing assumptions and results, investigated the relations between narrative, ideology and power (Jameson 1981; Hutcheon 1988; Lee 1990). There is a tendency in all this work, however, to ignore or underestimate one of the features of narrative that is most apparent in our ordinary experience of it, namely that narratives are events of communication. Stories have purposes as well as structures; they have, so to speak, intentional direction. Stories, in short, are always told to listeners and audiences, whether these be actual, intended, assumed, imagined or desired. This is not to reduce narrative to a form of communication, since it is a condition of narration, as it is of all verbal forms, that successful communication, in the sense of a transmission or making common of an intended meaning, can never be guaranteed. I prefer, therefore, to speak of the *addressive* nature and purposes of narration. I derive this term from the idea of the 'orientation towards the addressee' which is an important feature of the work of the Soviet philosopher of language Mikhail Bakhtin. Writing as V. N. Voloshinov in *Marxism and the Philosophy of Language* (1928), he proposes that, in all forms of utterance,

> the *word is oriented toward an addressee*, toward *who* that addressee might be: a fellow-member or not of the same social group, of higher or lower standing (the addressee's hierarchical status), someone connected with the speaker by close social ties (father, brother, husband, and so on) or not. There can be no such thing as an abstract addressee, a man unto himself, so to speak ... *Word is a two-sided act.* It is determined equally by *whose* word it is and *for whom* it is meant. As word, it is precisely *the product of the reciprocal relationship between speaker and listener, addresser and addressee.* Each and every word expresses the 'one' in relation to the 'other.'
>
> (Voloshinov 1986: 85–6)

Bakhtin's arguments about the force of the actual or implied participation of addressees and discursive partners in any utterance or communication cohere with the more generalised claims of the French ethical philosopher Emmanuel Levinas for the opening towards the Other that is at work in all language, a movement that he calls the 'vocativity' of discourse. Levinas sees this force operating against every attempt to reduce others to the condition of discursive objects. Speaking *of* others is always pulled awry by the implicit address *to* others:

> Language is a relation between separated terms. To the one the other can indeed present himself as a theme, but his

> presence is not reabsorbed in his status as a theme ... The knowledge that absorbs the Other is forthwith situated in the discourse I address to him ... In discourse the divergence that inevitably opens between the Other as my theme and the Other as my interlocutor, emancipated from the theme that seemed a moment to hold him, forthwith contests the meaning I ascribe to my interlocutor. The formal structure of language thereby announces the ethical inviolability of the Other.
>
> (Levinas 1991: 195)

Despite the promise of such work as that of Wolfgang Iser on the notion of the 'implied reader' (1974), and on the empirical and theoretical problems attached to the reading of fiction, little attention has been paid to the complex functions and effects of what I am calling the 'addressivity' of narrative. With this term, I mean to evoke not just the tendency of narratives to surmise or otherwise orientate themselves towards certain receivers or addressees but also the associated effects of recoil and redoubling, whereby the narrative may be seen to acknowledge, or even react against the knowledge of that address. It may be useful here to distinguish between 'address' and 'addressivity'. The addressivity of a text concerns not only the kinds of reader or reading it may seem to imply or require – for this I would employ the term 'address' – but also the manner in which the text may reflect on these acts of address. The analysis of addressivity would thus attempt to describe the recoil and impacting of the conditions of address upon the text itself.

The peculiarity of addressivity is that it exists neither fully in the text nor wholly outside it, but in some exchange between the two. The addressivity of a text is what opens or orientates a text to its actual reception in particular acts of reading, as well as the visible impress of this expectation on its language and form. The degree to which a narrative succeeds in summoning or installing its addressee in the posture required of him or her is one measure of its success as a narrative, though not the only measure. A text can achieve a high level of fit between the reader it seems to address and its actual reader – for example in some kinds of genre fiction and formula fiction – but in so doing actually make low demands of that reader. Another kind of novel may address itself to its implied reader in more uneven or complex ways and yet ask and achieve more of the act of reading precisely through the mobility of its forms of address. Although addressivity can sometimes manifest itself in explicit textual forms – in literal addresses to the reader, for example – it is not only or even most powerfully at work in such forms. The addressivity of a novel is always in a sense a matter of postulation rather than declaration. Often, a novel may feign to address one reader in order to address another. The addresses to the reader in Sterne's *Tristram Shandy* or Fielding's *Tom Jones*, for example, are intended as a sort of performance or simulation of address, which is put on for the benefit of another, more knowing reader than the one seemingly addressed.

The material conditions of the novel as a form encourage the highlighting in it of the question of addressivity. From its beginnings, the novel has been founded on an uncomfortable but enabling gap between its intended address and its actual readership. In the work of Daniel Defoe, for example, the novel represents itself as an easygoing, candid conversation between equals. But this utopian sense of the novel as perfectly achieved communication is undercut from the beginning by the fact and awareness of the mass distribution of the novel and the consequent erosion of any firm sense of expected readership. This uncertainty of address comes to be displaced and dramatised in such forms as the epistolary novel, in which the novel replaces the assumption of direct communication with a structure of oblique or intercepted address. Within this the reader must decipher letters written to other addressees (though by no means always delivered to or received by them), installing himself or herself in the crevices between the multiple lines of address set up by the novel. Such a form is the perfect compromise between intimacy and distance, the reliable assumption of known addressees and structures of address, and the uneasy sense of an unknown, inaccessible audience.

The founding conditions of the novel are such that its addressivity is always in fact a problem. The more successful the novel becomes, and the more its readership swells, the more improbable becomes the dream of perfect, uninterrupted communication between the author and reader and the more pressure is exerted on the question of address. The structure of address of novels is what binds them to their historical moments, as well as what opens them to different readers and readings at other historical moments. At different moments, the problem of address takes different forms and provokes different kinds of solution. If one can accept the largish claim that the novel is the form in which a modern society not only dreams its own integrated state but also addresses its constituent members in the name of that embattled integration, then it follows that, in a period when forms of narrative are fluid, the forms of its address will also be so.

In the twentieth century, the problem of address in the novel becomes complicated by the fact that the form must compete for attention with the very mass cultural forms with which it shares so much and which its example helped to foster: film, radio and popular fiction of all kinds. As Colin MacCabe has suggested, modernist writers compensated for their sense of alienation from their readers in the present by positing an ideal reader in the future, who would be perfectly equipped to read the obscure and demanding products of modernism (1993: 11). The more the modernist novel withdrew itself from actual address to current readers, the more the awareness of those current readers and their forms of reading returned to haunt the works of modernism. When Joyce parodies the cooing, teasing style of address of turn-of-the-century girls' romantic fiction in the 'Nausicaa' section of his *Ulysses* (1986: 284–313), the effect is both to separate his novel and readership from the degraded form it parodies and unexpectedly to disclose points of liaison and affinity between the two. That the notoriety of its trial meant that *Ulysses* itself sometimes turned up on the same kind of pornographic book-barrows as it shows Bloom and Stephen investigating in the streets of Dublin is only one sign of this uneasy affinity within antagonism.

With the multiplication of competing forms of attention and address after the Second World War, the assumption of the ideal, or even the adequate, reader came to seem increasingly difficult to maintain. As we will see in chapter 2, the postwar British novel was required to respond to twin imperatives. On the one hand, there was a certain limited disruption of patterns of social division brought about both by the experience of the War and by the tide of optimism that followed it, producing the sense of a renewed possibility of a unified or common culture which the novel might once again address. On the other hand, the effect of this loosening of the old forms of social division and cohesion, accompanied and accelerated by the increasing commercialisation of the culture industry and its promotion of multiple forms of consumption in unstable cycles of fashion, was to weaken the plausibility of such a collective address. For the postwar novel, it was necessary to deal with the problem of address in ways that acknowledged without wholly accepting the marginality of the novel in a world in which the authority of a literary culture was even more than ever compromised. We will see that, increasingly, novels looked for *rapprochement* with the forms, languages and modes of address of mass culture, as well as ways of distinguishing themselves from it. Many novels of the postwar period seem to be preoccupied with their addressivity, and reflect intricately on the possibilities of their modes of address. Novels of this period are characteristically driven (and sometimes instructively defeated) by the desire to build anew the ideal reciprocity between text and reader that seems to have been diffused by competing cultural forms and increasingly complex social differentiations. But they are also characteristically aware of how risky and uncertain this ambition is.

ECONOMICS, PUBLISHING AND READERSHIP

In order to understand this mingled sense of opportunity and anxiety, it is necessary to spend some time looking at the material conditions under which novels have been produced, circulated and consumed in the postwar period. Narrative is a central part of the cultural and economic life of any contemporary society. Indeed, it is hard to think of a single activity in which more time and resources are invested than the production and pursuit of narratives, in advertising, newspapers, and all aspects of media and broadcasting, as well as the more obvious cultural industries such as publishing. It is commonly said that contemporary history has seen a discrediting of the word; that we are moving from a print-based culture to a culture of images, from an 'alphabetic' to a 'visual' one (McLuhan 1967; Ulmer 1989). I will argue a little later that this is rather to be understood as bringing about more and more diverse forms of conjunction and cooperation between words and images. My present purpose, however, is to investigate the ways in which the authority and importance of the printed word, especially in the form of fiction, has been compromised, defended, and sometimes enhanced.

First of all, it is important to note that most evidence points to the fact that people in both the developed and developing worlds read more than ever before. In Britain, Ken Worpole reported a generalised survey of 1982, which found that 45 per cent of the people spoken to were currently reading a book of some kind; and, of all the books people read in the early 1980s, one-third was fiction (1984: 2). The fact that the numbers of books sold has continued to increase in the decade since then is a raw indication that the consolidation of video and information culture is far from having annihilated the activity of reading. The rise in the readership of fiction was brought about in postwar Britain and elsewhere by two interlocking factors: the development of mass paperback publishing and the growth of higher education. Central to the paperback revolution was the establishment of Penguin Books by Allen Lane in 1935. The imprint had already achieved considerable success by the outbreak of war, and with the gradual return of prosperity from 1950 onwards, Penguin paperbacks began to effect what was nothing short of a revolution in bookbuying and the consumption of literature. Contradicting traditional accounts of the standardising or levelling down of taste in the mass fiction market, Penguin Books managed both to enlarge and to diversify habits of reading. Penguins brought together a kind of 'crossover' market for crime, travel, biography and, most importantly, fiction, especially 'literary' fiction. Often, this was of a challenging or controversial kind, with works by Mailer, Nabokov and, most sensationally, D. H. Lawrence. The effect of the trial of the Penguin edition of *Lady Chatterley's Lover* in 1960 was to highlight both the desacralising of literature and its availability – troubling, of course, to many – to a much larger and more diverse readership. It also conferred respectability and style on the hitherto despised and demotic paperback (Sutherland 1978: 174). As Rachel Bowlby has remarked, the real significance of the notorious remark addressed to the jury by the chief prosecution lawyer – 'Is it a book that you would even wish your wife or your servants to read?' (Rolph 1961: 17) – lies in its acknowledgement of the huge and troubling power of an immoderately enlarged readership for fiction, and the incipient collapse of the ideally homogeneous culture of the past (Bowlby 1993: 30–2).

Initially, Penguin Books achieved its readership for classics and literary texts by not announcing them as such, thus removing both the barrier of price and the apparatus of semiotic exclusion which has often been a feature of the production and distribution of literature. Literary texts and, especially, literary fiction were marketed and sold by Penguin alongside other kinds of writing, and were not much differentiated in appearance or price. Undoubtedly, the symbolic flattening of hierarchies represented by the austere (yet also rather chic) functionalism of Penguin book design, along with their simple colour-coding (orange for fiction, green for crime and thrillers, blue for travel, and so on) accorded with the more inclusive cultural ideals abroad in the years after the War, up to the beginnings of economic revival and affluence in the mid to late 1950s. There is no doubt that, after this point, the continuing success of Penguin drew on the steady increase in education, especially in the USA, but also in Britain and Western Europe and the extraordinary centrality of English literature in schools and university curricula. John Sutherland has pointed to the importance of the American education market for writers of fiction during the 1950s and 1960s; when a novel such as William Golding's *Lord of the Flies* became a set text in colleges, in a system which had 10 million participating students by the late 1970s, and in which English courses were a compulsory gateway for nearly all first-year students, it achieved vast sales (Sutherland 1978: 34–6).

It is also true that, with the establishment of a continuing market for 'serious' fiction in the 1960s and 1970s, and the more aggressive pursuit not only of affluence but also of what Pierre Bourdieu has called the 'symbolic capital' that accompanies it (1984: 12–13), some traditional differentiations began to be reintroduced into this market. Following the establishment of the 'quality paperback' in the USA in the 1950s, an idea whose success depended on a hugely expanding college market, British publishers in the 1970s began to distinguish literary texts or classics from their other products by marketing them in larger format, more expensive editions and series, thus removing such books from the kind of distribution outlets where they had previously been available alongside other, less exalted kinds of reading. The effect of this was to widen the divide between 'literature' and fiction, the divide once (and still to a degree) symbolised through the distinction between hardback and paperback works. Serious literature tended to be shelved separately, or sold in a different kind of location altogether, the bookshop rather than the supermarket. Ken Worpole suggests that this differentiation was then reinforced by the fact that it left a gap in the paperback market, which was subsequently filled in again by various kinds of best-selling formula fiction (1984: 10). If this restricted the circulation of serious literature to some extent, it is important not to underestimate the sizeable market that remained for serious fiction, or for any kind of fiction linked to education or carrying associations of prestige or cultural authority. Novels by established twentieth-century authors such as Virginia Woolf, James Joyce or D. H. Lawrence, whose books might have sold a few thousand copies in their year of publication and a few hundred in subsequent years, can now be relied upon to sell annually in tens of thousands.

It is possible to tell a very depressing story about the publishing and circulation of fiction from the 1970s onwards. In a period characterised, especially in Britain, by the alternation of inflation and recession, the costs of publishing books, and fiction in particular, have soared. The problem with publishing is that so many different cooperating skills and processes are involved, from the writing of the book through all the other processes of editing, design, printing, marketing and distribution, and all are vulnerable to increased costs. Furthermore, the inflationary economies of the 1970s affected publishing in particular since it has traditionally been a low-turnover industry: if a supermarket expects to replace its stock almost daily, a bookshop may have single copies of certain texts palely loitering on its shelves for weeks or months. Furthermore, publishing faces problems of stock control and organisation that few other industries do. To borrow a comparison quoted by John Sutherland, where a manufacturer of cement may only need to produce and supply three different grades of his or her product to about 19 customers, a publisher such as the Oxford University Press may have 18,000 titles and up to 2,000 customers (Sutherland 1978: 25). The problems of marrying product to customer under these circumstances exact a potentially crippling cost.

A principal economic imperative in a period of inflation and overproduction is to shorten turnover time. When costs can be contained no further, or driven no lower, and prices can be raised no higher, the only way of maintaining profit is by shortening the time of circulation. For publishers to do this involves a number of potentially damaging effects on the diversity of the product produced and made available. First of all, it involves cutting the commercial lifetime of a book, by printing only as many copies as the market will bear, and not allowing the book to take up valuable warehouse and bookshop space once its rate of sale begins to dip away from its peak. It also means consolidating around titles that can be guaranteed to make money, or make enough money. Increasingly, the business of fiction publishing is a matter of matching product to consumer. At its most extreme, this has involved the aggressive marketing of 'formula' or 'category' literature, especially romance, crime and science fiction. The conditions which Janice Radway describes in American publishing after the Second World War began to apply almost everywhere:

> Category literature became a useful tool for publishing houses whose success depended on their ability to predict demand so exactly that the product not only sold but sold in the identical quantities projected at the beginning of the entire process. Because of the cost of overproduction, a sense of the size of the potential audience, an understanding of the preferences its individual members held in common, and the ability to embody those preferences in a product they would buy became essential to the editorial process. Success, in effect, became a function of accurate prediction. That prediction was ultimately dependent on the capacity to control the interaction between an identifiable audience and a product designed especially for it.
>
> (Radway 1987: 29)

A similar desire to homogenise and make predictable the readership for particular kinds of book led to the establishment and continuing success of bookclubs, offering selected titles at considerable discounts to a subscription readership contracted to purchase a certain number of books per year.

For some of the traditional publishers of 'quality' fiction in the 1970s, such as Jonathan Cape and Secker and Warburg, the long-established practice of subsidising quality unprofitable fiction by means of large sales of more successful titles continued for a while. Increasingly, however, it grew more and more difficult to do this, as the market for even fairly well-established writers began to decline. In Britain, where fiction was much more dependent than in the USA on library purchasing, the steady shrinkage in public spending from the mid-1970s onward exacerbated this effect. One other important factor has reinforced the move towards the publication of smaller numbers of works of fiction aimed at more predictable markets. Since the 1970s, British publishers, who had hitherto been able to resist the pressure of large American corporations, have become more and more vulnerable to takeovers and mergers. The 1980s saw a simultaneous increase in the size of publishers and a remorseless reduction in their number. Increasingly, publishing houses found themselves either part of large publishing conglomerates, which demanded high-volume sales from every unit of production, or part of multinational companies, whose publishing sections were only a small part of a range of different activities. If this sometimes gave publishers access to levels of capitalisation that they did not have before in the days of their poor but honest independence, it also meant that their product became increasingly difficult to distinguish from other commodities and the techniques used to promote and sell them. Most importantly, the rationalisation of the book market, and especially the fiction market which continued to grow in proportion to the rest, involved an unprecedented and dramatic rise in the importance of advertising and promotion.

The rise of television has accelerated this process. If it seemed initially as though television represented dangerous competition for publishers of fiction, it has become clear that television is largely fiction publishing carried out by other means. First of all, television provided a means of keeping writers in enough work to keep them alive from novel to novel, either by working on scripts, adaptations, and so forth or by working as reviewers (publishing has always depended on somebody else paying the author's wages while they produce their product). But, more importantly, television increasingly provided an easy medium of promotional access to enormous markets. Indeed, as the television 'tie-in' has become ever more important to fiction publishing, television itself helped to isolate and sustain the kind of preconstituted and predictable markets that had become so vital in modern high-volume and high-pressure publishing.

The result of this might seem to bear out the gloomy prognosis made by Q. D. Leavis in her *Fiction and the Reading Public* (1932), and repeated at intervals ever since: that the publishing of fiction would not be able to resist the general corruption of modern capitalism. Publishers would come to depend more and more upon low-quality formula fiction, designed to produce maximum sales in the shortest possible time, sales maintained by the crass stimulation and manufacture of markets by advertising and promotion. The power of global capitalism, and the necessity of exploiting markets as widely as possible, would result in a homogenisation of cultural diversity, and the swallowing up of national and cultural traditions. There is a poignant irony in this vision of the collapse of the novel into the market-place, since the novel has often been accorded a special role in resisting the levelling influences of the mass market and commodity capitalism. For D. H. Lawrence, the novel is 'the one bright book of life ... In the novel, the characters can do nothing but *live*' (1992: 147); for F. R. Leavis, announcing his Great Tradition (1948), and even for Raymond Williams in his early work (1970), the novel, more than any other form, preserves the possibility of that intensity and organic complexity of human experience which is increasingly under threat by the monstrous impersonality of industrial and economic processes in modern life.

Almost all commentators on the economic and sociological conditions of fiction publishing maintain a Leavisite sense of the fundamental antagonism between the fiction market and the literary novel. Most commentators, even such a moderate and pragmatic one as John Sutherland, take it as axiomatic that literary fiction or the 'quality' novel can only survive against the grain of contemporary publishing. Literary fiction is usually defined by negation – it is *not* formula fiction or genre fiction, *not* mass-market or best-selling fiction – and, by subtraction, it is what is left once most of the conditions that obtain in contemporary publishing are removed. Typically, though, the question of whether the literary novel will survive, or can be protected, tends to obscure questions about the relations between the literary (with its customary or conventional meanings, values and powers) and the commercial.

The sense of crisis that fuels such accounts also prematurely blocks off some unresolved questions about the nature and social function of fiction. Most strikingly, it encourages a regularisation of the relations between novels, their readers, and their readings of those novels. Mass-market publishers and academic commentators on the fiction industry share the assumption that there are distinct groups of people in society known as romance readers, thriller readers, science fiction readers, etc. They also seem to share the assumption that the particular kinds of reading these readers undertake on every renewed encounter with their chosen genre yields them the same kind of gratification. This is indeed the founding assumption of mass cultural marketing and it continues to have a certain functional value for the commercial publisher, for whom everything conduces towards, and only makes sense in relation to, the act of purchase. From the publisher's point of view, and probably even from that of the writer, the question of what else detective story readers may read or may do with themselves in their time off from being detective story readers is invisible and irrelevant, or relevant only to the degree that it can potentiate further acts of purchase; if it can be discovered that readers of Mills and Boon romances also tend to share an interest in bobsleighing and backgammon, this will suggest opportunities for new channels of publicity and distribution, but will not fundamentally shift the idea of the Mills and Boon 'reader' as a certain kind of composite person or type.

The idea of the homogeneous reader thus conditions the assumption that this reader will always read for much the same reasons and in more or less the same way. Here, academic critics are at risk of replicating marketing assumptions about the nature of the reader in their investigations. Janice Radway's *Reading the Romance* (1987), though it is an admirable and pioneering study of reading practices, is a case in point. The book focuses in considerable and instructive detail on the often highly articulate and self-conscious reflections of a group of women readers of romance within a small community of readers in the midwestern American town of Smithton. The group of women is treated as what Stanley Fish (1980) calls an 'interpretive community', on the assumption that

> whatever the theoretical possibility of an infinite number of readings, in fact there are patterns or regularities to what viewers or readers bring to texts and media messages in large part because they acquire specific cultural competencies [*sic*] as a result of their particular social location.
>
> (Radway 1987: 8)

Radway seems more than usually sensitive to the crudely levelling effect of identifying readers with the idealised readerships projected by publishers and cultural analysts alike. To regard such readers as being merely the artefacts of marketing strategies is really to write them off altogether, and Radway concludes her book by reminding us that 'commodities like mass-produced literary texts are relocated, purchased, constructed and used by real people with previously existing needs, desires, intentions and interpretive strategies'. She urges us to keep these unpredictable activities at the centre of interpretation, lest we blind ourselves 'to the fact that the essentially human practice of making meaning goes on even in a world increasingly dominated by things and by consumption' (Radway 1987: 221). Nevertheless, it is plain that Radway herself constitutes her group of readers as typical and internally undifferentiated. In this sense, she may be said, despite all precautions, to be repeating the mistake of turning commercial into ethnographic homogeneity. If it is indeed the case that the particular group of women studied by Radway is particularly unified in terms of shared social conditions and cultural preferences (though not much detail is given about this), this does not necessarily allow us to see such a group as typical of the readers of mass-market fiction.

The problem with Radway's enquiry is that it assumes, like many others of the same kind, a regularity of relation between the three stages of the reading process, namely, the object, the agent and the action of reading; or, put more simply, books, the people who read them and the way in which they read them. Romances are read not only by romance readers but also by readers who are not 'romance readers' (academics, for example), or who will not remain so, or who have not always been so, or who are only occasionally so, (though they may be intensely loyal during the periods when they are); to specify only these variables. But even if we grant the notion of the dedicated romance reader, who does hardly anything else with 'her' (the assumption of gender is important here) spare time but read romances, it is important to remember that reading does not take place all at once and under clearly delimited conditions. It is always possible for romance readers to read differently on different occasions, or even on the same occasion – indeed, it is hard to avoid this. Radway found that the group of women she studied were articulate and self-aware about how they read romances; but she does not seem to have investigated the difference that her enquiry might have been making to that reading. If her informants are converted from being merely readers of romance into readers of *the* romance, or, indeed, readers of their own readings of romance, are they still typical romance readers? And what of the prospect that such self-awareness is not merely induced by the enlightening appearance of the cultural theorist or ethnographic outsider, but is already a recurrent possibility within such a readership? Does this not suggest that it is difficult to define the typical ways, times and places in which reading is conducted, and that there is a kind of mobility built into the act of reading, even of such an apparently homogeneous group?

The same objections might be made to many studies of or commentaries upon the readerships and forms of reading of genre or formula fiction in general. In effect, studies of mass culture and responses to it have tended to replicate one of the ways in which modernist art, and its associated cultural theory, attempted to distinguish itself from mass culture, namely in terms of a contrast between the immobile, not to say fixated, appetites and reading habits of the consumer of mass cultural forms and the suppler, more ironically adaptive reader of literature or appreciator of art. Elsewhere, I have discussed the ways in which a theory of different kinds of reading and response hardens into an account of different kinds of reader (Connor 1992: 37–9). The distinction between art and mere entertainment is personified in terms of a distinction between the active and autonomous reader and a mere member of a readership. Such a notion underlies much educational theory and policy from the 1930s onwards. This idea is both contradicted and, in an intriguing sense, complemented by the modernist construction of the ideal reader of the future, to which I drew attention a little earlier. In its way, the modernist ideal reader is an exact counterpart to the idealised reader of mass fiction; though each is defined against the other, each is also imagined as a wholly self-identical category, with no possibility of traffic or fraternisation between the two kinds of reader or readership. The central principle of Leavisite close reading and the educational practices founded upon it is that of irreversible evolution; having become a sensitive and flexible reader, one is supposed to be incapable, except in the case of pathological relapse, of reverting to one's earlier condition. Even more unthinkable is the idea of the untutored reader, or habitual reader of mass fiction, who might nevertheless occasionally read different kinds of text, or pay them a different kind of attention.

It is no accident, perhaps, that such a theory of reading and cultural experience more generally should have had so much authority in the face of so many obvious objections, for so long. It proved strikingly adaptable to the purposes of the newly centralised forms of educational and cultural planning of the period following the Second World War. It proved so because it offered, even compelled, a statistical or distributional model of society, in which different communities of taste and forms of cultural participation could be demarcated, and the transition from one to another both promoted and regulated. The implications of the loosened sense of readership that I am urging are much more than statistical. If there ever was a moment in which it could be assumed that readers were identical with the readerships to which they belonged, or in which they electively participated by reading certain kinds of text or watching certain kinds of film, that moment has given way to a condition in which readers, or consumers of culture generally (since 1950, this is to say all of us), typically have multiple affiliations and participate in multiple readerships and forms of reading.

Since the 1950s, and especially following the appearance of work by Richard Hoggart (1957) and Stuart Hall and Tony Jefferson (1975), which stressed the vigour and value of certain forms of popular or working-class culture, the modernist anxiety about preserving high culture intact from the depredations of the market has modulated into an undoubtedly more democratic anxiety about the preservation of diversity. Increasingly, a postmodernist cultural politics has been defined in terms of such an attention to the value of plurality against the narrowing, standardising effects of the market on the one hand, and an oppressively monolithic account of high culture on the other. But the plurality valued by postmodern cultural politics tends to be conceived in ways which actually derive from a modernist view of mass culture. Everybody who considers the problems of publishing and the sociology of literary forms, for example, seems to agree on the value of preserving different kinds of text for different kinds of reader; but this diversity tends still to be measured in terms of the quantum of possible readerships, or species of reader. According to this measure, it is hard to avoid the conclusion that diversity has diminished. If there are more books produced now than previously, then, overall, it is pretty easy to show that there are fewer kinds of book being published, and therefore, it is assumed, fewer different kinds of reading constituency.

But this is to attend to the question in only a distributional way. If one pays attention to the internal differentiation of these forms of readership, and to the degree of mobility between or participation in different kinds of reading, it is possible to make out a rather different picture. Positing the existence of interpretative groups, or communities of taste, may be useful mostly in order to help to register the effect of the multiple allegiances which precisely work to dissolve the clarity of such groups. Such a perspective offers a more dynamic and three-dimensional way of evaluating contemporary culture, and may suggest that there is more diversity in the participation in cultural life than is easily observable with a distributive perspective.

For the last couple of decades, the reader of fiction, like the consumer of culture generally, has tended to become much more versatile in his or her tastes and forms of reading. This has a number of causes, including the possibility of class and cultural mobility brought about by the expansion of secondary and higher education in the 1960s, and, to a lesser degree in the late 1980s. As many have remarked, this produces not only an expansion of 'access' to high culture among social groups who would not previously have such access, but also a diversification of the very nature of the high culture to which these new student bodies were supposed to have access. The new students of the 1950s onwards were the products of the mass culture against which the universities and especially the English departments of those universities defined themselves. The effect of the passage through academic institutions which were themselves under increasing pressure to relax their mistrust of the world of mass culture was to create a newly hybrid kind of cultural consumer. Such a consumer possessed enough high-cultural nous and confidence not to feel intimidated or bored by art and culture, but was also enough of a participant in the world of advertising, TV and popular culture to be unimpressed by the more austere denunciations of mass civilisation that still emanated from certain quarters.

More important even than education has been the commodification of learning and high culture that has taken place more generally. From the 1960s onwards, it became plain that the careful quarantining of culture from commerce was unsustainable; from the early 1980s onwards, as more and more cultural institutions were taken out from under the wing of government and exposed to the tender mercies of the market-place, the dream of the autonomy of art from society and the culture industry survived only as nostalgic desire or utopian vision. This breakdown of the distinction between commerce and culture was assisted also by the extraordinary expansion of the culture industry. In the period immediately following the Second World War, a workable distinction could still be made between what belonged to the sphere of production – industry, commerce, goods – and what belonged to the sphere of reproduction and representation – films, books, advertising. In the last two decades, that distinction has become increasingly hard to maintain. By the 1960s, in what had already been christened the 'society of the spectacle' (Debord [1967] 1990), information, images, signs, services and lifestyles were no longer supplementary to the real business of manufacturing and distribution but were the very engine of such processes. It is hard to be sure whether this represents a final assimilation of the cultural to commercial and economic processes, or, on the contrary, a 'culturising' of those processes, for example in the increasing emphasis on consumption rather than production.

A modernist analysis would tend to emphasise the corruption or annulment of culture and authentic cultural value under such circumstances. When classical music begins to achieve mass popularity (for example, in the success of performers such as Nigel Kennedy, and the use of the voice of Luciano Pavarotti in connection with the promotion of the 1990 football World Cup in Britain) or when competitions such as the Booker Prize and the Turner Prize begin to generate substantial sales for writers and artists, critics and commentators may respond with a certain kind of defensive defeatism which would prefer the prospect of the death of culture to its enlargement to include a mass audience. Another reading of these effects is possible, however. According to this the enhanced visibility of certain cultural forms, through the marketing of high culture within mass culture, produces new and rather unpredictable kinds of reader and experiences of readership.

This is not to argue that the mass market and the commodification of culture have simply overcome the problems of exclusion which continue to dominate in the politics of culture. It would be fatuous to attempt to deny that mass marketing and broadcasting have homogenised and narrowed the range of different kinds of cultural experience they transmit, firstly by processes of selection and exclusion and secondly by making everything that is transmitted or becomes visible seem to be interchangeable and uniformly fungible. But it is important also to come to terms with the effects of loosening, compounding and overlayering that come from the mass visibility of different styles, products and forms of cultural affiliation.

For homogenisation and diversity are not necessarily mutually exclusive. The development of the mass culture industry since the Second World War depends, as we have seen, on the attempt to attain absolute correspondence between commodity and consumer: to predict, and increasingly to construct, desires and markets with sufficient accuracy to reduce storage and turnover time and thus to increase profit. One effect of this is undoubtedly to maintain cultural distinctions and hierarchies, to divide up the market-place into easily and effectively targeted consumers and constituencies of taste. Oddly, however, the very diversification of the market that this brings about tends to make it more difficult to achieve. The availability and (as a result of the growth of advertising) the increasing visibility of these different constituencies and commodities, one to another, has tended to create market volatility alongside and within market standardisation. Consumer society has created much less predictable patterns of consumption than society organised around production, since consumers tend to develop multiple affiliations and loyalties, which may – to some degree – cut across traditional notions of taste as determined by class, age, profession, sexuality or ethnic origin. The publishing industry, like the culture industry in general, has adopted more flexible, 'post-Fordist' models of production and distribution, in an attempt to control and respond to such fluctuations of taste. If the classical model of modern mass production was the single Ford or Volkswagen car, produced centrally in vast numbers by standardised techniques, then the equivalent in a post-Fordist era (which is characterised by more intensely stimulated but less easily channelled consumer desire) is the idea of the product range, running from the sensible family car at one end through to the sumptuous, high prestige or high performance model at the other end. As many have argued, the mobility or diversity of products is increasingly being matched by the mobility and flexibility of the production process; thus, the range of a particular model is likely to be built by various workforces in different countries, who may be hired, redeployed and abandoned with alarming rapidity. The principle of standardisation, which depends on economies of scale (the more of one thing that can be stockpiled, in one size and colour, the cheaper each one is) has given way to, or works alongside, the principle of articulation, which depends upon economies of scope. (Here, the more different things that are made, by flexible, small-batch and 'just-in-time' production of a variety of product types, the greater the range of consumers that can be reached, and the more protection there is against unpredictable markets [Harvey 1989: 177]).

There are some instructive parallels here between publishing and the fiction industry in particular and post-Fordist production processes more generally. First of all, producers of books now tend to associate themselves much less with a certain specialised or standardised product. Thus, academic publishers such as Oxford University Press find it necessary to maintain an extensive non-academic list. It would be a mistake to relate size to standardisation in any simple way. Although the most characteristic feature of publishing in recent years has been the agglomeration of smaller publishers in larger and larger corporations, this has not always been matched by simplification of product or by the elimination of unprofitable minority publishing. Large corporations tend to try to maintain a spread of products at different levels of the market (though in trying to define and control this spread, of course, they may very well end up by acting to constrain diversity). Similarly, production processes have been made subject to much more flexible contracting; books are now assembled in much the same way as cars, by different specialised and short-term workforces in widely separated locations.

Despite the survival of apparently very strong forms of stratification, both the reading and readerships of fiction have become more complex, hybrid and mobile in the postwar period than previously. Localised or specialised readerships have arisen alongside the previously established mass readerships for genre fiction. Women's and lesbian and gay fiction have enjoyed striking marketing successes. The availability and popularity of contemporary international fiction is increasing. Indeed, large international readerships have been built up for the 'Latin American novel' or the 'African novel'. Also significant has been the increasing permeability of British and American markets, such that it is now hard to be sure of what 'the British novel' may be said to consist. All of this suggests that the formal and aesthetic problem of addressivity may be related closely not only to a general sense of uncertainty about the reach and status of the novel as a cultural form, but also to more fundamental changes in the structure of the culture industries, in their increasingly determining effect on literary culture. One respect in which the novel may be seen to reflect on the nature of its involvement with the culture industry is in the conflict between print or reading culture and the visual culture which predominates in the new technologies of communication and information.

THE NOVEL AND OTHER MEDIA

From its beginnings, the novel has had an uneasy relationship with the mass media with which it is coeval. Like television and film, the twentieth-century mass cultural forms which depend on it so closely, the novel is defined not so much in terms of its characteristic subjects or styles or the forms of pleasure it provides, as in terms of the apparatus of its material production, distribution and consumption. Like television and film, too, the novel has maintained its energy and invention through its parasitism of other forms, rather than through any strong aesthetic principles of its own. Theory of the novel arrived comparatively late in its history, with the work of Henry James, critics before the end of the nineteenth century being little inclined to waste time on this most demotic, mendicant and aesthetically dishevelled of forms. But no sooner had writers begun to take the novel seriously and to advance aesthetic claims and definitions on its behalf than it found its prestige and particularity being challenged by the arrival of new mass media. The promotion of the novel to literary and cultural centrality in the critical writing of James, Lawrence, F. R. Leavis and others accompanied the rise of film during the modernist period so exactly as to suggest a more than contingent relationship between the two. In Britain in particular, the task of reclaiming the novel from the degenerating influence of mass culture was a miniaturised form of the more general task of securing an increasingly embattled sphere of high culture from absorption by mass culture. What was most important to modernist theories of the novel was that the aesthetic purity of the form be defined and affirmed, as part of a larger desire to protect against the promiscuous mingling of forms, languages and effects.

With the vast expansion, in the period since the Second World War, of the available range of forms of representation and reproduction, it grew more and more difficult to defend the claims of verbal narrative against the confidence, versatility and power of visual media of all kinds. The displacement of written fiction effected by television and media has been intensified by the rise of computer technology from the 1970s onwards, and an information revolution which has fundamentally reorganised the ways in which knowledge and experience are transmitted and preserved and narrated. It is not surprising that, under these conditions, novels and novelists have shown themselves uneasy about the influence of the electronic media. For many novelists writing in the 1950s and 1960s, during the rise and heyday of public service broadcasting in Britain, television proposed itself not just as a glamorous alternative to literary culture but also as a competitor in speaking for and constructing a common culture.

The title of Margaret Drabble's *The Radiant Way* (1987), which looks back over this period, plays between these alternatives of literary and televisual culture. *The Radiant Way* is the name of a pre-war reading primer, as Liz Headeland, a psychoanalyst, discovers at the end of the book when she is looking through the property of her dead mother. But we have first encountered the title of the book because it has been taken over by Liz Headeland's ex-husband, Charles, to be the title of a highly popular and influential television series with which he has made his name in 1965, a series arguing for the necessity of comprehensive education in the interests of creating a truly common culture. From the vantage point of the 1980s in which the novel is set, Charles's television programme, which shares its title with the novel in which it features, is not just an argument for such a common culture but also an enactment of its possibility in the very circumstances of its production.

> The Brave New World, it would be, and the new populist and popular medium of television would help to bring it into being. The team itself, with its mixed skills, its mixed social origins, its camaraderie, its common purpose, was a microcosm of what would come about: a forward-looking, forward-moving, dynamic society, full of opportunity, co-operative, classless.
>
> (Drabble 1988: 176)

The title of the television series, itself appropriated triumphantly from the class-divided culture of literacy, is subsequently appropriated by Drabble's novel. The effect is not to reaffirm the continuing centrality of the word, and especially the novel, in representing and sustaining a sense of collective life, but rather to acknowledge the uncertain rivalry between word and image, the public medium of television and the diminished but authentic privacy of the novel. I develop this discussion of *The Radiant Way* in the next chapter.

Other novelists have embraced the alleged degradation of the electronic media of the twentieth century with much greater alacrity. The brimming, rampaging farrago which Salman Rushdie's *Midnight's Children* (1981) makes of the post-Independence history of India depends heavily upon its homages to and imitations of the vocabulary and form of film. The borrowing of the idea of the voice-over, the rapid jump-cutting between 'scenes', the jolting conjuncture of melodrama and romantic movie with slapstick theology, and the lively inventiveness of legend, song and proverb all testify to the deep penetration of cinematic consciousness into literary and popular culture alike, both in the India which is Rushdie's subject and in the Britain which provided his primary readership. The central event in the novel itself depends upon a novelistic borrowing from another characteristically twentieth-century form, the radio. The hero and narrator of the novel, Saleem Sinai, discovers as a result of an accident that he has developed a kind of aural telepathy, in which he can pick up thoughts from and transmit them to all the other 'midnight's children', born around the time of the declaration of India's independence on 15 August 1947. Thus, the entry of India into the modern world of independent nation-states seems to be signalled and enacted in the very form of this novel. Benedict Anderson has pointed to the way in which the novel as a form has helped to define a sense of the regular, synchronised time necessary to the conception of the nation (1983: 30–40); but *Midnight's Children* suggests that the traditional form of the novel is not capacious or internally diversified enough to represent the teeming complexity of the different lives, cultures and languages suddenly brought into the schooled simultaneity of 'nation-time'. Instead, Rushdie's novel adopts and mimics the form of the electronic media that have been so important in defining and dissolving cultural identity in the twentieth century. In contrast to the dream of diversity brought into unity that lies at the heart of the ideas of the nation and the novel alike, Saleem experiences the capacity of modern electronic media to preserve and multiply incompatibilities.

> The inner monologues of all the so-called teeming millions, of masses and classes alike, jostled for space within my head ... The voices babbled in everything from Malayalam to Naga dialects, from the purity of Lucknow Urdu to the Southern slurrings of Tamil.
>
> (Rushdie 1982: 168)

The form of Saleem's narration follows the radiophonic telepathy of his miraculous gift. Like a radio scanning the frequencies, or drifting slightly out of tune, *Midnight's Children* is full of vocal interference, from different voices, styles and languages. Brought into being by the entry of India into the homogeneous time of modernity and nationhood, the 'polyglot frenzy' (ibid.) that throngs Saleem's head and narration testifies to the possibility of multiple chronologies and to the unreliability of the public calendar. Rereading his narrative, Saleem discovers an error in chronology; he has recorded Mahatma Gandhi's assassination on the wrong date. The error causes him to reflect on the relations between memory, narration and history in the light of his radiophonic consciousness, and to conclude that 'for me, there can be no going back; I must finish what I've started, even if, inevitably, what I finish turns out not to be what I began . . . *Yé Akashvani hai.* This is All-India Radio' (Rushdie 1982: 166; ellipsis in original). The irony of the radio metaphor in the novel is that it is at once the characteristic form of modernity, in its ubiquitous reach and universality of address ('All-India Radio'), and also the medium which preserves and transmits jaggedly incompatible kinds of truth and experience. The technology of modernity does not simply abolish the old world, but highlights the conflict between the modern and what it supersedes but only partially displaces. What characterises modern media, *Midnight's Children* seems to show, is a curious blend within it of the archaic and the modern, in which, far from abolishing the 'myth-life of India' (244), contemporary technology cooperates with and furthers it.

As Saleem grows more used to his nightly conferences with his 581 supernatural kin, he begins to try to organise them along the lines of the political organisation of India during the 1950s. Once he learns not only to receive but also to broadcast telepathic transmissions, he assembles his own MCC, or Midnight Children's Conference, 'in the *lok sabha* or parliament of my brain' (227). Slowly, the children fulfil the prophecy delivered by Prime Minister Nehru that they will become a 'mirror of the nation' (255), in their growing conflict and divisiveness. Rushdie exploits the forms and resources of the medium of radio, along with those of film and, in later novels such as *Shame* (1983) and *The Satanic Verses* (1988), of television and video, because such forms are the evidence of a fundamentally new relationship between public and private life. If the realist novel depended upon the interlocking difference of individual lives and the larger historical realities which they inhabit, and if it retained even in its most emphatic reconciliations of this difference an awareness of it *as* a difference, by contrast the forms of contemporary mass culture bring about a mutual permeation of the private and the public, such that the integrity of both is dissolved and a relationship of difference is no longer possible between them. *Midnight's Children* mimics a situation in which the individual self is no longer alienated from the world of public events but is ceaselessly traversed by them, even as those public events are themselves dependent for their existence upon their staging and projection by the new media followed by their consumption as images. Saleem Sinai seems to experience what Jean Baudrillard has described as 'the absolute proximity, the total instantaneity of things, the feeling of no defense, no retreat. It is the end of interiority and intimacy, the overexposure and transparency of the world which traverses . . . without obstacle' (Baudrillard 1988: 133). There is an instructive contrast here with Sterne's *Tristram Shandy* (1767), a novel whose vagrant, digressive structure and concern with the relations between physical impotence and the difficulties of storytelling is parodied throughout *Midnight's Children*. Where, in *Tristram Shandy*, the clear and orderly narration of a life and its events is thwarted by the unreliability of memory, the slipperiness of language and the insistent illogic of feeling, such that the connections between the world and the conscious subject are hard to establish and sustain, the difficulty for Saleem's narration lies in disentangling his own unreliable memories and reporting from the equally unreliable national memory. Even when Saleem thinks he has withdrawn from history, in conscious imitation of the buddha, into the repose of amnesia, he is in fact representative of a history that embodies itself in him. Having lost his memory and been recruited by the Pakistani security services as a kind of human tracker dog, 'this man with his nose like a cucumber and his head which rejected memories families histories' (351) replicates or anticipates larger events, since,

> by abandoning consciousness, seceding from history, the buddha was setting the worst of examples – and the example was followed by no less a personage than Sheikh Mujib, when he led the East Wing into secession and declared it independent as 'Bangladesh'.
>
> (Rushdie 1982: 351)

Again, *Midnight's Children* suggests that such transformations are best understood in the generic terms of popular media culture:

> With some embarrassment, I am forced to admit that amnesia is the kind of gimmick regularly used by our lurid film-makers. Bowing my head slightly, I accept that my life has taken on, yet again, the tone of a Bombay talkie; but after all, leaving to one side the vexed issue of reincarnation, there is only a finite number of methods of achieving rebirth. So, apologizing for the melodrama, I must doggedly insist that I, he, had begun again; that after years of yearning for importance, he (or I) had been cleansed of the whole business ... To sum up: I became a citizen of Pakistan.
>
> (Rushdie 1982: 350)

Nevertheless, despite the apparent collapse of distinctions between the novel, with its traditional vocation to discriminate, clarify and connect the lives of individuals and societies, and the turbulent, all-inclusive modes of modern media, *Midnight's Children* in fact continues to insist on and display difference within amalgamation. If it acknowledges and celebrates the superior explanatory power of media spectacle, farce and melodrama to explain the events of history, it does so with melancholic irony. *Midnight's Children* offers itself as a simulation rather than a replication of the media's powers of fable. If Salem's narrative airily distorts and forgets history, it does so partly as a kind of psychic defence and partly to display the more systematic distortion and forgetting of history in Indian and Pakistani political life more generally. At the heart of *Midnight's Children* is a curiously moralistic mistrust of the modes of the fabulous which it indulges with such zest. The novel banks on its power simultaneously to counterfeit and to offer for appraisal the operations of spectacle in the political life of a nation.

In recent years, a number of other novelists have attempted to negotiate and reimagine the uneasy relationship between the novel and the competing modes in which fiction is constructed and distributed in the contemporary world. Notable among these is Angela Carter. Like Rushdie, Carter attempts to reinvigorate the novel by enlarging its range and repertoire of effects. Her work eschews many of the conventions and consolations of the English realist novel, with its levelness of tone, its curbing of fantasy in close attention to the particular and the plausible, and its attempt to gather dispersed and separated events into unity and pattern, and favours instead a much more extravagantly pushy kind of narrative, full of the disrespectful energies of exaggeration, travesty and masquerade. Like Rushdie, Carter grafts into her narratives elements derived both from the prehistory of the novel form, including myth, legend, fairy-tale and other forms of oral narrative and popular fiction, and from its posterity in the technological forms of the twentieth century, namely radio, film and TV; like Rushdie, too, she sees much of the force (as well as much of the danger) of contemporary electronic media as lying in their power to preserve and unfold the powers of the fabulous.

In *The Passion of New Eve* (1977), Carter elaborates a particularly complex encounter between the forms of myth, cinema and the novel. The narrator of the novel, Evelyn, describes his movement from London to New York, and thence to the desert, where he is captured, first by a band of feminist guerillas who transform him into a woman and then by a male tyrant called Zero, who is obsessed by the belief that he has been telepathically emasculated by a film-star called Tristessa de St Ange during a showing of one of her films.

The novel depends upon a recurring contrast between linear time and cyclical time, the time of history and the time of myth. This contrast is emblematised in its opening paragraphs, which describes the figure of Tristessa de St Ange as she appears in the film of *Wuthering Heights* being watched by Evelyn:

> The film stock was old and scratched, as if the desolating passage of time were made visible in the rain upon the screen, audible in the worn stuttering of the sound track, yet these erosions of temporality only enhanced your luminous presence since they made it all the more forlorn, the more precarious your specious triumph over time. For you were just as beautiful as you had been twenty years before, would always be so beautiful as long as celluloid remained in complicity with the phenomenon of persistence of vision.
>
> (Carter 1982: 5)

The process of Evelyn's transformation from man to woman is represented as a passage from the phallic time of linearity to the spiral or recurrent time of the female. 'Time is a man, space is a woman', chant the women in Beulah, the underground society of radical feminists who effect Evelyn's transformation into Eve. 'Man lives in historicity; his phallic projectory takes him onwards and upwards – but to where? Where but to the barren seas of infertility, the craters of the moon! Journey back, journey backwards towards the source!' (53). But, if male or phallocentric time is identified with the aggressive onward drive of modernity – cities, wars, the space-race – then the novel also characterises this male modernity as mythical, which is to say locked in the straining sterility of self-construction and self-replication. If to be a woman is to be the negative of man, to be condemned to a mirror-life reflecting back male fantasies of femaleness, then it is equally true that, as Mother tells Evelyn, 'To be a *man* is not a given condition but a continuous effort'(63).

At the heart of modernity is the form of the cinema, which characteristically suspends time in illusion and repetition. Tristessa's house of glass in the desert, upon which Zero and his band mount a destructive assault, is imaged simultaneously as an insubstantial mirage, made and sustained in light, and as a vast rotating apparatus of reproduction, which is designed literally to spin around its own axis, like a gramophone or film projector. Tristessa's appearance in her coffin, when first seen by Evelyn, emphasises her retreat from time into deathly recurrence:

> It was as if all Tristessa's movies were being projected all at once on that pale, reclining figure so I saw her walking, speaking, dying, over and over again in all the attitudes that remained in this world, frozen in the amber of innumerable spools of celluloid from which her being could be extracted and endlessly recycled in a technological eternity, a perpetual resurrection of the spirit.
>
> (Carter 1982: 119)

The Passion of New Eve seems poised between fascinated identification with the self-replicating fantasies of modern life and mass culture and revulsion at their vacuity. From about half-way through, the novel itself seems to give up its commitment to the forward movement and starts to circle in on itself in a series of thickening concentricities. When Eve sets out to sea from the American west coast, it is unclear whether this is any kind of new beginning or merely another phase in the cycle of replications: 'All this strange experience, as I remember it, confounds itself in a fugue', says Eve

(191). To read a novel such as this, it seems, one needs the literary equivalent of the 'persistence of vision', upon which the illusion of film depends, the capacity to merge separated instants into continuous motion. However, if 'persistence of vision' is what allows isolated fragments of spatialised time to lengthen into duration, the novel's repeated use of this phrase also suggests the capacity to recall and replay images brought about by techniques of reproduction. Used in this sense, 'persistence of vision' comes to mean, not the turning of space into time, image into narrative, but the respatialisation of time, in the permanent, unchanging availability of images: Tristessa 'would live as long as persistence of vision', thinks Eve (119).

The two possibilities of meaning compounded in the idea of persistence of vision seem to encode the difference between cinema and narrative. Admittedly, this is a somewhat forced dichotomy, since, if films are repeatable, they nevertheless also occupy and move forwards in time in narrative fashion; and if novels are unavoidably sequential in form, they are nevertheless available in part and whole for rereading in just the same ways as film or other reproducible media. Nevertheless, in exploring the relationship between linear and recurrent time, unfolding and convolution, *The Passion of New Eve* seems to be exploring the opportunities and dangers for the novel that are represented by the example of film. Neither this nor any other novel can actually achieve identity with the forms with which it identifies. Indeed, as in *Midnight's Children*, a great deal depends on the fact that, precisely because it can only ever offer a translation or impersonation of film rather than an exact replication of it (film, as it were, in indirect speech) *The Passion of New Eve* offers a perspective upon film and the culture of the electronic media as well as emulating it. The resulting awkwardness of fit between novel and film is part of the point, since the novel here allows and requires a reading of the meaning and function of fiction in general.

Angela Carter's later fiction sustained and enlarged this enquiry, most especially in her last two completed novels, *Nights at the Circus* (1984) and *Wise Children* (1991), which run the form of the novel into unexpected collisions and collusions with circus, music-hall, pantomime, TV game show, popular song and Hollywood musical. The question of the legitimacy of cultural forms seems to be central to *Wise Children* in particular. The novel is narrated by Dora Chance, one of twin sisters who have spent their lives in show business. They are the daughters of Melchior Hazard, an aged Shakespearian actor of grand reputation, and are thus drawn into the complicated mock-Shakespearian plot of the novel, involving the search for true parentage, and accompanied by disguises, false trails and improbable revelations. The novel establishes a parallel between family lineage and culture, and embraces and celebrates the undersides of official culture just as it prefers the condition of uncertain or illegitimate parentage. Indeed, its repeated pairing of legitimate and illegitimate seems to suggest the inseparability of high and low culture. The respectable twins Imogen and Saskia Hazard, who are the legitimate daughters of Melchior Hazard but are biologically the daughters of Melchior's twin brother, the Falstaffian Peregrine Hazard, are balanced by Dora and Nora Chance, who are officially known as the daughters of Peregrine Hazard but are in fact the illegitimate offspring of Melchior. The kitschy vulgarity of the Hollywood version of *A Midsummer Night's Dream*, as summoned up by Carter's delighted account of it, conceals a serious point about the mutual contamination of literary culture and the mass culture of the movies and, later on, of television. From this point on, *Wise Children* seems to imply, the novel should give up its attempt to trace its lineage securely back to the sources of cultural value and prestige, and instead learn to admire and embrace the soiled vitality, the swift associativeness and transformational capacity of the 'bastard show' of the mass media (1991: 41). Thus, the meandering movement of Dora Chance's narrative is matched by the videotape of the game-show *Lashings of Lolly*, which is cut into her narrative with the aid of freeze-frame and fast forward.

But, as in *The Passion of New Eve*, there is also a kind of rivalry in this novel between the literary and the electronic media. Carter's novel strives in a certain sense not just to equal but to outdo the capacities of the media, to intensify and redouble their absurdities for ironic purpose. The climax of the farcical account of a double wedding performed on the set of the Hollywood production of *A Midsummer Night's Dream* reduplicates the comic confusion of Shakespeare's comedy and converts the tawdry glamour of Hollywood into a very image of magical transformation:

> I no longer remember that set *as* a set but as a real wood, dangerous, uncomfortable, with real, steel spines on the conkers and thorns on the bushes, but looking as if it were

unreal and painted, and the bewildering moonlight spilled like milk in this wood, as if Hollywood were the name of the enchanted forest where you lose yourself and find yourself, again; the wood that changes you; the wood where you go mad; the wood where the shadows live longer than you do.

(Carter 1991: 157–8)

Despite all the lurching inconsequence and boozy confusion of Dora's narrative ('There I go again! Can't keep a story going in a straight line, can I? Drunk in charge of a narrative. Where was I?'; 1991: 158), we should be struck by the poise and steady purpose of the narrative's impersonation of vulgarity. Like other novels that appear to have abandoned themselves to other media, *Wise Children* retains a hold upon its identity as a novel, exploiting the capacity which is paradoxically intrinsic to the form, to hold together different registers of experience and to inhabit intermediary conditions between the solemnly canonical word and its riotously vernacular counterparts.

Other, less mainstream and more 'experimental' novelists appear to have made greater demands on the form and on its readers. Michael Westlake, for example, has attempted to push the impersonatory capacities of the novel to a comic extremity in a series of novels. *Imaginary Women* (1987) in particular attempts to give to written narrative some of the agitation and affective density of film. The novel is a congeries of different narratives, chopped into short sequences and spliced together, most of them with women as narrator or principal character. The various sequences neither interlock coherently nor build steadily, though some narrative continuity is provided by a mock *film noir* plot involving a film-maker known only as Mac**ash, a Professor J. J. Case, who migrates between genders, sometimes appearing as 'Julius John', sometimes as 'Julia Jane', and a succession of foreign powers. The novel includes a number of elaborate accounts of the plots of classic thrillers and *films noirs*, including Polanski's *Chinatown*, Hitchcock's *North By North-West* and Welles's *The Lady From Shanghai*, bizarrely knitted together with the motifs of fish, glass and water, and overlaid with sophisticated readings of the films from critics and viewers. The novel also seems to combine and contrast the differing modes of literary and film narrative. At times, the narrative lags clumsily behind the films it treats, as in the deliberately laborious plot summaries:

> She makes her appearance in the scene Jake bursts into his office full of the story he's been told in the barber's shop to calm him down after he's been insulted by a fellow customer who accused him of being in a dirty business because of the front page story of the water commissioner's marital infidelity which Jake has investigated on the instigation of his wife, Evelyn Mulwray.
>
> (Westlake 1989: 20)

More often it deploys the resources and expectations of written fiction to overlay the experience of film with a kind of probing self-consciousness which is not available to the films themselves. In something of the manner of Robert Coover's *A Night at the Movies: Or, You Must Remember This* (1991), which is a series of parodies and nightmarish distortions of famous films and film genres, *Imaginary Women* borrows the intensity and excessiveness of film narrative precisely in order to exceed it in a narrative that then lies somewhere between script, performance and critical reading. Though the novel concedes much less to its reader than the work of Salman Rushdie and Angela Carter, and its academic knowingness is sometimes merely smart, it testifies to the capacity of the novel to conjoin the diverse pleasures and experiences of narrative with an investigation of narrative's nature and force.

Recent years have seen a number of attempts to investigate the nature of the challenge posed to the novel not only by the more established media such as radio, film and TV, but also by the information society more generally. Texts such as Russell Hoban's *The Medusa Frequency* (1987) and Sue Thomas's *Correspondence* (1991) use the established reading patterns and expectations of the novel, as a text which proceeds from an individual author to an individual reader, to embody and explore the much more complex and decentred forms of communication and exchange of information characteristic of computer culture. Nowhere has this confrontation between different forms of information and communication been more thoroughly enacted than in Christine Brooke-Rose's quartet of novels, *Amalgamemnon* (1984), *Xorandor* (1986), *Verbivore* (1990) and *Textermination* (1991). The most demanding and intriguing of the quartet is the first, *Amalgamemnon*. This assembles the thoughts, recollections and anticipations of Mira Enketei, a university teacher who is about to be made redundant. We follow her conversations and relationships with friends, students and lovers, her plans to start a pig-farm and her fantasies of kidnap by a terrorist group. But these broadly realistic concerns are mingled bewilderingly with others drawn from Mira's professional interests, notably the writings of Herodotus and the mythical narratives of Agamemnon, Cassandra and Orion (from which Mira decides to 'invent myself an alternate family, mythical magical multitudinous and play with names and thus anteprogenitize'; Brooke-Rose 1984: 37), as well as the voices of the contemporary media, especially the radio broadcasts to which Mira listens as she reads Herodotus.

The text is built around two founding principles, the metaphor of redundancy itself and the restriction of the novel to non-realised verbal forms, which is to say, principally future and conditional tenses and imperative and subjunctive moods. This means that it is very hard to distinguish what actually happens in the novel from what is surmised, desired or imagined. The indeterminacy of all the actions and events of the novel seems completely opposed to those qualities of coherence, definition and narratable sequence which are associated with the use of the past tense in narrative. In giving up the realised past, the virtual narrative of *Amalgamemnon* allies itself with the contemporary discourses of the media, which seem equally at home in an indeterminate space between the prediction of events and their realisation, as Brooke-Rose has herself explained in comments on the novel:

> The more I explored narrative in the future tense, the more I realized that we're living all the time in a kind of pseudo-mini future. A lot of news is given in the future. I don't mean an actual event that hasn't happened yet, but there's a tremendous amount of speculation like 'Tomorrow the Prime Minister will meet the President of . . . and they will probably discuss . . .' By the time they've met and discussed it, it's gone, and they're speculating about something else.
> (Friedman and Fuchs 1989: 85)

The dissolution of the authority of the past and the present in favour of an endlessly anticipated, but unarriving futurity links prediction to redundancy in the novel. A world which narrates the future so incessantly appears also to annul it; the future, when it ensues, has been so prepared for that it is little more than repetition, or redundancy. Nevertheless, redundancy, as Richard

Martin has noticed (1988), also proliferates in this novel. Constructed futures occur in many different forms and languages, ranging from sports reports, weather forecasts and political commentary to Mira's reading of Herodotus. All of these intrude repeatedly upon the 'central' narrative, which is itself made up largely of Joycean word-drifts and compounds:

> And so what shall I be, Io for instance or Europe – shall we ever make it? – or a swinegirl sighing for her swineherd to sexplode the Lawrence myth, becoming cyclonic in Fortes, snow, good, becoming poor . . .
>
> Meanwhile the ecopoliticonomists will fly in from everywhere and poke the entrails of the grunterranean fire and mutter smoothing pragnostications and stake out their statistics to announce the coming recovery, the summit in unemployment figures will be reached in about nine months and we'll all go on as if.
>
> (Brooke-Rose 1984: 16, 21)

But *Amalgamemnon* does more than reproduce what the American novelist Don DeLillo calls the pervasive 'white noise' of the contemporary communications and information overload. Although she seems to give over the consciousness of its central character, and indeed the very novel she inhabits, to the accelerating virtualities of contemporary discourse, Brooke-Rose actually retains a sense of the fixative and clarifying purpose of the novel form. In its very difficulty, in its creation of incongruity, oddity and blockage, the novel attempts both to replicate and to resist the frictionless slide of one discourse over another in media communication. The novel is placed at the point of transition between more traditional requirements and uses of narratives and the alarming dissipation of narrative into a culture of instantaneously renewed futurity. Its force and promise lie not so much in any revolutionary dissolution of the form of the novel as in the fact that the novel manages to capture and hold the process of its own dissolution.

Thus, even in work such as that of Michael Westlake or Christine Brooke-Rose and, outside Britain, in novels such as Don DeLillo's *White Noise* (1985) and William Gibson's *Neuromancer* (1984), which may seem to have surrendered the novel to the ceaseless, interrupting flow of mediatised discourse that jabbers across the jammed airwaves of the world, crucial differences remain between the discursive processes of the media and the framing of those processes in what most still feel content to call a novel. The novel that allows itself to be traversed by the discursive overload of contemporary media civilisation always aims to make that overload available to imagination and in some way narratable. These functions survive even when the purpose and the effect of the novel seem to be to undermine or abandon the possibility of narrative as such. One function of the novel is then to create a syntax of disorientation, to solidify and clarify the very sensations of impermanence, evanescence and inmixing.

In the light of the massive infiltration of written narrative forms by a multiplicity of idioms, registers and media, it may well be that the most important question to ask about the novel in this particular period of history is not what is specific to it, in terms of its concerns and capacities, but rather into what kinds of altered and altering contexts it has been drawn. To ask what the novel means in the contemporary world is to ask about the distinctive mutations that it has undergone in its relations with other cultural and technological forms. It is to ask about the meanings and values accorded to narrative fiction in general, whether this be in written, oral or visual form. If this may seem to evacuate the novel, or to spell its death, it may also be to attend to the diversified manner of its survival.

Earlier in this chapter, it was suggested that the function of addressivity was crucial to the postwar novel. It might seem as though this function is thrown into crisis if not altogether nullified by the conditions dealt with in novels such as those by Rushdie, Carter, Westlake and Brooke-Rose. In the irredeemably plural worlds represented and inhabited by these novels, and under the conditions of discursive saturation replicated in them, there might seem no further possibility of positing a reader, or reliable trajectory of address. The novel, it might appear, must be content to exist 'between', to borrow the title of an earlier novel by Christine Brooke-Rose (1968), caught in the ceaseless crossfire of representations. But even when it seems merely and passively to display the incommensurability of discursive forms and the worlds they instance, when it seems to be simply, as Susan E. Hawkins puts it, describing *Amalgamemnon*, 'a space in which a cacophony of voices, or discursive amplifications, or babble . . . enact their own sounding' (1991: 59), the novel implicitly poses the question of what kind of fictional world or narrative constitution might organise them or make them graspable. This is partly because, for all the splitting and scattering of its traditional lines of address, and communities of interpretation, the novel cannot avoid what we might call the impetus of addressivity, no matter what provocations it may deliver to, or demands it may make of, its addressee. In posing the very questions of what kind of novel and what kind of novel reading are still plausible in the contemporary world, as so many examples of the form seem to do, such novels are posing larger questions about the sort of world, and the sorts of imaginative inhabitation of it, that are still possible. The chapters that follow will consider the different ways in which the novel form since the Second World War has sought to consider and dramatise its own place in contemporary history, in terms, firstly, of its relations to the sense of national belonging and unbelonging and, secondly, of its complex relations to history, in the narratives whereby individuals and groups install themselves in or seek to secede from the narrative of the past.

2
CONDITIONS OF ENGLAND

If, as Homi Bhabha and others have recently suggested (1990b), the nation is closely implicated with the exercise of narrative in general – with the isolation of origins, the building and sustaining of continuity through time, the summoning of difference and divergence into a shared and 'organic' synthesis – then the novel has seemed an especially ductile form in which to elaborate the narrative idea of the nation. Timothy Brennan has associated what he calls 'the national longing for form' with the novel in particular, observing that 'it was the *novel* that historically accompanied the rise of nations by objectifying the "one, yet many" of national life, and by mimicking the structure of the nation, a clearly bordered jumble of languages and styles' (1990: 49). In nineteenth-century Britain, in the high noon of the social-realist novel, Dickens, Eliot, Disraeli and Gaskell all responded to the imperative to imagine and diagnose the 'condition of England', in novels the very teeming inclusiveness of which seemed to be both an enactment of the problem of imagining the whole of a nation and a utopian prefiguring of such a vision of healing unity. Modernist fiction of the interwar years in the twentieth century retained the perspectival ambition of nineteenth-century social realism, but shrank back from the arena of the nation into more circumscribed kinds of community. This may be seen, for example, in the generational struggles and mutations of a small group of characters in Lawrence's *The Rainbow* (1915) and *Women in Love* (1921); in the snapshot of a single day in Dublin which, in Joyce's *Ulysses* (1922), is both snatched out of shared, public history and painstakingly reinserted into a longer, mythical perspective; or in the interweaving of memories and perceptions which, in Woolf's *The Waves* (1931), provides a kind of psychologised public history.

It is sometimes said that the postwar novel in Britain is characterised by a conscious recoil from the stylistic and formal artifice of modernist fiction, and by a return to the demands and responsibilities of realism. Certainly, it appears to be the case that novelists after the war experienced a cautious return of the nineteenth-century aspiration to diagnose and display in fiction the 'condition of England'. In a rough and ready sense, it can be acknowledged that there was indeed a widespread dissatisfaction among novel writers with what was regarded as the asocial experimentation of modernist fiction of the years before the war, and that there was a willing return to a certain perhaps distinctively 'English' rendering of a closely-particularised can community, which, though circumscribed, can nevertheless be offered as a type of the social whole. Margaret Drabble's sentiments in a radio broadcast of 1967 are often taken as representative:

> I don't want to write an experimental novel to be read by people in fifty years who will say, ah, well, she foresaw what was coming ... I'd rather be at the end of a dying tradition, which I admire, than at the beginning of a tradition which I deplore.
>
> (Quoted in Bergonzi 1979b: 65)

In fact, the image of a simple retreat from modernist experimentation in fiction after the War is a good deal *too* rough and ready. The 'condition of England' novel in its postwar version shows the pressure of many of the same problems to which certain kinds of modernist experimentation were a response in the interwar years. Most particularly, such novels continue to respond to the sense of the author as socially marginal rather than socially central, and to cope with the uncertainties of audience, address and function which had partly prompted the defensive and triumphant transformations of novel form in the previous generation. In returning (in modest and sceptical enough fashion, to be sure) to the social-realist ambitions of the nineteenth-century novel, certain examples of the postwar novel are in fact furthering the debate carried on within the novel form throughout the twentieth century, as to its own adequacy to account for and answer to the disturbing social forces it took as its subject.

The particular 'condition of England' which postwar novelists were concerned to represent and analyse was indeed one of marked and troubling transition and redefinition. The establishment of the Welfare State and, following the period of austerity in the years immediately following the Second World War, the beginnings of the upswing in economic prosperity, which was to continue broadly unabated until the 1970s, brought about an extraordinary agitation of settled social forms and structures. As with the period immediately following the First World War, education in Britain underwent a considerable expansion and diversification, caused both by the return of a body of adult students who had served in the War, and thus had a much expanded range of experiences, expectations and demands, and by the generally increased participation in education, especially at university level, of lower middle class and even working class students who came from a (somewhat) wider regional spread than hitherto. Within a period of about ten years, from the late 1950s to the late 1960s, the number of universities in Britain doubled, and the number of undergraduates in course quadrupled. Growth slowed thereafter, but by 1985 there were nearly five times as many full-time students (almost 600,000) in higher education as there had been in 1955. This represents an increase in the proportion of the population in higher education from about 4 per cent to 12 per cent (Ball *et al.* 1989: 290–3). It is important not to overstate the effects of this, for it is true that, taken as a whole, the class background of students in higher education has changed little despite the increase of numbers (ibid: 281). Nevertheless, the perception of increased educational access in Britain, along with the belief in the opportunities for class and economic advancement offered by the new prosperity, combined to effect a decisive shift in cultural power and authority. The actual experience of this shift was rather more unsettling and conflicted than might be suggested by the rhetoric of postwar reconstruction, which represented the changes as an extension of the allegedly spontaneous sense of shared belonging and cooperative effort that characterised the War years. Effectively, what was happening in British society was not a refashioning of educational, communicative and governmental institutions, but rather their stretching to include different kinds of participant. The spheres of art and culture are good examples here. As Alan Sinfield has shown, the principle that operated during the first twenty years of postwar cultural policy was that the benefits of high culture should be extended, through the enlightening influence of such institutions as the fledgling Arts Council and the BBC, to a larger and more diversified population, not that culture should be transformed as a result of such widened participation (Sinfield 1989: 39–59). The result was more often bafflement, resentment and the clash of sedimented interests and perspectives than any shared or significantly transformed perspective on what art and culture meant for different classes and competing social groups.

This was reinforced by the effects of a fundamental contradiction within British society which was to become fully visible only with the breakdown of the postwar social consensus after 1979. This was the conflict between the centralist ideals of the Welfare State, producing attitudes that were often protective, constraining and inward-looking, and the more explosive forces of economic growth, which shook apart many of the structures of British society, not least in making it increasingly clear that Britain was dependent upon and vulnerable to the larger pressures of a newly globalised economy. The irony, it was to transpire in the late 1970s, was that, without the latter, the former could not in fact survive. Despite the attempts by the Labour government of 1945 and the Conservative governments that followed it to harness centralist planning to the engine of capitalist growth, the effects of this disjuncture between welfare state and capitalist process are already apparent in the 1950s and reflected in the novels of the decade, which tend to set the euphoria and sense of possibility consequent upon economic and social mobility against the sense of displacement, alienation and blockage.

Throughout such novels, an inherited ambition to represent England and Englishness goes along with – is even to a large extent driven by – the apprehension that the condition of England was resistant to the kinds of novelistic and narrative representation that had previously seemed adequate. At the same time, however, there is a powerful residual sense of the potential of the novel to imagine, project and preserve forms of national and collective identity. This sense of the potential fit between the form of the novel and the form of new social identity is borne out interestingly in a moment from Margaret Drabble's early novel *Jerusalem the Golden* (1967). Like so many novels of the 1950s and 1960s, this follows the social and cultural journey from the provinces to the metropolitan centre that is undertaken by its central character, Clara, who gains a scholarship which enables her to exchange her cramped and constraining life in the Northern town of Northam for what turns out to be the facile but still alluring sophistications of artistic and theatrical London. A passage early in the novel describes the imaginative prefigurings of her new life that she has encountered as a child. One of these is a hymn from which the title of the novel is taken, presenting a vision of 'Jerusalem the Golden/With milk and honey blest' (Drabble 1969: 32). Another is a book of fables, most of which point up their morals with a lucidity which Clara finds depressingly impermeable to qualification, but among which is one which offers her something of the 'complication, in the absence of conviction, that she was seeking ... the true brittle glitter of duplicity ... the warm shine of wider, more embracing landscapes; she looked for half-truth, for precious qualification, for choice, for possible rejections' (33). The fable, entitled *The Two Weeds*, offers, but does not resolve, an allegorical choice between short-lived beauty and more prudently conserved longevity. In its productive failure to resolve the choice, the fable offers not the simple wish-fulfilment of another life, but a more complex forming and framing of ambivalence and 'the shock of the new contained and expressed in the framework and the terms of the old' (35). A future that is open to possibility is here prefigured by the openness of the narrative form. In offering itself as an enlarged exploration of the forms of choice and possibility concentrated in the fable, *Jerusalem the Golden* establishes a strong continuity between the fashioning of new forms of class and national identity and the form of the novel itself. One significant irony here is that, though it sets the moral maturity of the novel against the abstract simplicity of other forms of representation, *Jerusalem the Golden* cannot itself avoid falling into the simplistically allegorical mode from which it distances itself; the stages of Clara's story, her scholarship to London, her meeting with a dazzling Hampstead family and her affair with the golden boy Gabriel, which ends in disappointment but increased insight and maturity on Clara's part, themselves follow through the stages of an abstract social fable.

During the decades that followed *Jerusalem the Golden* Drabble was to produce a series of novels which quite explicitly project and analyse the condition of England at various points in its postwar development, and I shall be considering two of them, *The Ice Age* (1977) and *The Radiant Way* (1987), a little later. Other writers, too, attempted to deploy the resources of the realist novel to respond to the transitional postwar condition of England. In many such novels, the desire to provide an adequate report upon a particular passage of contemporary history is accompanied by a troubled preoccupation, similar to that of *Jerusalem the Golden*, with the possibilities of the novel in history.

Among the most explicit of these is Angus Wilson's *Anglo-Saxon Attitudes*, first published in 1956. Wilson's title compresses many different ironies. As the novel's epigraph makes clear, it alludes to the comic contortions of the messenger in Lewis Carroll's *Alice Through the Looking Glass*, as a way of characterising the neurotic and foolish inflexibility of many of the established institutions of English life: 'The Messenger kept skipping up and down, and wriggling like an eel, as he came along, with his great hands spread out like fans on each side... "He's an Anglo-Saxon Messenger – and those are Anglo-Saxon attitudes"' (Carroll 1970: 279). But this is an England which, for all its continuing disdain of foreigners, is being rapidly forced to recognise its marginality in the growing internationalism of the postwar years. In the 1950s, the Englishness (or Britishness, for the terms are, of course, often interchangeable, though irregularly and problematically so) which had been so triumphantly preserved against the threat of Nazism, was now under threat from the very forces which guaranteed its victory, namely, the new dispositions of international military and political power. This irony is signalled in the fact that the attitudes and identities of the 'Anglo-Saxons' are themselves a matter of uncomfortable adjustments to and relationships with other peoples, even and especially with the 'Saxon' adversary who seemed the opposite of the principles of Englishness. The uncertainty in the title as to whether the attitudes are the attitudes of the Anglo-Saxons themselves, or the mutually defining attitudes of the English and their national 'others' and antagonists, is re-enacted in the historical puzzle which is at the centre of the story. Gerald Middleton, Professor of Medieval History, needs to ascertain the truth about the discovery early in the century by his own academic mentor, Professor Lionel Stokesay, of a pagan figure buried in the Christian grave of a renowned Bishop. The discovery is variously accounted for throughout the novel, but what is at stake seems partly to be the authenticating force of historical origins in a narrative of Englishness. Responding to that wave of historical patriotism of the war years that is represented most notably by Lawrence Olivier's film of *Henry V*, Wilson's novel suggests that such appeals to origins always run the risk either of fraudulence and self-delusion (Gerald Middleton guards the suspicion that the pagan figure may have been placed in the grave by Gilbert, Stokesay's son, as a deception) or of the discovery that, at the point of historical origin, where identity should spring single and entire, it is in fact composite and compromised.

Like the nineteenth-century novels it parodies, (it is not plain quite how seriously) *Anglo-Saxon Attitudes* attempts to engineer a formal and structural solution to the problems of divergence, complexity and contradiction in social life. The central character is named 'Middleton', aptly enough perhaps, given the fact that he mediates between so many different forms and levels of social life in this, a novel that itself seems sometimes to masquerade as a miniature, mid-twentieth-century *Middlemarch*. The novel asks us to accept the equivalence of Middleton's personal turmoil with the deceits and conflicts within his family and widely distributed circle of friends and, beyond that, with the much deeper and more systematic conflicts within modern social life. The first part of the novel centres around two gatherings, a lecture given by a historian at the Historical Association of Medievalists, and a family Christmas celebrated at the house of Ingeborg Middleton, Gerald's estranged wife. These two gatherings act as a focus for the personal process of integration that Gerald involuntarily begins to undergo, in a number of detailed passages of retrospection that are intercut with the conversations between characters at the gatherings. The parallels are made clear: the process of articulating, in its senses both of expressing and of connecting, the different, disjointed stages of Gerald's own life is offered as a model for a much larger act of cultural self-understanding. Such self-understanding is necessary, both to connect the past with the present in a significant and honest fashion, and to loosen the condition of historical fixation that is comically evoked throughout the novel in the form of constipation, indigestion and variously impeded speech, most notably in the silence about the question of the effigy which is preserved by the paralysed (and inaptly named) Barker. Historical fixation of this kind results both in an unhealthy lingering on the past and in that loss of relation between past and present which is described by the garage-owner Derek Kershaw when he meets Gerald:

> Perhaps you can tell me what happened in history after the Tudors. We never got any farther than Francis Drake and his bloody bowls at school. The glorious Armada, and back we

went each year to the Ancient Britons in their woad. Not a word about why things were like they are now.

(Wilson 1992: 82)

In all of this the allegedly pagan figure is associated with different kinds of divided identity, or blocked self-knowledge. In the most obvious sense, it stands for the division between a disruptive sexuality and the forms and requirements of social life, as seen in the various sexual irregularities and infidelities upon which Gerald broods – notably his own affair with Dollie Stokesay, the daughter-in-law of his mentor. It also suggests the possibility of a more lethal darkness that threatens Englishness at the very point of its origin, in the violent paganism of the 'Dark Ages' that, as luridly evoked by the novelist Clarissa Crane, prefigures both the Second World War and the prospect of an even greater annihilation:

> those extraordinary dark centuries, the faint twilight that flickers around the departing Romans and the real Arthur, the strange shapes thrown up by the momentary gleams of our knowledge, and, above all, the enormous sense of its relation to ourselves, its nowness, if I can call it that. The brilliant Romano-British world, the gathering shadows, and then the awful darkness pouring in.
>
> (Wilson 1992: 18–19)

It also stands for the distorted and partial acknowledgement of the relations between academic history and politics, as instanced in the simmering suspicions about Professor Stokesay's pro-German feeling in the years before the Second World War. These suspicions are borne out somewhat by the fabricated extract from Stokesay's *The Making of England*, said to have been published in 1930, which Wilson provides in the appendix to his novel. There Stokesay dismisses the claims of the historians he dubs 'Little Englanders', the 'romantic souls, the adherents of the Celtic cause', such as the dishevelled Rose Lorimer; they reflect, he says, the failure of the Celtic church to fall in with the 'Roman' qualities of 'political sense . . . worldly wisdom, authoritarianism . . . collective organization' which were necessary for England's greatness. The complexity of Stokesay's view of Englishness, which not only is defined against the distortions and vulgar excesses of German history but also borrows from and replicates some of its mythology of national origin and racial superiority for its account of 'the making of England', finds its parallel in the irony he points to regarding the reburial of Bishop Eorpwald's coffin to protect it from the invading Northmen:

> How terrified they would have been could they have stood with me on that marshy land on a warm July morning over one thousand years later and seen that their precious burden was a temple to the same unspeakable idol as was worshipped by the terrible barbarians from which they were fleeing.
> (Wilson 1992: 342)

If the invading Northmen are one form of hidden otherness buried at the origin of Englishness, then the Celt is another; and another parallel for the effigy within the novel is the pathetic misfit Larrie Rourke, an Irish juvenile delinquent who is taken up by Gerald Middleton's son John as his homosexual lover and is eventually driven out of the Hampstead circle to his comic-grotesque death.

The buried pagan figure also seems to stand in the novel for the failure to confront difficulty, guilt and evasion at the level of the individual psyche, as it is described by Gerald's son John:

> 'If you really care about this famous spiritual vacuum,' he said, 'I doubt if information is going to help. I think you will have to touch people at an unpleasantly personal level . . . Something we all guard desperately . . . The level at which we all prefer emptiness, because to fill it would mean facing something we prefer not to.'
> (Wilson 1992: 129–30)

Wilson works hard in the novel to produce the sense of typicality and inclusiveness appropriate to the depiction of the condition of England. Among its different competing constituents are the world of scholarship and the values associated with it, in Professor Clun's hypocritical evocation of 'that general standard of culture, that breadth of humane study which commands literary ability, worldly experience, and all the other penumbra of scholarship' (184), and the values of commerce, as embodied in the figure of Gerald's industrialist son Robin Middleton and cynically described by the arid sociologist Donald Consett: 'We live in Leviathan; expediency and power must presumably be our guides . . . If your only truth is jungle law, then the greater must devour the lesser' (103). John Middleton, in his role as media crusader on behalf of those abused by impersonal bureaucracy, seems to represent the embattled principle of individualism, even though it is plain that his power and influence are fatally entangled with the corporate power of publishing and the media. The novel also assumes the presence and force throughout of the centralised bureaucracy of the welfare state, though interestingly it never provides a dramatic instance of this constituent of postwar social life. And it attends to two distinct groups of deracinated or culturally transient persons. At one end of the scale, participating in high culture, but culturally high and dry, are the refined but declining *émigrés* such as Marie-Hélène Middleton, Gerald's daughter-in-law, and Stéphanie Houdet and her international wastrel son, Yves, with his slippery improvisation of languages and identities. At the other extreme are the various sexual and cultural outsiders, prostitutes, homosexuals, Irish and West Indians, who gather in Frank Rammage's Earl's Court lodging house. In a sense, nothing holds this group together other than their shared failure to belong to the Englishness which the novel aims to anatomise. Their homogenisation as the category of those who lie outside recognisable social-novelistic categories is both the concealment and the acknowledgement of the limits of the social imaginary in *Anglo-Saxon Attitudes*.

Gerald's problem in ascertaining the truth about the Anglo-Saxon figure is associated both with the problem of his chaotic personal life and with the problem of encompassing some more general truth about the nature of Englishness after the crises, conflicts and entanglements of the twentieth century. As with much nineteenth-century realist fiction, truth in this novel is a matter not of correspondence to facts but of perspective. What matters to the novel is the establishment of an angle of vision, or vantage point, from which widely separated issues and experiences can become commensurable, or graspable, as aspects of each other. Gerald's personal and professional paralysis at the beginning of the novel seems to come from his inability to bring together the two dimensions of truth:

> He had long felt that detailed scholarship such as Clun favoured was insufficient, disreputable, crossword-puzzle work, and historical generalizations were an equally disreputable pseudo-philosophic moralizing of the kind that old Stokesay had indulged in at the end of his life. All this seeking for the truth of the past should be in abeyance until we had reached some conclusions about the truth of the present. In

any case, who was he to dabble in truth-telling when he had evaded the truth, past and present, for most of his life?

(Wilson 1992: 15–16)

The bifurcation here between the detail and the whole is dramatised in the novel in a number of rather complex ways. The desiccated, dyspeptic Professor Clun, who is Gerald Middleton's rival, argues that the requirement for successful historical writing is 'depth of scholarship tried over years of organized research work' (183). Here, specialism is allied to a certain dream of cultural wholeness, but in a way that suggests not organic synthesis but a unity achieved by what it excludes or ignores. The opposite to Clun's austere fact-crunching might be the fabled Professor Stokesay, whose later career is summoned into Gerald's reminiscence by an exchange between his two sons about the problem of reconciling the particular and the general:

> 'I was always careful to say what was true,' said John.
> 'Oh! I've no doubt,' Robin stirred his coffee furiously; 'all sorts of little pinpricking, puking bits of candour that matter to nobody set against the wider truth of the situation the country's in.'
>
> (Wilson 1992: 99–100)

The words he hears remind Gerald of Stokesay's specious justification of his support for the policy of negotiating with Nazi Germany:

> Don't think I can't appreciate what you feel, Gerald – integrity of scholarship and so on. I don't at all like some of the nonsense our friends in Germany call history nowadays myself. But that sort of thing, one's distaste for this and that, has all got to be set against the wider truth of the situation the country's in.
>
> (Wilson 1992: 101–2)

For Gerald, it is precisely this apparent attention to 'a wider and wider canvas', the openness to larger structures of relationship and connection, which condemns Stokesay to dishonesty, compromise and complicity. But Gerald's disgust at Stokesay's naive recruitment to Nazi appeasement produces in him a recoil which is an equal and opposite kind of disconnection from the real:

> Lionel Stokesay had gone on and on and up and up. As

though he was running away from reality. And as Stokesay's gas balloon had floated away into outer space, Gerald had found himself shrinking from his own high aspirations, refusing the wider implications of his own work, all out of distaste at the spectacle of such empty eminence.

(Wilson 1992: 102)

The problem here is not just that the particular and the general have fallen apart from each other; it is that, in its extreme form, each perspective can loop into the other. Dogged particularism of the kind demanded by Professor Clun, or practised by John Middleton in his campaigning for the isolated individual, can itself become abstract, formulaic and glassily idealised. This is shown when John Middleton's secretary explains saltily to Gerald that their campaigning office never meets the individuals whose causes they espouse, since they are 'concerned with injustice to individuals. Nice abstract individuals – Pelican the wicked bureaucrat and Cressett the exploited little man. We don't want to get mixed up with personalities' (61). On the other hand, an attention to the 'wider truth' is always vulnerable to a kind of irresponsibility that is itself partial and fragmenting.

Gerald's struggle to achieve a truthful, or at least inclusive, perspective on his personal and professional difficulty acts out a problem of social meaning and interpretation which, while scarcely unprecedented, was taking more and more intensified forms in postwar Britain. On the one hand, social and political realities were becoming more and more tightly organised and administered than ever before, and the impingement of the impersonal upon individual lives was becoming more and more marked. At the same time, there was a growing apprehension that, despite the forging of a revived sense of national purpose, the real centres of power and influence were irreversibly elsewhere. This is the period of the vogue for French existentialism in Britain, an ethical philosophy which, in its popularised forms, dramatised exactly the split between the impersonality and inauthentic *en-soi* itness of abstract structures of power and the absolute, because absolutely absurd, self-definition of the estranged individual.

For the F. R. Leavis whose *The Great Tradition* had been published in 1948, it was plain where we were to look for a restoration of the organic wholeness that the forces of modern capitalist rationality were so remorselessly sundering and stultifying. For Leavis, the novel was the form in which wholeness of design can penetrate and harmonise every atom of particularity without blunting or thwarting any of their rich precision. If it is true that Leavis had little confidence in the capacity of the contemporary novel to speak on behalf of life against the technocratic, bureaucratic nightmare that he saw building every day, his grandiose claims for the novel as a form pervade the period, and stimulate the sense both of aspiration and of niggling unease within postwar novels about England. Q. D. Leavis paid more attention to the contemporary novel than did her husband, but was even more disdainful of it, and nostalgic for the specifically English mixture of humane inclusiveness and experiential minuteness that she found in the work of George Eliot and other nineteenth-century realists. The waning of the English novel, or of what Q. D. Leavis could still in 1981 call the 'Englishness' of that novel, is due to the loss of what she believes to be a specifically English condition of unified and interconnected national life, to be replaced by the conditions of contemporary squalor catalogued in this booming indictment:

> The England that bore the classical English novel has gone forever, and we can't expect a country of high-rise flat dwellers, office workers and factory robots and unassimilated multi-racial minorities, with a suburbanized countryside, factory farming, sexual emancipation without responsibility, rising crime and violence, and the Trade Union mentality, to give rise to a literature comparable with the novel tradition of so different a past.
>
> (Q. D. Leavis 1983: 325)

Nevertheless, she speaks for many in her conviction that 'the novel is the art most influenced by national life in all its minute particulars' (ibid: 303), and in her explicit identification with the form of the novel with the form of national consciousness itself.

If *Anglo-Saxon Attitudes* protects itself with a wry, self-mocking irony against this aspiration to unify the forms of novel and nation, it does not altogether suppress it. Novels and novel writing in general come in for a certain amount of ridicule throughout the book. Clarissa Crane in particular functions as a sort of negative self-image, an example of the vacuously sentimental generalisation from which Wilson's comedy of exact discrimination wishes to distance itself. It does so partly by means of its reiterated – though also repeatedly undermined – contrast between fiction and history.

Despite the sniffy disavowal of Rose Lorimer ('we think Gerald Middleton's a great stylist,' said Rose, and added archly, 'but then we're not novelists'; 21) and the fastidious sneer of Professor Clun reviewing her book ('her book, in the last resort, is more a fit subject for the critic of historical fiction than for the historian proper'; 345), and despite the scornful portrait of the Gallic historian Armand Sarthe, with all his pseudo-historical gossip about the mysterious essence of 'Woman' through the ages, there is a continual interchange between history and fiction in the book. Indeed, the professional practice of history acts as a displaced way of talking about the function of narration, since its crises of procedure and perspective so closely match those of the novel itself.

The problem is that the irony that works to protect Wilson's novel against falling into vulgar commitment to a particular position, or a particular diagnosis of the condition of England, also disallows the claims of the genre with which the work uneasily identifies itself. There are hints through the novel that the work of Dickens is being projected as a model. This is evident in some of the discreet symbolism, such as the references to pervasive fog that, borrowing from the opening descriptions of Dickens's *Bleak House* (1853), establish the inertness and nullity of metropolitan cultured life: 'Fog seemed to have seeped into the Regency dining-room. Marie-Hélène's complexion and the bottle-green evening dress seemed full of it. The pretentious food tasted of it' (33). But there is also a complicated moment when the presence of Dickens, and the great encompassing social novel that the middle period of his work typifies, becomes quite manifest in *Anglo-Saxon Attitudes*. When John Middleton refers to his brother's plan to provide a safe haven for the civil servant driven from his post by John in one of his campaigns against bureaucracy, he evokes Dickens's exposure of the relations between commercial and political corruption in *Little Dorrit* (1857):

> What a partnership! Robin Middleton, the head of our greatest steel-construction business, the champion of 'more free-enterprise houses for all', and Selwyn Pelican, one of our top red-tape manufacturers, the champion of that rousing slogan, 'Every brick laid means a civil servant paid'. With their combined pull on the noose, who dares to say old England won't be hanged? It's Merdle and the Barnacles all

over again, and, by God, we need another Dickens to blow them off the face of the country.

(Wilson 1992: 108)

Here, Wilson not only identifies his work with the very possibility of a totalising critical and moral grasp on a complex and fragmented society that *Little Dorrit* seems to represent but also carefully distinguishes his work from it; the grandeur and ambition of such a novel must be backed away from if this novel is to retain its seeming ironic flexibility.

This is the mark, really, of the failure of *Anglo-Saxon Attitudes* to provide either the satiric anatomy or the healing wholeness of vision to which it aspires. If the novel as a form seems to have imprinted in it the expectation that an adequately inclusive vantage point on a complex social reality is always achievable, then the unavailability of such a perspective seems to have become a structural feature of the contemporary social conditions to which Wilson's novel attends, with its own kind of defeated fidelity. This results in a number of uneasy irregularities in the book's narrational manner: the relaxed, elastic voice that can nevertheless harden into icy distance, as in the brutal disposal of the ne'er-do-well Larrie Rourke (305); the swings between the vagrant familiarity of the narrative eye, and a more austerely Jamesian adhesion to Gerald's unifying, but restricted point of view; the uncertainty of fit between the novel's delight in farce and grotesque caricature and the serious and respectful attention paid to Gerald's not very dramatic seeming personal problems; the simultaneous seriousness and triviality of the central preoccupation of the book, which is offered at once as a complex symbol of the uncertainties of English and British identity and as a self-conscious pretext or organising device. Perhaps most notably, there is the odd relation between the cosmopolitanism or hybridity that the novel seems at least implicitly to recommend over the narcissistic fixation upon the defence of Englishness, and its own tendency to rely for comic effect on comic stereotypes of national character, even where it appears to be offering such judgements as examples of an undesirable narrowness of sensibility. The novel is also stiflingly restricted in social range, offering as 'typical' an assortment of social groups and connections drawn from a markedly narrow social, ethnic and regional band. This is the more striking given the intermittent but regular acknowledgement in the novel of the importance of the local or regional as against the centralised or national view of social and political truth. The novel is able satirically to suggest the necessity of an opening outwards of Englishness, but replicates some of the self-absorbed enclosure of its characters in being unable to accommodate, except in the form of admittedly sometimes affectionate caricature, working class or non-English characters, especially female characters, such as Mrs Salad. Thus, although it recommends the advantages of turning Englishness inside out, or of opening it to various sorts of otherness, the novel remains locked within the very narcissism and fixation it discloses.

The novel, in fact, depends upon the maintained authority of the omniscient voice, or the 'view from nowhere', against all the evidence that it itself amasses. There is, however, one moment when the appearance of smooth authority is allowed to fracture. It comes during the description of how Ingeborg Middleton attempts to persuade a reluctant little boy to sing at her Christmas party:

> When no sound came from his terror-struck mouth, she bent down from the heavens above and placing her huge doll's face close to his, she asked, 'What is the matter, Maurice? Have the trolls bewitched your tongue?' so creating a deep psychic trauma that was to cause him to be court-martialled for cowardice many years later in World War III.
>
> (Wilson 1992: 86)

This is the only moment when the narrative voice is allowed to display this degree of command by projecting us beyond the confines of the novel to which it belongs. In doing so, it also dramatises its own hubristic undoing, for the claim to the long perspective that could include the next world war is a demonstration of its unlikelihood. If the comment is evidence of how quickly a sense of the inevitability of another war had established itself after 1945, its comedy depends upon the widespread apprehension that the imminence of another war might mean the end not only of all history but also of any possibility of narrative from any surviving point of view. (The challenges to narrative representation represented by the prospect of nuclear annihilation are discussed in chapter 6, below.)

More emphatically than Wilson's comically and perturbedly qualified evocation of Englishness, Margaret Drabble's *The Ice Age* (1977) announces itself from the outset as an anatomy of the malaise of the nation. Like *Anglo-Saxon Attitudes*, the novel centres on the experience and perceptions of one character, who is caught, as the novel begins, at a point of symbolic transition. As a middle-class Oxford graduate, Anthony Keating has drifted first into the fringes of the entertainment industry and then into the BBC. His subsequent movement into the world of property development has acquainted him with the exhilaration of success and the devastation of financial collapse and near ruin, accompanied in his case by a heart attack. Anthony's transition marks a more general cultural conflict and transformation, as the still powerful, but ever more embattled traditional forms of cultural authority represented by linked institutions such as Oxbridge and the BBC are challenged and disrupted by the nakedly brutal values of competition and no-holds-barred 1970s free enterprise. The novel isolates Anthony classically at his, and the nation's, moment of choice, offering in the prospect of his transformation or adjustment a larger story about the condition of England: 'A senile Britain casting out its ghosts. Or a Go Ahead Britain, with oil-rig men toasting their mistresses in champagne in the pubs of Aberdeen? And himself where? A man of the past, the present, the future?' (Drabble 1978: 201)

So the novel seems to have the apparatus necessary for a contemporary condition of England novel: the allegorical character in transition, facing the dual prospect of ruin and recovery; the concentric circles of characters ranged about him, with their various interconnections and thematic echoes, the balancing and mutual illumination of the small and the large, the slow *pavane* of complication yielding to resolution, in the building consummation of the design. But the striking feature of *The Ice Age* is that there is so much interior resistance to this classical structure. I have suggested that, in the condition of England novel of the postwar period, there is an intensifying, if subterranean concern with the condition of the novel form itself. In *The Ice Age* there is a sense of strain and uncertainty, as the novel has to be forced to run in its assigned channel. Certain of the elements seem ineffective or terminally implausible: most notably the confidence in the capacity of the novel to identify the typifying cluster of particulars, to maintain the balance between contingency and thematic purpose which is essential to this kind of novel. Consequently, *The Ice Age* ends up as a poker-faced but nevertheless rather desperate simulation of the novel it would like to be.

The result is a novel that does not fall short of its ambition to measure the life of the individual and the life of the nation but

CONDITIONS OF ENGLAND

instead desperately overshoots that ambition. At strategic moments, the novel is perforated by passages of Dickensian denunciation, as though to summon by sheer prophetic fervour the nationhood that otherwise dumbly eludes articulation:

> Not everybody in Britain on that night in November was alone, incapacitated or in jail. Nevertheless, over the country depression lay like fog, which was just about all that was missing to lower spirits even further, and there was even a little of that in East Anglia. All over the nation, families who had listened to the news looked at one another and said 'Goodness me' or 'Whatever next' or 'I give up' or 'Well, fuck that', before embarking on an evening's viewing of colour television, or a large hot meal, or a trip to the pub, or a choral society evening. All over the country, people blamed other people for all the things that were going wrong – the trades unions, the present government, the miners, the car workers, the seamen, the Arabs, the Irish, their own husbands, their own wives, their own idle good-for-nothing offspring, comprehensive education. Nobody knew whose fault it really was, but most people managed to complain fairly forcefully about somebody: only a few were stunned into honourable silence.
>
> (Drabble 1978: 62)

The problem here is not just one of novelistic tact, in the sudden wrench away from the scrupulous, moderating, free indirect style of the novel into prophetic rant, though this is relevant. What is revealed in the sheer implausibility of passages such as this one is the panicky desire for a fusing intensity of crisis which is continually diffused by the numbed banality and lowered affect of the condition Drabble is describing. A little like *Anglo-Saxon Attitudes*, the passage borrows some historical authority from its passing allusion to the omnipresent fog of *Bleak House*, but the imaginative poverty of its evocation of Britain, with its crude sneering and deliberated carelessness of distinctions, displays a kind of narrowness that seems curiously of a piece with the malaise it demands that its reader acknowledge:

> there they all were in their large houses and their small houses, with their first mortgages and second mortgages, in their rented flats and council flats and basement bedsits and their caravans: stuck, congealed, amongst possessions, in

attitudes, in achievements they had hoped next month to shed, and with which they were now condemned to live.

(Drabble 1978: 63)

The deadening grip of the narrative on its subject here enforces the very homogeneity it denounces.

The problem of perspective is also a problem of voice. The kind of panoramic sweep that the novel seems to force itself into also requires a vatic, or prophetic, voice which is painfully at odds with the cautious contingency of the realistic narrative voice that dominates in the novel. Such a voice, if it were to be procured, might also magically requisition its own raptly consenting audience. A little later on, indeed, the passage attempts to borrow such a voice:

> A huge icy fist, with large cold fingers, was squeezing and chilling the people of Britain, that great and puissant nation, slowing down their blood, locking them into immobility, fixing them in a solid stasis, like fish in a frozen river.
>
> (Drabble 1978: 62–3)

The allusion is to the passage from Milton's *Areopagitica* (1644) which Drabble supplies as the epigraph to her novel, which renders the vision of 'a noble and puissant Nation rousing herself like a strong man after sleep, and shaking her invincible locks' (Milton 1959: 557–8, quoted in Drabble 1978: 5). The point here is precisely that the voice is a borrowed one, its cultural portability undoing its authority.

In a sense, the homogenisation of the subject and the homogenisation of the novel's address are closely equivalent. The vision of England (or Britain – the novel seems to vary its designations according to whether it wishes to signal declining contemporary political or economic conditions, for which it refers to Britain, or to summon a more mythical conception of the nation, in which case it will refer to England) is also a kind of apostrophe, which is addressed to the personified form of the nation it has as its subject. If on the one hand the passage issues a reproach to the nation for failing to cohere in the shared subjectivity which would make it a fit addressee, on the other hand its attack on the nation and its drearily identical inhabitants itself again brings about a sort of levelling unification. The vehement rhetoric of the reproach issued to the absent addressee thus squeezes it into factitious existence.

Accompanying and assisting these forms of homogenisation is

the novel's insistent use of symbolism. The subjugation of the national will and the narrowing of its spirit is suggested throughout by images of ice and cold, from the lack of heating in Anthony Keating's country cottage to the frigid conditions in the prison that houses Anthony's unscrupulous associate, Len Wincobank. The images of cold, suggesting lowered vitality and a generalised rigor mortis across the nation, often cooperate with images of confinement or immurement, as in the story remembered by Anthony of an old woman, buried in her cottage by snowfall for two days (41). These images of cold and deathly disconnection are predictably countered by images suggesting the heat of activity, for example in the search for 'fiercer and fiercer condiments' shared by Anthony and Len when under stress. The possibility of change, revival and renewal is suggested especially in images of birds: the pheasant which, in the opening lines of the novel, plops improbably and emblematically into Anthony's frozen pond after having suffered a heart attack, gives way to the rare, annunciatory bird which Anthony sees as 'a messenger from God, an angel, a promise . . . fluttering away its tiny life' (287) in the course of his enlightening imprisonment, at the end of the novel, in a camp in the East European country of Wallachia (287).

The point about such images is that they act as a displacement of, or compensation for, the cohering, inclusive picture which the novel seems to feel unable to supply in any other fashion. But *The Ice Age* ends by acknowledging its own limits. It is able only to hint at the possibility of happiness and rebirth for Anthony in his austere confinement in the Wallachian camp. The complicity of the 'we' that is summoned up in the narrative is weakened by the very circumscription of the novel's scope:

> This book too, like Anthony's, could have been about life in that camp. But one cannot enter the camp, with Anthony Keating. It is not for us; it is not, anyway, now, yet, for us. But we must acknowledge, we must pay our respects, within our limitations. Into some of Anthony's experience, we can enter.
> (Drabble 1978: 286)

Even bleaker is the sense of retraction in the final lines of the book which leave Alison tending her handicapped daughter Molly: 'Alison, there is no leaving. Alison can neither live nor die. Alison has Molly. Her life is beyond imagining. It will not be imagined. Britain will recover, but not Alison Murray' (287). The offhanded suggestion of Britain's economic recovery is in fact undermined by the novel's acknowledgement of the unrepresentability of individual lives within Britain. The real problem with Britain, these lines seem to suggest, is not so much its unprofitability or powerlessness but its unimaginability, its incapacity to be pictured and integrated.

The recession years that followed the boom of the mid-1970s were characterised by an obsessive debate about declining national prestige and prosperity, involving mourning and reparative narratives of all kinds. Far from providing a vital and cohering vision to a nation deprived of it, *The Ice Age*, along with Margaret Drabble's later novels, such as *The Middle Ground* (1980) and *The Radiant Way*, falls in altogether too unresistingly with the characteristic generalisations, national personifications and self-designations of the period (indeed its metaphor of the ice age resurfaces in the idea of the 'winter of discontent' of industrial conflict in 1978–9). Drabble has acknowledged in an interview that 'the whole idea [for *The Ice Age*] came from reading papers', and pointed to the gap between representations of Britain in the public media and in fiction, remarking that 'there was an enormous amount of economic analysis in the papers, but nothing on the subject of declining Britain in fiction at all' (Drabble 1978: 48). In this, there is an interesting development in the twenty years or so that separate *Anglo-Saxon Attitudes* from *The Ice Age*. In the period following the Second World War, there was a narrative problem in matching the diversifying social and political experience to an increasingly unconvincing prolongation of the state of national unity produced not wholly artificially during the War. This disjuncture provides *Anglo-Saxon Attitudes* with a difficulty and a comic opportunity. For Drabble's novel, the problem lies not only in the state of decline and conflict affecting the nation but also in the overdefinition of the condition and nature of the nation, in that excessive self-production in fantasy and media facsimile which is the proof of its disappearance.

Drabble's *The Radiant Way*, written a decade or so later, looks back on the years following on the period dealt with in *The Ice Age*; beginning on New Year's Eve, 1980, after a few months of the Conservative government elected to power in 1979, it follows its characters through to the mid-1980s. The novel shares many concerns with *The Ice Age*. Like the earlier novel, it measures and is in a sense structured around the tension between the postwar ideals of a national common culture, as they were embodied in the Welfare State and in economic, educational, arts and broadcasting policies more broadly, and the marked return to *laissez-faire* economics and the corresponding abandonment of such assimilatory cultural ideals from 1979 onwards. This was a period of renewed class and cultural division which seemed to many to be not merely a byproduct of Thatcherism but also the systematic effect of a top-down class antagonism.

The diagnosis of the conditions of British life offered by *The Radiant Way* is bleak enough. The novel centres on the interlinked lives of three women, each of them graduates from Cambridge during the same period shortly after the War: Liz Headeland, who has become a successful psychoanalyst with a judicious blend of National Health and private practice, Esther Breuer, whose Jewish family fled from Central Europe before the War, and who maintains a certain detachment from English life as a freelance art historian, and Alix Bowen, who teaches English part-time in a rehabilitation centre for delinquent girls. With considerably more subtlety and differentiating range than *The Ice Age*, *The Radiant Way* establishes the intermediary position of the three women. At Cambridge, they are linked by their sense of shared displacement, 'a sense of being on the margins of English life, looking in from a cold street through a lighted window into a warm lit room that later might prove to be their own' (Drabble 1988: 90). But as their lives develop, and as they move inwards to the geographical and cultural centres of British life, their interrelationship, and the web of further family and professional relationships that ramifies from and between them, is offered as a pattern of British life. The novel attempts in this way to offer a general portrait of the condition of England without collapsing the particularity of specific groups and forms of community. The focus on the shared experience of women's lives is significant here. It links closely with the growing confidence of women and women writers and the increasing visibility and dignity of forms of female collectivity during the 1980s in Britain and elsewhere, which had themselves stimulated and been stimulated by representations of women's individual and collective lives in forms such as the novel. The ambivalent or mobile position of middle-class women, as simultaneously participants in and marginal to authoritative cultural institutions and professions, provides the particular perspectival advantage that Drabble requires in this novel. The condition of England (here it is England,

and not Britain, for the 'other' of metropolitan life is Northern working-class English life) is glimpsed or connoted obliquely, without overstatement or impatient homogenisation, but equally without abandoning the orientation toward wholeness and inclusiveness. The novel begins with an account of a New Year's Eve party in Liz Headeland's house, the description of which suggests the tenuous, but still persistent possibility of relationship between the inside and the outside, observer and participant. An important connection is made in this scene between Drabble's novel of the 1980s and the oblique female perspective which is so important in many Victorian and Edwardian novels. Preparing for her party, Liz Headeland remembers how 'as a child, reading her mother's collection of Victorian novels, Edwardian novels, she had wondered how women could bear to renounce their position in the centre of the matrimonial stage' and she substitutes a more hopeful view of the female observer, which places her at the centre of a rich network of generational continuity and social relatedness:

> No, the observer was filled and informed with a quick and lively and long-established interest in all those that passed before, in all those that moved and circled and wheeled around, was filled with intimate connections and loving memories and hopes and concerns and prospects. Nor was the observer impotent, for it was through the potency of the observer that these children took their being and took the floor. Actual children, children of the heart and the imagination, old friends, new friends, the children of friends, they circle, they weave, and the pattern is both one's own and not one's own, it is the making of generations. One is no longer the hopeful or the despairing guest: one is host in the house of oneself.
>
> (Drabble 1988: 14)

Where her earlier work had identified itself closely with the forms and ambitions of the realist novel, Drabble's later work has supplemented this with narrative forms and techniques that owe more to the female modernist novel associated with writers such as Virginia Woolf and, more recently, Sara Maitland. The beginning of *The Radiant Way* builds up the sense of social solidarity through a slow participial incrementation which aims to intimate affinity without prematurely imposing wholeness; there is a striking similarity between such descriptions and equivalent evocations of connectedness in the representation of social gatherings in Virginia Woolf's *Mrs Dalloway* (1925) or *The Years* (1937):

> Liz, moving from group to group, surveying from the stairway, engaging and disengaging, tacking and occasionally swooping, was pleased with what she saw. They were mixing and mingling, her guests; the young were speaking to the old, men were speaking to women, Left was speaking to Right, art unto science.
>
> (Drabble 1988: 26)

Two central motifs of *The Radiant Way* embody the alternatives of unity and division. First of all, there is the 'radiant way' itself, which is the title of a television series produced by Charles Headeland in 1965, which is said to have encouraged the move towards comprehensive education by the Labour Government. The narrative reports a little enviously on Charles Headeland's ambition, apparently still a feasible one in 1965, 'to speak to the whole nation, in a language the whole nation would understand: the language of film' (179), and, as we saw in chapter 1, on Charles's memory of the production team that collectively brought it about, which he sees as a microcosm of a common culture. The image of the radiant way is contradicted progressively through the novel by images of severed heads, stimulated by periodic reports of the 'Harrow Road Horror', a series of murders in which the victims are decapitated. These are accompanied by Esther Breuer's dreams of being spoken to by a severed head. The severed head images the conditions of division and conflict that the novel shows developing through the 1980s. These reach a climax at a political level with the struggles of the miners' strike of 1984–5 and at a personal and sexual level with Liz Headeland's partial intuiting of the secret kept hidden through her childhood of her abuse by her father. The secret comes to light at the same time as she unearths a copy of another work with the title *The Radiant Way*, a child's reading primer whose title Charles had ironically borrowed for his utopian TV series (384–5). Britain, poised at the beginning of the 1980s as the novel opens, can still be pictured as an hospitable house, connecting, if only temporarily, the different areas of national life. By the end of the novel, this ideal image has shrunk back, as we see Alix, Liz and Esther 'becalmed, enisled' (366) in the back room of Esther's flat, while the police move in to arrest the Harrow Road murderer, the unknown 'monster under your roof' (368) who occupies the upstairs flat.

The bleakness of the diagnosis of the state of British life contained in this novel, as it is mediated through the perceptions of Alix Bowen, has much in common with that of *The Ice Age*: 'The nation is divided as never before, the Labour movement is in ruins, the self-deception of some of Brian's friends has reached the proportions of mass psychosis' (391). It is true that there is a greater complexity and expansiveness in the design of the novel, along with the enlargement of technique and perspective mentioned earlier. There is a more nuanced sense of the relations between written narrative and visual media such as TV, and a subtle and ironic sense of its realist predecessors, for example in the slowly dying palm tree owned by Esther Breuer, which recalls the stubbornly surviving core of suburban Englishness imaged in the aspidistra plant of George Orwell's *Keep the Aspidistra Flying* (1936). All of this suggests an augmented confidence in the power of the novel to forge a cohering vision of the social whole. At the same time, it must be said that the novel's formal development and confidence in its powers are blunted by the same movement of imaginative retreat to be found at the end of *The Ice Age*. As in that earlier novel, the divisions of society come to be an assault not merely on social ideals of collectivity but also on the aesthetic ideal of imaginative reach and assimilation that is embodied in cultural forms such as the novel and, at its utopian moment of inclusiveness, the TV. Charles Headeland has been lured away from programme production into media management and we hear at the end of the novel that he has gone mad, imagining he hears voices in the sky; he has been driven to it, Liz suggests, by 'the dish receiver' (353). The failure of connection is envisaged precisely as a failure of the power to envisage:

> Once, thought Alix, I had a sense of such lives, of such peaceable, ordinary, daily lives. I could envisage interiors, clothes drying on fireguards, pots of tea in the hearth, a pot plant on a window-sill. Now I see them no more. I see horrors. I imagine horrors.
>
> (Drabble 1988: 337)

In a similar way, Liz reads through the newspaper cuttings that she discovers after her mother's death and is unable either to put them plausibly together or to relate them to her life: 'The mess of paper jumped and swam before her eyes. One could make any story out of these fragments... One could rearrange these pieces as one wished, like the jigsaw scraps of an experimental novel' (383). *The Radiant Way* here seems pushed to the odd expedient of including within the frame and fabric of the realistic social novel a modernist or postmodernist registering of disjuncture or unrepresentability. In its anxiety about its own capacities, the novel succeeds, oddly, in acting out with fidelity more general misgivings about the retreat or failure of the 'social' which have proliferated in the last couple of decades.

One of the most remarkable developments in postwar British literature has been the rise of university fiction or the campus novel. The usefulness and attraction of the university campus for the novelist is in many ways easy to account for. The university is a closed world, with its own norms and values, which is thick with the possibilities of intrigue. Indeed, the very restriction of elements in the academic world, the stock characters, with their cosily familiar routines of evasion and abstraction and their conspicuous, if always insecure, hierarchical structures, and the well-established situations and plot-lines, seem to generate a sense of permutative abundance. Given this, the prosperity of a sub-genre such as the university detective novel, as exemplified in Dorothy L. Sayers's *Gaudy Night* (1935) or in the novels of 'Amanda Cross' or Colin Dexter, is hardly surprising. However, if it were just the boundedness of the university setting that made it so irresistible, we would expect to see much more than we do in the way of military fiction, monastery fiction and other fiction set in enclosed worlds. There are instructive overlaps here, however, for example in the military academy novel popular in the USA, and the case of a novel such as Umberto Eco's *The Name of the Rose* (1980), whose monastic setting is what allows it to operate as a mediaeval campus novel; and it is clear that the donné of the collection of schoolboys marooned on a desert island allows William Golding to write a sort of primitivist campus novel in *Lord of the Flies*. In fact, the university or academic setting has been useful for postwar novelists precisely because the membrane of self-satisfaction that surrounds it is never sufficiently worldtight but, on the contrary, is permeable by the alien and disruptive forces of politics, sexuality and crime. The occupants of these worlds are thus subject to threats from the outside, and the fact that the majority of the university's inhabitants are there only temporarily gives the academic institution itself a structural impermanence and vulnerability.

The academic novel therefore has two principal narrative structures, though they are typically combined with each other in varying proportions: the one concerns the disruption of a closed world, and the gradual return of order and regularity to it, while the other concerns the passage through this closed world of a character who must in the end be allowed to escape its gravitational pull. The one is institutional, and allied to what Roman Jakobson called the paradigmatic axis of selection; the other is individual, and skewed towards the syntagmatic axis, or axis of combination. Typical of one is the detective story, in which the aim is to neutralise the menace of an enigma; typical of the other is the *Bildungsroman*, or novel of development, in which the aim is to define the terms of a freedom.

But the academic novel can perform another, rather more historically concrete function, in imaging the more general condition of the nation. The academic novel offers interesting opportunities to explore conflicts and transitions between competing values and structures of belief as well as between different ideological time-scales. As Terry Eagleton has observed, the university in contemporary British society is both inside and outside society (1988: 93–4); both an asocial enclave, protected from the uncertainties and excesses of the social, and yet also an exact scale model of it, a burnished surface on which the dangerous and unpredictable lines of force of the social and political world may be seen faintly but finely incised.

All this responds to some of the marked changes in the university life in Britain after the war. With the marked and steady increase in the provision of university places, along with the widening of aspiration to and of participation in higher education among lower middle class and working class students, the university in postwar Britain began to become something rather more than the repository of privilege. Although the universities remained overwhelmingly middle-class institutions, it seemed to many that they were the very sign and symbol of the levelling of class distinction promised by the postwar cultural consensus. Kingsley Amis, himself the author of one of the most influential of campus novels, *Lucky Jim* (1953), was quite clear about the cultural decline that he associated with this egalitarianism: 'More', he mourned, 'means worse.' But if for some the passage through the universities and on into the cultural and political institutions of the country of more and different kinds of student meant the disastrous elimination of distinction, for those experiencing the transition, it usually meant something very different; the abrasion of different worlds, and the stubborn, troubling persistence, even the reassertion, of difference. Thus, many of the most significant campus novels highlight the problems of survival and adjustment of the various kinds of displaced person who are their heroes – from Jim in Amis's *Lucky Jim*, through to Tom Sharpe's *Porterhouse Blue* (1973) and others.

It is this which allows the campus novel or academic fiction to present miniaturised versions of the condition of England theme. But there is another, less often remarked advantage offered by the academic novel. As we saw in chapter 1, the readership of literary fiction was increasingly being defined by its relationship to education, and especially to the teaching of English literature which had come to be the principal vehicle for imparting cultural distinction and competence in the university curriculum. Here, the teaching of English had already undergone something of the same revolution that the universities underwent as a whole in the postwar period and for some of the same reasons. Spurred largely by the arrival in the ancient universities after the First World War of lower middle class and grammar-school educated children such as F. R. Leavis, English literature began to define itself in violent dissent from the gentlemanly, belletrist traditions that dominated in Oxford and Cambridge. From being a channel for the spontaneous and intuitive reproduction of class and cultural distinctions, English literature became a laboratory for the dissection of values and the distinctions that were related to them. Ironically, the more the cultural criticism associated with F. R. Leavis and the *Scrutiny* group after the Second World War entered the cultural mainstream, as more and more students who had encountered the ideas of Leavis or his associates began to teach in schools, the more bitterly it represented itself as embattled and marginal. Leavisite criticism, with its fiercely aggressive nostalgia for an epoch in which the values of culture were central rather than peripheral, was egalitarian in essence, and easily modifiable to a set of educational practices in schools and universities that depended on intelligence and learned skill rather than intuitive inherited sensibility. But it derived much of its critical force from the gloomy resentment about its own increasing irrelevance in the modern world, in which the demands of the market were coming more and more to define the aims and outcomes of education. This resulted in the irony of an egalitarianism which expressed itself in terms of a defensive maintaining of standards and cultural distinctions. Such an irony corresponds exactly, of course, to the position of many of the new participants in higher education after the War. Their own experience made them suspicious of the sedimented power of tradition and cultural authority, but also anxious that the forms of cultural distinction which gave them their own newly achieved and precarious social and professional authority should be defended against the levelling effects of mass culture and the market.

The fact that many of the novelists concerned with the narration of the condition of England have been closely associated with university life is not coincidental. This is not just because of the actual and symbolic centrality of the university as an index of social changes and pressures, but also because of the concern about the nature of national and cultural identity within the universities during the postwar period. As Brian Doyle has argued, the apparent institutional success of English as a subject in the universities has actually been achieved at the cost or even, in some quarters, the relieved abandonment of the link between English literature and Englishness as such. This came about partly as a precondition of the postwar adaptation of the universities to the demands for a more flexible kind of intellectual training (Doyle 1989: 77–8) and partly as a necessary response to the diffusive effect of the arrival of large numbers of students wishing to study English but not possessed by background or training of the kind of receptive sensibility apparently necessary to the fostering of a sense of Englishness (ibid.: 112–13). Nevertheless, it is plain that the diversification of the universities and their simultaneous integration into and separation from broader social contexts, as they became more and more governed by economic demands while less and less ideologically serviceable to social and political life as a whole, has produced complex reactions not only within academic life and theory but also within the contemporary literary and fictional forms in which Englishness has been imagined and reimagined. There are in fact queer and striking correlations between the attempt to narrate the contemporary condition of England in fiction and attempts to construct or reexamine ideas about the Englishness of English writing. The problem of representing England, and, as I shall say, of finding a plausible or appropriate audience and form of address for such a representation, is closely related to the seemingly more parochial problem of how, if at all, the social value of literary representation itself is to be defended. It is for this reason that my account of the condition of England novel will need to consider in a moment the particular variant of this form of fiction represented by such a campus novel as David Lodge's *Nice Work*.

The fact that most campus novels tend to be about English teachers or students has not gone unremarked, but is of course not very surprising, even given the hostility to traffic or fraternisation between the critical and creative realms characteristic of the teaching of English literature since the War. What is less often remarked is what this implies about the addressivity of such novels, which is to say, their sense of their readership and the different attitudes to it that they may have. In the case of the campus novel, we may say that there is a simultaneous sense of confidence and uncertainty in this structure of address. The campus novel appears to be addressed to an ideal audience constituted by the more generalised experience of higher education, an audience who can be flattered, entertained and reassured by recognition of a familiar world and by their sense that, after all, the experience of higher education was still available only to a small minority of the population. But it is also addressed to the outsider or non-participant in university life. This is not just a matter of an awareness of (at least) two different kinds of typical reader for the academic novel; it is a sense of the dividedness of actual readers, who may feel that they both do and do not belong to the academic world through which they may or may not have passed. This sense of divided address is often explicitly thematised in the conflict of academic and non-academic values in the campus novel, as, for example, in Malcolm Bradbury's *The History Man* (1975) and *Rates of Exchange* (1983) and David Lodge's *Changing Places* (1975), *Small World* (1984) and *Nice Work* (1988). Sometimes this conflict takes an endogenous form, as in *The History Man* and *Small World*, in which an easygoing, leisured English academic life is disrupted by the alien competitiveness of US-style academic professionalism. Sometimes – and more frequently in campus novels produced during the 1980s, the period when British university life was under most economic and ideological assault – the conflict is between academic values and the values of the world 'outside', often the industrial or commercial world. As we will see, this is especially the case with *Nice Work*.

Interestingly, the sense of divided or compounded address also affects such novels' sense of their own status and function. For

Leavisite literary criticism, as we have seen, the novel occupied a special place; dangerously poised between the realms of the mass market and high culture, the novel stood as the guarantee of a culture unified around human values rather than the abstractions of modernity. One may imagine that the very complicity with the market-place and its pacified mass readerships that delayed the novel's acceptance as a serious literary form was what in part recommended it to a Leavisism which was itself socially and politically divided between a suspicious elitism and a more enlarged and inclusive sense of culture. The novel, we may say, was the visible sign of the possibility of the redemption of mass culture, of the sacramental transformability of pleasure into intelligence, mere mass into the distinctions of form.

We should therefore not be surprised to find that the specific versions of the condition of England theme to be found in the form of the academic novel encode interesting ambivalences. These concern not only what may be called the addressive range of the novel, which is to say, its power to address enough readers and to address them in a direct enough way to make good its imaginative and analytical claims, but also the status and function of the narrative and the novel itself. David Lodge's *Nice Work* may serve as an example of this. The novel sets out explicitly to provide a late twentieth-century version of the industrial novels of the nineteenth century, such as Charlotte Brontë's *Shirley* (1849), Charles Kingsley's *Alton Locke* (1850), Charles Dickens's *Hard Times* (1854) and, most particularly, Elizabeth Gaskell's *North and South* (1855). The awareness of this rewriting is driven home by the fact that one of the novel's two central characters, Dr Robyn Penrose, is an academic who specialises in exactly the industrial novels that *Nice Work* is using as exemplars. Robyn Penrose's lecture on *North and South* establishes with painful explicitness the 'two nations' theme that is to govern the novel, because the 'Shadow Scheme' that is to involve Penrose professionally and erotically with Vic Wilcox and the engineering works of which he is managing director will require of her the same incongruous intimacy with manufacturing process and the world of business as Margaret Hale has in her relationship with the local mill-owner Thornton in Gaskell's novel.

The sleight of hand that this systematic parallel both conceals and to some degree acknowledges is the suppression of all the important differences between the nineteenth and twentieth century condition of England and thus also of all of the differences between the functions of the novel at these different moments. For one thing, it enforces a misrecognition of the actual economic conditions that prevail around the Midlands manufacturing region that is the novel's setting. If there are superficial similarities between the kind of *laissez-faire* capitalism prevailing in the mid-nineteenth century and the boom years of the 1980s, there are also dramatic differences. The relative simplicities of the economic antagonisms between owner and worker in *North and South* are here mapped on to a much more various and multiaccentual political and economic situation. Far from being at the centre of economic power, Midlands manufacturing industry is in decline, and the relative dispositions of State, industry, financial and educational institutions are strikingly different; there are no nineteenth-century equivalents, for example, for the powers of 'fictitious capital' represented by the financial markets which feature in *Nice Work*, or for the curiously intermediary position of such State-run institutions as a university, which is at once culturally central and ideologically under attack from the centres of political power.

The parallels here are not wholly serious, of course, and are mischievously undercut, for example in the fact that where Robyn Penrose claims of *North and South* that 'the interest Margaret takes in factory life and the processes of manufacturing . . . is a displaced manifestation of her unacknowledged erotic feelings for Thornton' (Lodge 1989: 79), her own, not very considerable interest in factory life is as a confirmation of her rather naive political theories, and not at all as an erotic displacement. Indeed, the apparent stifling of Robyn's natural sexual affections by her intellectualism, evidenced in the fact that she is able to dismiss so easily the one-night stand which comes as the consummation of her relationship with Vic Wilcox, is the cause of a number of ironic rebuffs delivered to her through the course of the novel. At other times, the novel protects itself against identification with its nineteenth-century originals by manipulating parallels to the point where they become ironically over-complete. In her lecture, Robyn pours scorn on the fact that 'all the Victorian novel could offer as a solution to the problems of industrial capitalism were: a legacy, a marriage, emigration or death' (83). The magically contrived ending to *Nice Work* in fact seems to offer Robyn versions of each of these evasive outcomes in turn: she is offered a job in an American university; she inherits a sum of money large enough to enable her to live in comfort, or, as it turns out, to invest in Vic Wilcox's new business venture; she is offered marriage and financial security by her long-term lover; and as for death, well, she does decide in the end to stay on at Rummidge when she is offered the prospect of re-employment. We seem to be ironically instructed that such wish-fulfilling fairy-tales are not adequate to the complex demands of contemporary life.

Nevertheless, these variations serve to protect rather than to disable the central parallel established between this contemporary novel of two nations and its nineteenth-century predecessors. The specific parallels with *North and South* are filled out by a series of epigraphs and allusions to other nineteenth-century industrial novels which suggest that, though conditions may have changed, the structure of perception that belongs to the nineteenth-century novel may still be reliable and appropriate. In sly revenge on Robyn Penrose for her determination to subject Dickens's novels to deconstructive readings that refuse their surface truths or apparent meanings, the novel quotes little instructional snippets from *Hard Times* to suggest the immaturity of her perspective. For example, Gradgrind's words about the insufficiency of the disembodied intellect stand at the beginning of chapter 5, just before the narrative of Robyn's and Vic's love-making:

> 'Some persons hold,' he pursued, still hesitating, 'that there is a wisdom of the Head, and that there is a wisdom of the Heart. I have not supposed it so; but, as I have said, I mistrust myself now. I have supposed the head to be all-sufficient. It may not be all-sufficient; how can I venture this morning to say it is!'
> (Dickens 1969: 245–6, quoted in Lodge 1989: 265)

Elsewhere, after she has read a letter from her boyfriend Charles explaining that he is giving up academic life to become a merchant banker, Robyn's mingled feelings are glossed in the bewildered words of Stephen Blackpool from the same novel: 'There were things in this letter which struck a nerve of reluctant assent, mixed up with things she found false and obnoxious. 'Twas all a muddle' (314–15). The instability of the citational mode employed in the words ''Twas all a muddle', which makes us uncertain whether it is an instance of Lodge mischievously translating Robyn's feelings into the sentimental formula she finds so evasive and unsatisfactory, or his rendering of a translation which Robyn is to be imagined as having effected herself, covers over any implausibility that the suture of nineteenth- and twentieth-century narrational modes might otherwise have.

Most importantly, this structure of allusive identification allows *Nice Work* to borrow in its own characterisation of the condition of England something of the integrating reach and perspectival authority it ascribes to its predecessors in social–realist fiction of the nineteenth century and afterwards. As in Drabble's *The Ice Age*, much depends upon the expressive force of setting and its evocation. Particularly significant here are the descriptions of the car journeys taken by Vic Wilcox and Robyn Penrose through the post-industrial landscape of the Midlands. As Vic Wilcox drives to work, the narrative uses the information that he 'knows a little of the history of this region, having done a prize-winning project on it at school' to develop a compressed history of the area, complete with quotations from Carlyle and Dickens. Robyn Wilcox's journey to the same destination does not stimulate the same synoptic sweep in the narrative, which lingers in much less visionary fashion on the dull and squalid details of the contemporary: 'a cinema converted into a bingo hall, a church converted into a community centre, a Co-op converted into a Freezer Centre' (97). Robyn sees the scene through literary precedent, and its description compresses together allusions both to the scene of muddy slithering that opens Dickens's *Bleak House* and to Lawrence's *Lady Chatterley's Lover* (1928):

> The people slipping and sliding on the pavements, spattered with slush by the passing traffic, look stoically wretched, as if they expect no better from life. A line from D. H. Lawrence – was it *Women in Love* or *Lady Chatterley?* – comes into Robyn's head. *'She felt in a wave of terror the grey, gritty hopelessness of it all.'*
>
> (Lodge 1989: 98)

The allusion so casually planted here is in fact to chapter 11 of *Lady Chatterley's Lover*, in which Connie Chatterley is looking with horror and despair at the dismal mining town of Tevershall and seeing it as representative of the state of England:

> Tevershall! That was Tevershall! Merrie England! Shakespeare's England! No, but the England of today, as Connie had realized since she had come to live in it. It was producing a new race of mankind, over-conscious in the money and social and political side, on the spontaneous, intuitive side dead, but dead.
>
> (Lawrence 1990: 159)

The novel that narrates Robyn's response to the desolation of the urban scene seems, for all her knowingness, to know more than she does. The fragmentariness of Robyn's perception here is in contrast to the grasp and sweep claimed by the narration in its association with authoritative literary precedent. What is not apparent to Robyn is that she would be included in the accusation levelled in novels such as *Lady Chatterley's Lover* at the hypertrophy of the intellect at the expense of the feelings. When, a moment or so later, the narrative reclaims her literary borrowing for its own purpose, it is again to suggest both the limitation of her perspective and its own inclusiveness: 'How strange it is, strange and sad, to see all these tropical faces amid the slush and dirty snow, the grey gritty hopelessness of an English industrial city in the middle of winter' (Lodge 1989: 99).

Occasionally, Robyn's perceptions are allowed to rise above the level of the fragmentary or superficial, but when they do it is only to substitute another kind of myopia or partial vision:

> Shocking, somehow, to come across . . . a gloomy Victorian gaol in the middle of an ordinary suburb where double-decker buses pass and housewives with shopping bags and pushchairs go about their mundane business. Prison is just a word to Robyn, a word in a book or a newspaper, a symbol of something – the law, hegemony, repression (*'The prison motif in* Little Dorrit *is a metaphorical articulation of Dickens's critique of Victorian culture and society' – Discuss*). Seeing it there, foursquare in soot-streaked stone, with its barred windows, great studded iron door, and high walls trimmed with barbed wire, makes her think with a shudder of the men cooped up inside in cramped cells smelling of sweat and urine, rapists and pimps and wife-beaters and child-molesters among them, and her heart sinks under the thought that crime and punishment are equally horrible, equally inevitable – unless men should change, all become like Charles, which seems unlikely.
>
> (Lodge 1989: 97)

The narration here attempts to supply the abstractive deficiency in Robyn Penrose's outlook, by filling out her habitual metaphor with the immediacy of metonymic detail. That this contrast is keyed into the contrast maintained in the novel between the ugly, but substantial virility of the 'real' world of industry and the comfortable, effete unreality of the academy is suggested by the scene towards the end of the novel in which Vic attends one of Robyn's tutorials. Robyn overrides Vic's suggestion that Tennyson's reference to 'the iron grooves of change' in *Locksley Hall* is a metonymy, and therefore evidence of Tennyson's lack of grasp of the real, since he did not know that trains run on rails rather than grooves. She informs Vic primly that 'It's a metaphor . . . The world moving through time is compared to something moving along a metal track' (337). In the privileging in *Nice Work* of what he has in his own critical writing characterised as the more realistic mode of metonymy (1977), Lodge is concealing the abstraction of his own mode of writing, which would really much better be characterised as 'metonymy inside a metaphor', to borrow the formula Robyn Penrose devises in grudging acknowledgement of Vic Wilcox's argument. The shreds and scraps of the 'real' condition of England offered in the evocation just quoted and in others through the novel are in fact made to stand for a complete picture, made available in its completeness to the panoptic eye of the novelist, and the reader his confederate. In this and in other respects, the gentle forms of anti-realist hedging that the novel offers (including the cute introduction of Robyn Penrose as 'a character who, rather awkwardly for me, doesn't herself believe in the concept of character'; 39), are really only diversions from the process by which the novel installs itself in a position from which to speak of the condition of England, and defends itself from the otherwise irresistible charge of having compressed and simplified that condition to one of fable or fantasy.

Much the same purpose appears to be served by the other twitches of self-reflexivity that occasionally trouble the comic composure of the novel. The two nations and the two thematic worlds of the novel are also projected as two potentially different readerships with their corresponding modes of reading. The inhabitants of the real world, such as Vic Wilcox, and his colleague who guffaws vulgarly about whether Robyn has read *The Thorn Birds*, are shown both as realist and as escapist readers: Vic insists doggedly on the necessity of getting realistic detail right and yet also finds it incomprehensible that reading could ever be seen as a kind of work.

The question of what is involved in the reading of a novel connects with the central issue on which this novel meditates, namely the question of what constitutes valuable or productive work. The title of the novel is picked up on a number of occasions, and seems to encode the opposition between, on the one hand, fulfilling and valuable labour – 'The foundry has a lot of potential. It's a good workforce. They do nice work,' says Vic admiringly at one point (37) – and, on the other hand, the assumption of wasteful, self-indulgent idleness that elicits from Vic the snort, 'Well, it's nice work if you can get it' (346). The novel manufactures a neat reversal between the workshy inhabitants of the academic world for whom reading – even the reading of this novel – is a kind of labour, and the inhabitants of the 'world of work', for whom, as Vic puts it, 'Reading is the opposite of work . . . It's what you do when you come home from work' (334). As the novel circulates different readings of the question of work and of the work of reading, the dual orientation of the novel is made part of its subject by addressing an academic or quasi-academic audience who are on the inside of the academic world looking out, and a non-academic audience who are outside that world, looking in at what it feels like to look out.

It is in this respect that *Nice Work* both belongs to and is historically split off from the nineteenth-century realist tradition of the novel. For that tradition, the worlds of work and leisure are conceived as stark opposites, as in the splitting of the factory and the circus in *Hard Times*, to which *Nice Work* multiplies allusions; and the nineteenth-century novel, though caught up inescapably in the world of commodity production and exchange, derives its critical power from its claim to speak for the 'human', apart from the world of work. One way of describing the developments in the condition of England that separate the late twentieth century from the middle of the nineteenth century is in terms of the systematic disruption of the relations of work and play. The rise of forms of commodified leisure of all kinds and the growing centrality of cultural consumption in an economy that, far from disdaining the wastefulness of play, puts it eagerly and systematically to work, in advertising and in all forms of the culture industry, is what lies behind the economic collapse of Pringle's engineering works in *Nice Work*. The real competitor for the world of work as represented by Pringle's is the world of finance capital into which Robyn's ex-boyfriend Charles is drawn, a world that is simultaneously less real and more real than the gritty actuality of the work represented by Pringle's. As Charles writes to Robyn:

I regard myself as simply exchanging one semiotic system for another, the literary for the numerical, a game with high philosophical stakes for a game with high monetary stakes – but a *game* in each case, in which satisfaction comes ultimately from playing rather than winning, since there are no absolute winners, for the game never ends.

(Lodge 1989: 313)

Though Charles' position is scarcely endorsed, one problem for a novel about such a condition of England is that it makes its own function so uncertain. Addressed to an academic audience as a kind of knowing game, readable both as entertainment and as serious fiction, but also participating in the culture industry for which entertainment is such conspicuous big business, *Nice Work* is designed never to be quite sure of the position it occupies or of the function it fulfils as a novel.

Interestingly, there are one or two moments toward the end of the novel when the possibility of a different economy of work and play is entertained. When Robyn is forced to reappraise her values and beliefs in the face of Vic's scepticism and her own growing professional difficulties, she fantasises a Morrisian vision of the university as

the ideal type of a human community, where work and play, culture and nature, were in perfect harmony, where there was space, and light, and fine buildings set in pleasant grounds, and people were free to pursue excellence and self-fulfilment, each according to her own rhythm and inclination.

(Lodge 1989: 346)

Seen in these terms, the novel seems for a space to be offering itself and the pleasure of its reading as a prefiguring example of the oxymoronic redemption of 'nice work', or nonalienated labour. In fact, however, this vision is discredited almost as soon as it is offered in the novel, since it belongs to the feminised scheme of academic values over which hangs the grim shadow of the reality principle. By the end of the novel, Robyn is forced to waken from this dream as, observing the mutual distance maintained between a group of students and a black gardener, she must acknowledge, in a kind of Forsterian 'not here, not yet', the persistence of the two nations:

There is no overt arrogance on the students' part, or evident resentment on the young gardener's, just a kind of mutual, instinctive avoidance of contact. Physically contiguous, they inhabit separate worlds. It seems a very British way of handling differences of class and race. Remembering her Utopian vision of the campus invaded by the Pringle's workforce, Robyn smiles ruefully to herself. There is a long way to go.

(Lodge 1989: 384)

Though apparently alive to the ironies involved in the question of work, and to the structural connection between the question of whether a novel is for work or for play, and the question of how a novel may grasp and integrate different modes of life and readership, *Nice Work* is unable in the end to do more than hover in indecision about these questions. The apparent split between two worlds, two nations, two forms of novel and readership is really the mechanism that the novel employs to fantasise its own power to encompass and analyse. The definitional anxiety over the question of work, and in particular the kind of work performed by such a novel as this, makes intermittently visible a new set of conditions of England which would seem to require more inclusive, more exploratory forms of the social imaginary than are provided by the sharp, yet soothingly distinct binarism of the two nations in *Nice Work*. During the 1980s, this kind of binarism, and the novel that claims to be able to reconcile it, comes to appear increasingly unsatisfactory to different writers. The novels of such writers often derive their perspectival authority not from an inwardness with Englishness but from an awkward, displaced sense of its partial, precarious and always narrated nature. In their work, some examples of which I consider in the next chapter, rather different views of the condition of England and the condition of the novel that represents it are elaborated.

3

OUTSIDE IN

Novels which attempt to affirm or summon the condition of England in the postwar period must look in two directions at once. To centre on the question of national identity and belonging is to turn inwards, imagining the nation as a secure, interior collective space, which is both a retreat and a matrix for the social monad. Such novels extend the cohering and habituating functions of narrative, in that work of symbolic transformation which, as Brian Doyle has suggested (1989: 9), is one of the most important social functions of fiction: the transformation of confusion into order, contingency into typicality, conflict into resolution, strangeness into familiarity, diffuseness into collectivity. Such novels depend upon a certain kind of making common, drawing into commensurability sundered areas of social experience and staging them in the thickened space and time of national identity. Benedict Anderson has suggested that the particular kind of simultaneity of experience premised in the 'meanwhile' of novel narration, in which characters and events may share no knowledge of or connection with each other but can nevertheless participate in an imaginary synchronicity, belongs to the emerging sense of the nation, which equally depends upon the idea of 'a sociological organism moving calendrically through homogeneous, empty time . . . a solid community moving steadily down (or up) history' (1983: 31).

But the turn inwards to the imagined community of the nation is always the positing or projection of an exterior too; formless, alien, unknowable as it may be, what stands outside the experience of national belonging always in some insistent sense belongs to, or bears upon, the apparently spontaneous reciprocal relations between a nation and those who are sheltered and recognised as its subjects. Narratives of the condition of England in the twentieth century as a whole have tended to be drawn outwards, in an attempt both to achieve perspectival distance on the question of national belonging and to confirm the integrity of the various boundaries that mark the nation off from its opposites, adversaries and others. Time and again, in modernist fiction of the first half of the century, the attempt to know and name a sense of national belonging seems to involve a defining movement of evacuation or expatriation, whether in Joyce's famous flight from Ireland, and in Beckett's repetition of the same trajectory; or in Forster's supplementation of the securely grounded, if also internally conflicted England of *Howard's End* (1910) with the narrative of a passage, to and through the imperial margins of India in *A Passage to India* (1924); or in Lawrence's restless absconding from the constricting yet also abidingly fascinating nightmare of English society and politics; or in George Orwell's internal flight, in documentary works such as *Down and Out in Paris and London* (1933) and *The Road to Wigan Pier* (1937), to an alien and unrecorded England that is both concealed within and yet also lurks menacingly outside official England. In all of these cases, the movement outwards proves to be a crucial and indispensable supplement to the condition and narrative of inhabitation. It is a supplement that cannot be construed simply in terms of the model of growth and development suggested by the *Bildungsroman*, which typically leaves its hero poised, as at the end of Joyce's *A Portrait of the Artist as a Young Man* (1916), on the brink of a personal autonomy achieved in a self-extrication from the clinging matrix of the homeland; in such novels, the movement away, outwards or beyond is neither linear nor irreversible but tends to circle back in actual or metaphorical homecoming. Thus, there is the paradoxical movement of works such as Conrad's *Heart of Darkness* (1902), which moves simultaneously out from the imperial centre of London and into its heart, or Joyce's exile from Ireland the better to take possession of it, or Orwell's interior recolonisation of an England that is both inside and outside, an uncanny double of the England he both leaves behind and advances upon.

Such works have sometimes been interpreted as a desirable remission of the imaginative investment in the nation, or in collectivity as such, and an opening on to difference or otherness. There is a strong, if rather vague connection between this modernist internationalism and the generalised condition of movement and displacement of peoples from their homelands throughout this century. As Edward Said has observed, there is an important difference between voluntary and involuntary exile, such that one cannot simply identify the forced eviction of peoples with the cultural picaresque of cosmopolitan artists and intellectuals; but strange and unpredictable kinds of commerce between the two forms of unbelonging are also possible (Said 1993: 402–3). If a parochial recoil from the excursive movement of modernism is discernible in postwar British fiction, then one can also point to a repetition of the modernist pattern of movement outwards from the centre. As in the early twentieth century, economic factors have a considerable part to play in this; whereas modernist writers such as Joyce, Beckett and Rhys may have left England in order to live cheaply enough to build an *œuvre* and reputation, postwar British writers have tended to leave England at the moment when they have gathered enough wealth to feel the constraints of the exacting tax regimes of the 1970s, or have begun to feel that their major markets are no longer to be found in Britain. As John Sutherland observes, the marked expansion and internationalisation of theme to be found in the work of writers such as Angus Wilson, Muriel Spark, John Fowles and, less straightforwardly, Graham Greene, is therefore in part a fairly direct response to the economic conditions of postwar publishing (Sutherland 1978: 58–62).

Nevertheless, I think that the movement outwards in much postwar fiction does perform something of the same function as the equivalent fictional evacuations of the first half of the century. In both cases, there is an opening of the inside to the outside, an imaginative (and also sometimes imaginary) travelling, the purpose of which at least in part is to focus attention back to the point of departure; the fiction of the earlier and later twentieth century unhouses in order to disclose and illuminate more permanent forms of dwelling. My purpose in this chapter, however, is to draw attention to a certain reversal or counter-movement to the inside-out movement of the narrative of the condition of England in exile. For many of the most striking and significant explorations of the conditions of national identity in the postwar British novel have been the product not of inside-out excursion but of an outside-in recursion, as outsiders who were previously held spatially and culturally at a distance have returned or have doubled back to the distant imperial centres to which they had previously been connected, as it were, only by their separation. Werner Glinga, borrowing a phrase that he attributes to the Jamaican poet Louise Bennett, calls this process 'colonization in reverse' (Glinga 1986: 117). In the hands of returning exiles such as Doris Lessing or of reverse colonists, such as Timothy Mo, Salman Rushdie and Kazuo Ishiguro, the condition of England and the fictional conditions necessary for representing it come to seem very different. In their work we encounter, in a heightened and tautologously tightened form, a brooding over the nature of the narrative processes necessary not only to represent the experience of national belonging but also to enable the nation to constitute itself. In fact, if the novelistic narration of the nation is really only a shadowing of a process of nation-formation that is already an act of narrative, then the novel may come to be regarded as one of the principal agencies by which the nation constructs itself in this, anyway fabular, always-narrated, 'first place'. To put it in the terms suggested by Homi Bhabha, the narration of the nation as a given, pre-existing entity is interrupted and embarrassed by laying open to view the performative present-tense of that activity of nation-making narrative which 'intervenes in the sovereignty of the nation's *self-generation* by casting a shadow between the people as 'image' and its signification as a differentiating sign of Self, distinct from the Other or the Outside' (Bhabha 1990a: 299). Under these conditions, Bhabha suggests, the barrier or borderline which marks the defining limit of national identity, and which maintains the clarity and self-evidence of distinctions between the nation and its others, is folded back into the heart of the nation, such that 'the barred Nation *It/Self*, alienated from its eternal self-generation, becomes a liminal form of social representation, a space that is *internally* marked by cultural difference and the heterogeneous histories of contending peoples, antagonistic authorities, and tense cultural locations' (ibid.).

The paradoxical intensification described by Bhabha is in theory possible at every historical moment in the achievement of the condition of nationality. But his is in fact a remarkably suggestive account of the particular processes undergone in imperial and ex-imperial nations in the late twentieth century, and perhaps especially in Britain in the postwar period. These were the years of rapid 'decolonisation', in which, within a very short space of time, Britain variously jettisoned, disentangled itself from and propelled to independence most of its imperial dominions, in Asia largely in the period 1945–48 and in Africa largely during the early 1960s. Although one of the aims of decolonisation was to trade imperial rule for the benefits of indirect British political and commercial influence, in fact this latter advantage was not to be realised (Darwin 1988: 334–5). This converged with events such as the Suez Canal Crisis in 1956, when Britain threatened to go to war with President Nasser of Egypt in an attempt to force him to open the Suez Canal and was only deterred by United Nations action, to bring about a sense of political decompression in a Britain that felt itself to be increasingly marginal in a world governed by the two great superpowers and the neocolonialism of multinational corporate capital. Alan Sinfield describes without really analysing the contradictory situation this produced. On the one hand, there was a centrifugal flow outwards from the declining centres of Western imperial power, facilitated by the steady increase in the speed of transportation and communications, along with the growth of internally diversified, globally extensive multinational corporations and the opportunities they created for swift and adaptive movements of capital to wherever profits could be maximised. This outwards flow reproduced the nineteenth-century imperialist habit of expelling social problems to the colonies, by moving investment to the Third World and other areas of cheap labour and reliably authoritarian government, thus exporting the industrial, political and ecological problems that proved so intractable in the USA and Western Europe. On the other hand, the movements of decolonisation and neocolonisation produced a massive feedback of previously colonised peoples into their 'home' countries. During this same period, Britain experienced a steady influx of immigrants from ex-colonies, notably in the Caribbean, who were consciously recruited by the Health Service and London Transport during the 1950s; from India and Pakistan and, during the late 1960s, from Kenya, after President Amin expelled many of the Asians living there (Sinfield 1989: 125). Though often represented as an overwhelming tide, in fact the numbers of immigrants have always been much less dramatic than the periodic spasms of public panic since the 1950s would seem to suggest. The number of West Indian immigrants in 1954 was 11,000. This rose within a couple of years to an annual rate of 17,000, but dropped back after the restrictions of the Commonwealth Immigrants Act in 1962 to 7,000 per year. The numbers of Indian and Pakistani immigrants jumped from 8,400 in 1960 to 48,850 in the following year, fuelled by speculation about the restrictions impending in the 1962 Act, but settled back thereafter. In 1988 the total number of members of all minority ethnic groups in the population was only about 2½ million, or less than 5% of the total population (Hiro 1991: 15, 114, 133).

These imports of labour were extremely useful to the British economy during periods of growth and prosperity. During the economic crises and recessions of the 1970s and 1980s, however, resentment and hostility grew, and were sometimes artificially provoked, at the fact that 'British' people were having to compete with first-generation immigrants for jobs, or, since such groups were actually much more likely to be made unemployed or to suffer economic deprivation, at the intolerable drain on national resources said to be consequent upon supporting such groups when their labour was not required. The irony of the latter is particularly grotesque, since the sustained growth of the Welfare State up until the 1970s, especially in the National Health Service, would have been unthinkable without the contribution of immigrant labour.

This dual directionality produced a special kind of cultural turbulence. British industries found themselves threatened by competition from products produced with Third World labour and, increasingly during the 1980s, Britain also experienced the humiliation of being treated as a peripheral zone itself by powerful corporations attracted by workforces who had been softened up and demoralised by unemployment, especially in North-East England and South Wales. Despite the fact that Britain retained considerable levels of prosperity and a political influence much in excess of its actual wealth or power, an anxious sense of fragmentation or depletion of national selfhood set in. At the same time as Britain felt marginalised, or emptied out, sections of British society also began to feel the inward crowding of internal contradiction, which could be relieved only by the erection of symbolic barriers against outsiders, such as the various forms of immigration legislation passed in 1962 (Commonwealth Immigrants Act), 1968 (Kenyan Asians Act), 1971 (Immigration Act), 1981 (British Nationality Act) and 1988 (Immigration Act), and by occasional re-assertions of the telescopic geopolitics of the past, such as the Falklands campaign, which seemed for a while to expel or discharge many of the symbolic tensions and contradictions affecting British life. But this movement of purgative exteriorisation was steadily and unstoppably contradicted by the feeding back into British life of the lives, peoples and histories that were supposed to belong to the outside. The condition was thus one in which a sense of national self-identity was both emptied out and crowded out, as every attempt to expel what was extraneous or foreign to British life returned in the form of more complexity and interior self-division. At the same time it must be recognised that the movements of new peoples into Britain also brought about enormous cultural invigoration and opportunity for self-transformation. During the late 1970s and 1980s, the effect of the increasing political organisation, self-affirmation and resulting cultural visibility of immigrant groups – now, of course, represented largely by second-generation black Britons – combined with the arrival of a diverse range of cultural and ethnic groups deriving from other regions than ex-British colonies, made the challenges of imagining a multicultural future for Britain unignorable. As so often proves to be the case, the threat from the 'outside' had also brought to light the fragile and unsatisfactory integration of what purported to be the inside. With the diversification of British cultural life produced by immigration, and, more recently, with the unevenly encouraging example of the newly independent states of Eastern Europe, there has also been an energetic revival of the sense of cultural difference in different regions of Britain, including Scottish and Welsh nationalists and, of course, Ireland.

There are a number of novels written since the Second World War which both give voice to and themselves help to fashion these feelings of unsettlement and opportunity. Characteristic of such novels is a sceptical dissatisfaction with the inherited forms in which the condition of England had been represented in novels, combined with a continuing faith in the capacities of narrative to effect kinds of collective symbolic transformation and solidary connections. This gives the lie in two different ways to Q. D. Leavis's vision of the essential integrity of the nation sustained by the English novel (1983: 320–1); firstly by seeking to add to that picture of harmonious interdependence some awkwardly unassimilable facts and experiences, and secondly by wagering the possibility of forms of mutual belonging which do not depend upon such a smooth annulment of conflict and difference.

One option, to be sure, for the novel concerned with a divided condition of England is to abandon most of what might have seemed to be the traditional requirements of the novel. Such a route is taken by Colin MacInnes in the three novels of his 'London' trilogy, *City of Spades* (1957), *Absolute Beginners* (1959) and *Mr Love and Justice* (1960). These novels represent the life of bohemian teenage London in the 1950s, but with a deliberate refusal to concede to the novel's tendency to typify the particular. The middle novel of the sequence, *Absolute Beginners*, moves without apparent purpose or structure through a series of incidents and characters, all the time favouring the local explosion of colour, idiom or interest over the slow thickening of narrative, the sharply isolated glimpse over the wide and differentiated perspective. It deliberately confines itself to the outlook and experiences of its unnamed narrator and central character, claiming in its title not that his experiences are representative but that they are in some sense primary, even innocent. The narrator remains through the novel an 'absolute beginner', his narrative animated by each new and seemingly unprecedented shock of violence, comedy, or strangeness that he encounters, while he himself remains impervious to and untransformed by the telling, unwilling to gather any kind of generalised significance from it. This obstinate fragmentariness is also a feature of the novel's address. It has the directness of monologue, which acknowledges the reader and aims the discourse directly and explicitly at him or her, and a melting disregard for narrative or discursive decorum:

> So what I am, is a photographer: street, holiday park, studio, artistic poses and, from time to time, when I can find a client, pornographic. I know it's revolting, but then it only harms the psychos who are my customers, and as for the kids I use as models, they'd do it all down to giggles, let alone for the fee I pay them. To have a job like mine means that I don't belong to the great community of the mugs: the vast majority of squares who are exploited. It seems to me this being a mug or a non-mug is a thing that splits humanity up into two sections absolutely. It's nothing to do with age or sex or class or colour – either you're born a mug or born a non-mug, and me, I sincerely trust I'm born the latter.
>
> (MacInnes 1980a: 17)

This form of narrative address simultaneously excludes and recruits its reader: the casual references, the unexplained argot, the swift transitions of topic, all give a sense of an enigmatic private code whose purpose is to remind the reader that he or she does not speak the language in which he or she is being addressed, while also in a sense educating the reader and drawing him or her into it. From the very opening words, the reader is, so to speak, included in the fact of his or her apartness from this self-sufficient world, which springs into being with its narrative telling or even consists wholly of it:

> It was with the advent of the Laurie London era that I realized the whole teenage epic was tottering to doom.
>
> 'Fourteen years old, that absolute beginner,' I said to the Wizard as we paused casually in the gramophone section to hear Little Laurie in that golden disc performance of his.
>
> 'From now on,' said Wizard, 'he's certainly Got The Whole World In His Hands.'
>
> We listened to the wonder boy's nostrils spinning on.
>
> (MacInnes 1980a: 11)

The novel depends upon this incommensurability of narrator and readership, and on the sense it conveys of an entire subcultural world that has only occasional points of overlap with the larger adult world of employment, economics and politics. It is, as Alan Sinfield has suggested, a kind of utopia (1989: 170), whose outlandish visionary force depends upon the fact that it has so little continuity with the condition of the England it inhabits. *Absolute Beginners* seems to suggest an abandonment of the large, assimilative perspective of the nation-novel and the novel-nation in favour of the self-inventing and self-legitimating communities of style that were increasingly generated by the explosion of pop and youth culture in Britain from the 1950s on. The self-inventing community is often the marginal community, drawing the vigour of its self-definition from its skewed relation to the mainstream. In his other novels, as well as in much of his journalistic writing, MacInnes celebrated the advantages of the outsider's off-centred perspective. As a homosexual and as what he declared himself to be in the *Jewish Chronicle* in 1960, 'an "English" London-born, Australian-reared Scot' (quoted in Gould 1983: 138), he himself shared and, it must also be said, energetically cultivated such a perspective. He found other examples of this perspective in unexpected places, for example in the work of the German art historian Niklaus Pevsner, whose studies of English art and architecture seemed to MacInnes to be

> an exploration by a curious, courteous, cultivated stranger of an inexplicable people, half Yahoo, half Houyhnhnm. And in spite of his later self-identification with us (to our own immense profit and enlightenment), I still feel that Dr

Pevsner has preserved the rare and enriched dual vision of a thoroughly inside outsider.

(MacInnes 1961: 122)

While allying itself with the complex obliquity of this perspective, *Absolute Beginners* nevertheless retains in its form a kind of memory of the generalising function of the realist novel. (Though it reads at times like a film, or a monologue, we remain aware that it is a novel which is borrowing from or simulating these idioms.) We are never quite sure whether we are to read the novel as a display, parodic or exemplary as it may be, of such an address. (In this, MacInnes's work foreshadows that of Martin Amis, and especially novels such as *Money* (1984) and *London Fields* (1989), which similarly address the condition of England via flagrant violation of every requirement of the condition of England novel.) Seen as such a display, the novel – and indeed the two others that follow it in MacInnes's 'London' sequence – becomes readable partly as a reflection on the conditions under which such a narration or form of narrative address might come to emerge. Read in this way, the apparent self-sufficiency of this fictional world seems increasingly to be fractured by oblique, perplexed acknowledgement of the larger social world that it seems deliberately to exclude. In *Absolute Beginners* this is a consequence in particular of the narrator's experience of violence inflicted upon blacks, in a series of incidents based upon the actual racial attacks that took place in Nottingham and Notting Hill during August and September 1958. Abruptly, the narrator's self-sufficient monologue turns into a vision of some more extensive possibility of address:

> I dusted my arse, and rode down Wood Lane to the White City, where the old BBC's building that splendid modernistic palace, so as to send their telly messages to the nation. And I looked at it and thought, 'My God, if I could get in there and tell them – all the millions! Just take them across the railway tracks, not a quarter of a mile away, and show them what's happening in the capital city of our country!' And I'd say to them, 'If you don't want that, for Christ's sake come down and stop it – every one of you! But if that's what you do want, then I don't want you, and for me, it's good-bye England!'
>
> (MacInnes 1980a: 179)

This passage sets up an interesting criss-cross of achieved and thwarted address. The actual words recorded in this narrative are addressed only to an imaginary audience, the new mass audience for the TV which is both in a technical sense more accessible and in a human sense more remote than any other kind of audience; though the reader of this text is given the actual words that the narrator would have said, and may in a sense feel addressed by them as reader, or constructed as their audience, he or she remains differentiated from this audience, aware that the true addressee, which expands to become 'England' itself, remains elsewhere.

The final pages of the novel show the narrator planning to leave England in earnest, accompanied emblematically only by a hold-all containing his father's handwritten *History of Pimlico*. Looking out at the scene, he reflects, 'standing there looking out on all this fable ... what a time it's been in England, what a period of fun and hope and foolishness and sad stupidity' (202) and runs through the rain to greet and embrace a group of immigrants from Africa. The gesture is sentimental, though the narration of it is not necessarily so. The embrace here seems to point to the possibility of – or at least the desire for – some connection between the outside-in novel, which celebrates the condition of the internal exile and so mistrusts the annulling generality of official English culture, and the dream of some more encompassing collectivity and inclusive address.

Much of the dash and surprise (and quite a lot of the boring self-regard) of *Absolute Beginners* derives from the fact that it refuses two aspects of the social novel. Firstly, it flattens and simplifies the conventional dialectic of character and context. The unnamed narrator is nothing more than the period of history through which he lives and which his narration mediates and reenacts; the novel scarcely concerns itself with the forming influence of his contemporary culture on the narrator, or with any response to or interiorisation of the culture on the narrator's part. Narration and the cultural experience which is its subject are seized together instantaneously, forming and at each moment renewing each other in a rich, celebratory narrative spill. Secondly, the novel thwarts the expectations of extension, development and growth. If the narration does show signs of hardening into character and consciousness at the end of the novel, this is not an unfolding of implicit meanings from earlier in the novel; it is almost, in fact, as though the novel comes to an end out of the need to avert such a tendency towards development and finality.

This double refusal, of connectedness and extension, is part of a more general refusal of the novel as a genre, and, embodied within that, of the implied continuity between the form of the realist novel and the form of social life itself. Neither entirely abandoning nor entirely remaining with the form of the novel, *Absolute Beginners* attempts to maintain its authentic exteriority, as it were, on the inside of the form whose expectations are so uncongenial. This can only be done by repeated acts of disaffection from the form within the form. As such, *Absolute Beginners* anticipates and predicts some of the very different transformations wrought upon novels that set out to represent not just the changing conditions of social life in postwar Britain and the world, but also the transformation in the very idea of the social; more recent examples here would include the work, again, of Martin Amis and also of James Kelman.

Absolute Beginners also provides a significant precedent for certain novels that set out to deal with the conditions of divided or ambivalent ethnic belonging in Britain. One example of such a novel is Hanif Kureishi's *The Buddha of Suburbia* (1990). From its very first lines, *The Buddha of Suburbia* simultaneously summons and rebuffs the *Bildungsroman* with its typical equations between self and society, the growth of the individual and the cementing of social meaning:

> My name is Karim Amir and I am an Englishman born and bred, almost. I am often considered to be a funny kind of Englishman, a new breed as it were, having emerged from two old histories. But I don't care – Englishman I am (though not proud of it), from the South London suburbs and going somewhere. Perhaps it is the odd mixture of continents and blood, of here and there, of belonging and not, that makes me restless and easily bored. Or perhaps it was being brought up in the suburbs that did it. Anyway, why search the inner room when it's enough to say that I was looking for trouble, any kind of movement, action and sexual interest I could find, because things were so gloomy, so slow and heavy, in our family.
>
> (Kureishi 1990: 3)

The writing here signals and declines a number of generic affiliations – the novel of intercultural conflict (Forster), the novel of class mobility and sexual discovery (Sillitoe, Braine, Drabble). Within its short compass, this opening paragraph seems to play out the characteristic swings of the novel as a whole, between serious political speculation and an offhand, slightly caught-out, but also somewhat arch deflection of serious enquiry into pose, performance and the disorderly pulsations of the body. A little like *Absolute Beginners*, *The Buddha of Suburbia* flaunts the contingency of its structure, replacing the slow uncoiling dynamism of development with the sputtering, discontinuous energy of episodic renewal. The novel covers the years of Amir's late youth, through the years of the 1960s and 1970s, beginning with the already *démodé* hippie lifestyle of Amir's parents (this surely a little premature, according to the time-scheme of the novel) and moving, as Amir himself moves, through the alternative culture of avant-garde experiment, the arrival of punk and new wave. Like *Absolute Beginners*, the novel substitutes the intensity of popular style and culture for the coherence of public history of a more official kind, revealing in fully developed form what is only incipient in *Absolute Beginners*, namely the way in which, for postwar children, the succession of popular–cultural moments or periods has become an authoritative and shared common language for linking personal and generational memory. (Indeed, this is the period in which the idea of the generation acquires its full explanatory and organising force for the first time.) Surrounding Amir are his father, who one day throws over his job in the Civil Service to become a freelance esoteric guide and spiritual adviser to the Bromley middle class (he is the 'buddha of suburbia' named in the title of the novel); Eva, the scarfed and kaftanned woman with whom his father has a long-standing affair; Jamila, the childhood friend and regular sexual partner of Amir; her arranged husband Changez; and Charlie, the English golden boy who is both object of desire for the bisexual narrator and the model of effortless success and perfection, as lover, rock musician and successful actor. If the characters are types, then much of the energy and comedy of the narration derives from its patient, wry attention to oddities and incongruities that complicate the type. A clear example of this is Amir's father, whose elaborate spiritual performances are offset by his dominating, but strangely innocent narcissism:

> Sometimes I dreaded seeing Dad. If you weren't in the mood for him, or able to fend him off, his personality could club you down. He could start pinching your cheeks and tweaking

your nose and stuff he thought was the funniest thing he'd
ever seen. Or he'd pull up his jumper and slap out a tune on
his bare stomach, urging you to guess whether it was 'Land of
Hope and Glory' or 'The Mighty Quinn' in the Manfred
Mann version.

(Kureishi 1990: 193)

The delight in the conjoining of incongruities, the deflection of
expectation and the lopsided disordering of pattern which is
embodied in Amir's father characterises the book as a whole.

Unlike *Absolute Beginners*, however, *The Buddha of Suburbia* is
unable to maintain the displacement of developmental time into
the suspended intensity of the personal or cultural epoch. This has
much to do with its retrospective first person narrative, which
makes it much harder to avoid drawing out significance and
developing judgements on the experiences offered. In the end, the
novel lurches, with something of the awkward abruptness of *Absolute
Beginners*, into a sort of summation, and ends, rather improbably, by representing the entire career of the narrator, along with
its ramshackle, opportunistic narration, as a kind of sentimental
education. 'I could think about the past and what I'd been through
as I'd struggled to locate myself and learn what the heart is. Perhaps
in the future I would live more deeply' (283–4), declares Amir right
at the end of the novel, in words whose offhand flatness scarcely
succeeds in holding the novel from collapse into a routine kind of
emotional piety.

Such a conclusion also does scant justice to the long-delayed re-emergence of the concern with cultural identity that characterises
the second half of the book. This concern is relayed mostly through
Karim Amir's experience as an actor, in his first role as an absurd
Mowgli in what its director thinks of as an expressionist version of
The Jungle Book (covered with body make-up to make him look the
right colour, he looks 'like a turd in a bikini-bottom'; 146) and his
involvement with an experimental improvisational company. For
the first time, Karim Amir and his narration begin to reflect upon
the political and ethical force of artistic representation. At one
point, Amir is asked to develop a character based upon someone
from his own experience. Amir responds to the benignly stereo-typing racism of Pyke, the director, who gently insists 'We need
someone from your own background ... Someone black', with a
gesture of comic disaffiliation which is typical of the novel: 'I didn't

know anyone black, though I'd been at school with a Nigerian. But I wouldn't know where to find him' (170). But only a short while later, Amir is being told that his Uncle Anwar, whom he has chosen as the basis for his character, has lost his wits and begun to starve himself to death in anger and helplessness after a racial attack. Amir's lesson about the responsibilities of performance and imitation is rather clumsily transmitted in the novel, through a denunciation by a black actress in Amir's company of his theatrical appropriation of Anwar's plight:

> Your picture is what white people already think of us. That we're funny, with strange habits and weird customs. To the white man we're already people without humanity, and then you go and have Anwar madly waving his stick at the white boys.
>
> (Kureishi 1990: 180)

But there is an interesting self-reflexive link between the concern with the responsibilities of theatre and the question of narration. As Alamgir Hashmi has noted, cultural and personal identity are seen as a kind of performance throughout *The Buddha of Suburbia* (1992: 89). It is not just black characters who are condemned to empty and futile mimicry, since, later in the book, Amir's hero Charlie begins 'selling Englishness' to American audiences as an actor specialising in Cockney roles (247). Amir's rendering of the comic eccentricities of the characters who surround him is in a sense to be included within the denunciation issued here, and Kureishi himself seems to be poised uneasily between identification with Amir's performative irresponsibility and concern for the effects of such performances. Late in the novel, Amir reflects on the difficult difference between belonging and cultural self-invention:

> I did feel, looking at these strange creatures now – the Indians – that in some way these were my people, and that I'd spent my life denying or avoiding that fact. I felt ashamed and incomplete at the same time, as if half of me were missing, and as if I'd been colluding with my enemies, those whites who wanted Indians to be like them.
>
> (Kureishi 1990: 212)

But a moment or so later, he admits that 'If I wanted the additional personality bonus of an Indian past, I would have to create it' (213). This issue connects with the rather broader problem which this novel is not able to resolve; the problem of how to resist the effects of typification, rendering the oddity and eccentric particularity of Indian Britons without freezing them into emblems or allegorical types of themselves; how to celebrate hybridity without regularising it as a form. Like other novels of this kind, *The Buddha of Suburbia* cannot altogether resist the lure of generality, and the desire to abstract and connect, even though this is to align it with some of the traditional ambitions of the novel from which it seems otherwise so ironically detached.

Timothy Mo's *Sour Sweet* (1982) differs from other 'outside-in' novels in a number of respects, but most importantly in its deliberate restriction of scope and its relatively unobstructed faith in the representational powers of the novel. The novel follows the fortunes of Chen, a Chinese restaurant worker in London, and his family, consisting of his wife Lily, her sister Mui and their son Man Kee. Chen becomes entangled with the Soho lodge of the Hung triad, a secret Chinese gangster organisation, and attempts to escape them by setting up a restaurant of his own in a remote part of South London, but is discovered and killed; the triad continue to support Lily with anonymous donations of money, and she survives partly persuaded that her husband is sending her the money from abroad. This intimate domestic plot alternates with an episodic narrative of various stages in the establishment of the Hung triad in London.

The novel's concern is with the capacity of Chinese living in London to maintain themselves in almost complete isolation from the English cultural life around them. The 'sour sweet' of the title is a characterisation of the swinging back and forth of the narrative between the small-scale domestic concerns of Lily and her family and the complex ceremonial and violent activities of the triad, but the novel is also concerned to establish continuities between the two levels of life. Contrary to the judgement of John Rothfork, who believes that the novel sustains a clear contrast between the male, violent and mercenary world of the Hung triad, which cannot adapt to British life, and the 'feminine . . . unconscious and procreative' power of the Chen family, which stands a chance of growth and development (1989: 52), the novel demonstrates, rather uncomfortably, that, in the cases of both the Hung and the Chen families, transplantation to a foreign country calls for adaptation and adjustment, though of a subtle and fundamentally conservative kind. In the Hung triad, the ways of Red Cudgel, who believes in enforcement of gang territory and rule by means of open and emphatic shows of force, prove to be unworkable in London and he is deposed in favour of a more moderate policy of coexistence with rivals. Lily, who has been trained in youth as a fighter by her champion boxer father, attempts to defend her business and her Chinese traditions in something of the same way as Red Cudgel and in some of the same ways is forced to accept a measure of adaptation. The parallel between the domestic and the criminal is understated but extensive. Lily is prepared to defend the integrity of her domestic sphere against the outside world, for example by teaching her son techniques of street fighting similar to those we see imparted to the new recruits to the triad. This is answered by the fact that the triad's world of extortion and violence also functions as a kind of family, a medium of the complex, displaced, withdrawn but tenacious interconnectedness of Chinese expatriate life. The novel is pointing in fact not just to what seems like the obvious contrast between the nourishing continuity of family life and the destructive violence of criminal life, but, more disturbingly, to their interdependence. Like the family, the triad is both public and secret, sustained by rules, codes and ceremonies and yet possessed of an intuitive capacity for change.

The power of the triad and its intertwining with the individual or family life is suggested by the emphasis throughout the novel on food, and especially on the processes of digesting and balancing diet. The ideal of the balance of opposites which Lily maintains in the food she provides for her husband ('sweet too soon after salty could upset the balance of the system, disturb the whole relationship of *yin* and *yang*'; Mo 1990: 252) seems to apply to the very alternation between and interdependence of the violent and the familial that structure both Chinese expatriate life and the novel itself. When Red Cudgel undergoes brutal revenge punishment, the narrative focuses attention on the interruption of the process of digestion: 'Most of the foot had been blown away. Red Cudgel began to vomit white noodles into a pool of blood. The sourness rose and mixed with the harsh, choking powder fumes' (241). This is recalled in a moment that focuses Lily's grief for the loss of her husband, after he has been killed on Red Cudgel's orders:

> Little things could be distressing. Going through her pantry, she upset a jar at the back and out poured a rattling flood of

the tiny red beans Husband had loved boiled in sugar. She picked up a handful, letting them run through her fingers one by one, as if they were the days of the life she had shared with Husband, until there were none left and she looked at an empty palm, still slim and shapely but now badly work-roughened. She looked at the beans again and they were red as blood, the bitter tears of blood she could shed, she thought.

(Mo 1990: 267)

Here, the alternation of sourness, sweetness and bitterness suggests both conflict, with its interruption of the smooth processes of balancing signalled in digestion, and the very principle of balance necessary to that process. Digestion also functions more generally through the novel as a metaphor for adaptation without loss of continuity, as in the description of Chen's family, which, presented with difficult changes, 'shuddered like jelly on impact with the obstacle but jelly-like suffered no damage, poured itself round the problem, dissolved what it was able to and absorbed what it could not' (228). On the other hand, the novel seems to acknowledge some ironic limit to its largely benign or encouraged view of the balance of adaptation and continuity in Chinese transplanted culture, in its wry discussion of the representative sweet and sour pork dish served by Chen with such success in his restaurant, which in fact 'bore no resemblance at all to Chinese cuisine' and produces a discoloration of the urine which shocks and alarms Chen (105). This is one of the few points in the novel where the maintaining of Chinese identity is threatened not so much by the otherness of the British as by a kind of involuntary self-mimicry, which is the effect of the image of Chinese identity reflected back on its bearers.

Sour Sweet draws back from the large and inclusive historical perspective developed, for example, in Mo's later novels, *An Insular Possession* (1986) and *The Redundancy of Courage* (1991). Rather it seems deliberately to mimic the condition of defensive enclosure or self-absorption which marks the culture with which it deals. Indeed, the novel comes close to suggesting that, if there is any such thing as a typical English life, then it is apprehensible only in odd, rather distorted fragments, which are themselves readable only by a sort of translation, for example in the soap operas which Mui watches:

The situations were universal enough ... and not so far

removed from the stock contexts of Cantonese drama as to be totally unintelligible; although the conventions could be very different. Mui was not able to retain the names of the leading characters but they were none the less real to her for that. She gave the characters names of her own devising; Boy, Hairnet, Drinker, Cripple, Crafty, Bad Girl. The composite picture she was able to glean of the British population was an alarming one.

(Mo 1990: 10)

This deliberate constriction of view, and the lack of any serious interest in the conflict or overlap of Chinese and British cultural worlds suggests powerfully the autonomy, density and complexity of Chinese inhabitation of the shared spaces of social belonging, as a kind of radial network of connections which neither overlaps with nor is seriously impinged upon by the more visible, more official versions of British life. Nevertheless, Mo's sense of the density of this form of cultural belonging is not wholly conservative or merely defensive, for his novel acknowledges the necessity of painful transformation. This is focused mostly upon the enigmatic figure of Man Kee, Lily's son, who begins to absorb more Western influences than Lily approves of. His gradual assimilation to British life is symbolised by the mango plant which he succeeds in getting to root in the unpropitious soil of the family garden. Lily's fundamental resistance to change is dramatised in an episode when, angered by hearing Man Kee say that he would like what Lily thinks of as the demeaning occupation of a gardener, she rips up the plant, rooted as it is with a surprising tenacity, with 'a subterranean tearing, the sound of small roots, tendrils and delicate fibres shearing and snapping' (255). But the snapping of the temporary continuity is also imaged as a kind of birth ('She strained, fighting the plant with her whole body. With louder vegetable groanings it began to come out of the earth'; ibid.). This recalls an earlier episode of gentle symbolism when Lily's attempt to pull a new jumper down over Man Kee's over-sized head is presented as a thwarted parturition (238). Mui, who at the end of the novel is to have been sufficiently assimilated into her new world to have a baby, to take out British citizenship and to lay plans to start a fish and chip shop, eases the painful transition for her nephew by cutting the neck of the jumper and sewing in more generous elastic (ibid.).

The idea of an integration into British life never rises in *Sour Sweet* to full and explicit narrative consciousness, but is expressed only in oblique and metaphorical hints. The exclusive emphasis throughout is on Chinese life, with only occasional reference to or even acknowledgement of the British life that surrounds them and, in marked contrast to *An Insular Possession*, a deliberate refraining from embodying any countervailing 'native' perspective. Habituated as we may be to such forms of blindness to indigenous populations and cultures in British novels about expatriates, exiles and travellers, this makes an effective reversal. By reflecting back to its British readership a sense of the strangeness and arbitrariness of all that seems familiar to them, British self-identity may be both imperilled and enlarged. But if the novel's refusal to dramatise a British perspective upon the Chinese in their midst is disturbing, the assumption of British life simply as an undifferentiated background actually runs the risk of suggesting that Britishness is a mere given, always in place and, in a sense, beyond or immune from the kinds of historical mutation required of the immigrant Chinese. This becomes particularly striking when one remembers that this is a novel published in 1982 about the experiences of immigrants during the 1960s, though the novel makes no attempt to register or contemplate the differences and similarities between the moment of writing and the moment that is being written about. Understandably enough, perhaps, the novel seems to assume that the most important question is how the immigrant is to adapt to the adopted culture, not what responsibilities and possibilities there may be for that receiving culture to transform itself.

However, there is a dramatic disproportion between the apparently uncompromising restriction of scope, subject and point of view to the Chinese characters, and the narrative mode of the novel. The novel addresses itself directly, exclusively and seemingly without self-consciousness to a British reader. The novel enforces an absolute trust in its own powers to explain, interpret and translate whatever is strange or idiomatic in the Chinese immigrant life that is its subject, and thus mediates in its form the mutual incomprehension, or non-impingement, of cultures that is suggested by its content. The narrator intervenes strategically to offer the reader ethnographic information about the pasts of the characters, about the codes and conventions of Chinese social life, about the complexity of familial vocative usages (the subtle differences between 'husband' and 'Ah Chen', for example; 40) and, most notably, about the secret intricacies of Hung ceremonial and history. It is easy to see how this accommodating openness to the reader could lead Michael Gorra to his judgement that Mo's achievement in *Sour Sweet* is 'not the creation . . . of his own world, but of a world that he makes part of everyone's' (1986: 671). Gorra is surely right to praise the way in which Mo here 'extends the range of material with which the novel as a genre can deal' and to approve the way in which he uses the form of the novel 'to make accessible to others the world one knows, and to do it so completely that the reader accepts the characters' point of view and begins to see London as an alien place' (ibid.). However, there remains something disquieting about the serene confidence in the novel that seems to underpin Mo's expansion of its possibilities. *Sour Sweet* suggests that it is possible to augment the novel's repertoire of subjects without needing to perturb or renovate any of its forms, languages and conventions. Often, the very clarity and authoritativeness of the narrative language works to divide the telling from the told, the experience of the characters and the reader for whom that experience is communicated:

> PRIVATE, proclaimed a notice in Mui's best block capitals above the particle-fall of swaying beads. TRESPASSER WOULD BE PROSECUTED. Outside, under Lily's and Chen's bedroom window, they slung a six-foot white plank, five-inch red English letters, four-inch black Chinese ideograms: DAH LING RESTAURANT, after the girls' home village. Natural attrition saw it become the Darling restaurant, of course, and the girls the two Darlings. About three months after they had moved in, the reason for the customers' strange jollity and their obsession with languidly repeating the name of the restaurant out loud dawned on Mui. She didn't tell Lily.
> (Mo 1990: 95)

The privacy and interiority of the world Mo is here mediating are both preserved and trespassed upon by the novel and its language. As in other novels with which I have been concerned in this book, the question of address relates to the wider issue of the possibilities of the novel form itself to register and resist cultural conflict and exclusion. If the challenge of *Sour Sweet* lies both in its deliberate refusal to take the large view of a condition of England, lest this should shrink the particular experiences of the immigrant Chinese community to invisibility, and in its determined decentring or internal alienation of Englishness, the very authority of this challenge rests oddly upon a continued faith in the synoptic powers of novelistic narration and the unifying mode of its address to a readership which, despite the novel's refusal to represent that readership or its interests, is thereby mirrored back to itself whole and entire.

On the face of it, Kazuo Ishiguro's *The Remains of the Day* (1989) hardly seems comparable to the other novels considered so far in this chapter. Certainly, Ishiguro occupies the same culturally intermediary position as Hanif Kureishi, Timothy Mo and Salman Rushdie, having been born in Japan but brought up in Britain. But unlike those writers, Ishiguro does not give the question of divided cultural identity visibility as a subject in his work. *The Remains of the Day* is certainly in one sense a meditation upon the nature of national consciousness and identity, but seems not to show much interest in the kind of doubled, convoluted, or outside-in consciousness and experience evoked in the other novels discussed in this chapter. *The Remains of the Day* is the narrative of Stevens, a butler, once in the employ of Lord Darlington but now working for the American who has bought up his house. Stevens is persuaded to take a trip to the West Country, in order ostensibly to discuss with Miss Kenton, who had previously worked alongside him as housekeeper at Darlington Hall, the possibility of returning to service. Like Ishiguro's other novels, *A Pale View of Hills* (1982) and *An Artist of the Floating World* (1986), the narrative maintains a parallel between a present tense and a past tense that is gradually but unreliably retrieved in reminiscence as the narrative proceeds. In *The Remains of the Day*, Stevens keeps a kind of journal of his trip down to Little Compton where Miss Kenton now lives, and intercuts this account with reflections on his past and the historical place of Darlington Hall. As his narrative proceeds, he gradually and grudgingly reveals two converging areas of hurt and defeat in his life, one personal, the other political. Stevens has in fact, though he scarcely knows it himself, been in love with Miss Kenton; and the employer whom he so admires has been a Nazi sympathiser who used his influence to try to forge an Anglo-German alliance in the years before the Second World War.

The novel maintains a clear parallel between the slowly, reluctantly enlarging awareness of Stevens, and the sense of Englishness as a whole. The disavowal of feeling, the strict partition between the private and public realms, the stiffening of the will to maintain conventional appearances, and the concomitant fear of the collapse of distinctions – everything, in fact, that is summed up for Stevens in the quality he calls 'dignity' – is also identified as essentially English: 'when you think of a great butler, he is bound, almost by definition, to be an Englishman', he declares (1989: 43). Englishness is embodied spatially and geographically. Stevens in fact knows little about his own country, and intends to do his sightseeing largely with a guidebook entitled *The Wonders of England* by a Mrs Jane Symons, but early on in his journey he encounters some surprises. First of all, he experiences a sense of unease as he passes beyond familiar landmarks, 'the feeling that I was perhaps not on the correct road at all, but speeding off in totally the wrong direction into a wilderness' (24). Almost straight away, he meets an enigmatic old man who advises him to follow a steep and winding path which delivers to him a panoramic prospect of the English countryside. The symbolism of this episode is restrained, but palpable, for Stevens is indeed entering an unpredictable and emotionally dangerous wilderness. Nor is this symbolic quality hidden from Stevens himself. Nevertheless, the marvels of the view upon which he dwells prompt only the most ordinary and unenraptured description from him:

> What I saw was principally field upon field rolling off into the far distance. The land rose and fell gently, and the fields were bordered by hedges and trees. There were dots in some of the distant fields which I assumed to be sheep. To my right, almost on the horizon, I thought I could see the square tower of a church.
>
> (Ishiguro 1989: 26)

When he returns to the question of this landscape a little later, Stevens projects his own understatement on to the landscape itself, suggesting that its greatness consists in 'the very *lack* of obvious drama or spectacle . . . as though the land knows of its own beauty, of its own greatness, and feels no need to shout it', as opposed to the 'unseemly demonstrativeness' of African or American landscapes (28–9).

There is an intriguing complexity here. Stevens praises the landscape for its coincidence with itself, for its tempering of that surfeit of spectacle allegedly characteristic of foreign landscapes. The English landscape presents an absolute correspondence between its appearance and its meaning. But at the same time, it is this very quality of reserve which gives the landscape a certain surplus of unaccounted-for meaning, in the fact that it becomes the sign and symbol of reserve itself. Such is also the case with the stories of exemplary dignity and greatness in butlers upon which Stevens broods. The parallel between the dignity of the English temperament and the quality of the English landscape is insisted on: 'It is with such men as it is with the English landscape seen at its best as I did this morning: when one encounters them, one simply *knows* one is in the presence of greatness' (44). The very elusiveness of the ideals that Stevens attempts to pin down, and the fact that he has to resort to symbolic parallels and expositions, always implies the necessity for some kind of interpretative supplementation in order to make clear and available the qualities of Englishness that are said to be immediately apprehensible and self-interpreting. Englishness is held to be a perfect fusion of the outside and the inside, surface and depth, symbol and meaning; but the only way to demonstrate this fusion is by breaking into it, by using symbols and exemplars that do not spontaneously deliver up their meanings, but whose very fullness and self-evidence can become troublingly enigmatic. For Stevens, the very act of analysis is a disturbing violation of the calm, self-sufficiency he requires of truth; at the same time, such self-sufficiency irresistibly demands the activities of understanding and interpretation.

It is for this reason that Stevens seems so driven to the acts of retrospection that make up his narrative. He longs to prove to himself that, as Darlington's butler, he has come 'as close to the hub of this world's wheel as one such as I could ever have dreamt' (126), but this still centre of achievement, identity and fullness of being is perpetually flung out to the circumference of history, change and the movement of recapitulation; the narrative of the achievement being the very sign of its falling short. It is no wonder, therefore, that Stevens's intrinsic, essential Englishness should come to seem so tenuous and lacking in stability, as in the passage in which he confesses to playing the part of his dead master in front of an audience of locals in Moscombe (180–94), or in the slightly disturbing episode in which his new master questions his credentials:

> I mean to say, Stevens, this *is* a genuine grand old English house, isn't it? That's what I paid for. And you're a genuine old-fashioned English butler, not just some waiter pretending to be one. You're the real thing, aren't you? That's what I wanted, isn't that what I have?
>
> (Ishiguro 1989: 124)

However, although Englishness is revealed at such moments to be conflicted and even constructed, there seems to be no doubt that it is Englishness that is at stake or under analysis in this novel. It seems worth making this observation, since so few readers have been able to accept it. In fact, most of the reviewers and commentators of the novel have assumed that the admittedly striking continuity of theme between this novel and Ishiguro's two earlier 'Japanese' novels, both of which deal, in the same meticulous, elegiac way, with the unreliability of memory and the difficulty of self-knowledge, means that all three must be concerned with fundamentally the same question of Japanese identity. Thus, there is the alarming explicitness with which Gabriele Annan identifies the message of *The Remains of the Day*: 'Be less Japanese, less bent on dignity, less false to yourself and others, less restrained and controlled' (1989: 4). Claude Habib similarly reads the apparent Englishness of the novel as a dissimulation of Ishiguro's real concern with Japanese identity. Despite the fact that there is no mention of Japan or of the Japanese in the novel, Habib believes that, in *The Remains of the Day*, 'Ishiguro has managed to translate into purely British terms the crucial problem of Japanese identity: what happens to the values of perfectionism when confronted with the values of democracy?' (Habib 1991: 117–18, my translation). Pico Iyer's review of the novel is also sure of the novel's real intentions:

> *The Remains of the Day* may seem just a small, private English novel done to – Japanese – perfection; a vale from a valet. To anyone familiar with Japan, however, the author's real intention slips out as surely as a business card from a Savile Row suit.
>
> (Iyer 1991: 586)

There is something a little disturbing about this critical unanimity that, since Ishiguro is not himself British by birth, and has not before written about being British, he can only be doing so here as a kind of strategy. This reading works alongside other readings of the work of writers not born in Britain or writing English as a second language (as Ishiguro is not) as a form of cultural repatriation. Salman Rushdie has remarked of 'commonwealth literature', for example, that it is a condition of its entry into critical acknowledgement in the metropolitan centres of literary taste that it stick to its 'own' subjects, rendering for the benefit of English readerships 'authentic' experiences of other locations and cultures (1991). But when Ishiguro is read as a Japanese writer concerned wholly and necessarily with Japanese themes, he is 'returned' to an identity that was never his own. The purpose and result of such a deportation is the maintaining of distinction and imagined distance between home and abroad, the self and the other. 'Translating the most Japanese of virtues into terms we recognize as our own,' writes Pico Iyer, 'he brings their foreign features home to us' (1991: 588). Here, the uncertainty of a hybrid, or outside-in, rendering of Englishness is made tolerable and coherent by being represented itself as a translation, an opening out of Japanese identity to us for inspection (Ishiguro allegedly being equipped 'to create an utterly convincing Japanese from the inside out'; ibid.). Thus, the foreignness within Englishness is 'brought home' to us, precisely by being first sent home to itself.

There is an element of risk in Ishiguro's writing to which such critics and reviewers are responding without necessarily having to recognise it. Very obviously, *The Remains of the Day* is a kind of performance, maintained with an impassive levelness that is a strange mixture of the understated and the demonstrative. In other words, there is a close equivalence between the kind of temperament that is being displayed by the book, and the book's own manner of displaying it. Stevens's watchfully precise language, which never allows itself to depart from decorum and correctness, is rendered in a narrative that equally encircles itself with restriction, never allowing itself the licence of other voices or idioms. It would appear that the parallel between the two performances is not exact or complete, however. The book does not merely imitate Stevens's language, it also exhibits it for us; by briefly revealing what Stevens cannot know or consistently acknowledge about his repressed love for Miss Kenton, his cruelty to his father, and his employer's guilty political past, the book unpicks the seamless self-possession of Stevens's language.

Such a distinction between the language that Stevens uses and the imitation of that language by Ishiguro has the advantage of maintaining coherence, for the book and for its reader. However, if there is no exact fit between the language that Stevens uses and the imitation of that language by Ishiguro, neither is there any reliable or continuous distinction between the two languages or levels. Ishiguro's language cannot be thought of simply as an impersonation, just as Stevens's language cannot be thought of simply as his own. Ishiguro's impersonation is of a language that is itself already an impersonation, a borrowed language which is extravagant in the extreme degree of its reserve, as well as in occasional muffs or misfires – such as the split infinitive with which the book actually concludes: 'I should hope, then, that by the time of my employer's return, I shall be in a position to pleasantly surprise him' (Ishiguro 1989: 245). The 'typical' Englishness of Stevens's language is in fact what makes it wholly unrepresentative of any type, marking it as something like the borrowed language of the kind of foreigner or outsider that, in class terms and historical terms, Stevens has so conspicuously become. If Ishiguro is imitating the effect of imperfect imitation, then there is always a risk of confusion between what Wittgenstein called 'use' and 'mention' in language, between serious and ironic language, between *ipsissima verba* and reported speech. More specifically, there is a risk – and it is one that, by definition, Ishiguro's writing must both exhibit and itself be exposed to – that one will not be able to tell apart Englishness and the foreignness that reconstitutes it from the outside in.

This strange reversibility seems to be dramatised in the novel in a cutely ludicrous interchange between Stevens and Miss Kenton concerning the position of an ornament. Miss Kenton is determined to make Stevens acknowledge that his elderly father, himself a distinguished butler in his day, is losing his grip and beginning to make mistakes about the house:

'Mr Stevens, that is the incorrect Chinaman, would you not agree?'

'Miss Kenton, I am very busy. I am surprised you have nothing better to do than stand in corridors all day.'

'Mr Stevens, is that the correct Chinaman or is it not?'

'Miss Kenton, I would ask you to keep your voice down.'

'And I would ask you, Mr Stevens, to turn around and look at that Chinaman.'

'Miss Kenton, please keep your voice down. What would employees below think to hear us shouting at the top of our voices about what is and what is not the correct Chinaman?'

'The fact is, Mr Stevens, all the Chinamen in this house have been dirty for some time! And now, they are in incorrect positions!'

'Miss Kenton, you are being quite ridiculous. Now if you will be so good as to let me pass.'

'Mr Stevens, will you kindly look at the Chinaman behind you?'

'If it is so important to you, Miss Kenton, I will allow that the Chinaman behind me may well be incorrectly situated. But I must say I am at some loss as to why you should be so concerned with these most trivial of errors.'

'These errors may be trivial in themselves, Mr Stevens, but you must yourself realize their larger significance.'

(Ishiguro 1989: 58–9)

The comedy of this scene has much to do with the ponderous precision with which the growing anger of the participants is both disguised and discharged. There is also some significance in the details of the scene being evoked. Stevens maintains his post in front of and with his back to the figure whose incorrect position stands for the catastrophic entrance of error and misjudgement into this meticulously regulated world. The fact that the contrast between orderliness and disorderliness is posed in terms of the contrast between the English and the Oriental gently registers the link between domestic space and the global space of Empire. (It is his father's error that has resulted in the incorrectly positioned Chinaman, but it is as though the entrance of the Chinaman brings with it a risk of spontaneous pollution and the disruption of space.) In both domestic and global space, power and identity are dependent upon the maintaining of distance. The 'larger significance' of the shifting Chinaman appears to be larger even than Miss Kenton divines, since it reflects the fundamental shifts in international dispositions of power both before the Second World War and after it (*The Remains of the Day* is set judiciously in 1956, the year of the Suez Crisis which saw the emphatic beginnings of Britain's decline as a world influence). This seems to be confirmed by a certain shiftiness in Stevens's own narration of the episode, for he cannot be sure on reflection that all of the phrases he has attributed to Miss Kenton, and especially her last phrase about the larger significance of trivial errors, were really hers:

> In fact, now that I come to think of it, I have a feeling it may have been Lord Darlington himself who made that particular remark to me that time he called me into his study some two months after that exchange with Miss Kenton outside the

billiard room. By that time, the situation as regards my father
had changed significantly following his fall.

(Ishiguro 1989: 60)

The dislocation of time and narrative here oddly matches its
subject, the mis-situated Chinaman which portends the fall of
Stevens's father. It also parallels the shifting international situation
which provokes Lord Darlington to convene his conference and to
ask Stevens to remove his father from the scene as a potential cause
of embarrassment. The narrative, in other words, concerns and
enacts shift and dislocation, in a way that may suggest obliquely the
larger cultural migrations and relocations that characterised the
postwar years; Ishiguro himself arrived in England only a few years
after this novel is set.

Under such conditions it becomes possible to read *The Remains
of the Day* as a rather more knowing and complex investigation of
the historical conditions of Englishness than it has hitherto been
given credit for. Rather than simply looking back on a moment
when the apprehension of English self-identity was still safe and
reliable, the novel draws attention to its own act of historical
performance in constituting its idyll of uninterrupted identity and
to the performative nature of that Englishness in itself and at its
allegedly authentic moment. It is not just that the alien eye of the
Japanese immigrant writer discloses a once-present but now lost
essential Englishness, because that eye reveals the ways in which
Englishness is already constituted on what it cannot fully know
about itself, namely its dependence on what lies outside (passion,
poverty, violence, foreignness). In many ways, *The Remains of the Day*
is less aware of itself and its own novelistic form than most of the
other novels I have been considering in this chapter and, indeed,
Ishiguro has spoken of his irritation with the techniques of self-
consciousness in fiction:

> The kind of book I find very tedious is the kind of book whose
> *raison d'être* is to say something about literary form. I'm only
> interested in literary experiment insofar as it serves a purpose
> of exploring certain themes with an emotional dimension. I
> always try to disguise those elements of my writing that I feel
> perhaps are experimental.
>
> (Ishiguro, in Mason 1989: 346)

Nevertheless, there does seem to be a striking parallel between

The Remains of the Day and some other outside-in novels, in the close relationship it maintains between the representation of England and Englishness and its exploration of the possibilities of its own form. The restrained exercise in chamber realism in this novel is just as much an impersonation as anything else about it, and in fact represents an ironic dramatisation of the impossibility of the closed circuit of writing, reading and interpreting that the kind of novel it purports to be would require. As in other novels, this is enacted crucially through the ambivalence of the novel's address. At times, Stevens's narration seems deferentially to assume a reader who is in the position of power and responsibility that his previous master has been, seems to assume therefore the kind of world which has passed away with the demise of Lord Darlington, with its easy concourse of the private and the public, the domestic and the international. At other times, his narrative seems to address an imaginary equal in age and experience, in its discussion of the Hayes Club and its regulation of standards among butlers. But, as the book goes on, Stevens has more and more to face the possibility that there is no plausible addressee at all to his narrative; that the fictional world conjured and sustained by the fact of the narration can never encompass the 'world' of public affairs in the way it has fantasised. The novel ends in the acknowledgement of this failure of connection, with Stevens deciding that

> The hard reality is, surely, that for the likes of you and I, there is little choice other than to leave our fate, ultimately, in the hands of those great gentlemen at the hub of the world who employ our services.
>
> (Ishiguro 1989: 244)

But, in this deliberate, narcissistic shrinking down of his world, Stevens actually repeats the error of his past, in failing to acknowledge the possibility, the necessity even, of multiple, mutually impacting and transforming worlds. The purpose of the performance of national identity that is *The Remains of the Day* is therefore to let in what such a restricted imagining of identity relies on keeping out. It aims to enlarge the possibilities for narrating identity across and between cultures and their alleged essential characteristics and conditions by performing the impossibility of a more constrained, coherent imagination of Englishness.

One of the many grotesque effects of the worldwide controversy sparked by Ayatollah Khomeini's denunciation in February 1989 of *The Satanic Verses* (1988) and its author, Salman Rushdie, was that

OUTSIDE IN

it produced a narrowing and simplifying retrenchment of cultures and cultural identities; the effect is grotesque because anyone who reads the book with any attention (and *The Satanic Verses* must be the most discussed but least read book of recent years) cannot fail to be struck by its determination to throw such clarity into turmoil. When it has been read at all, the novel has been read almost entirely in the terms enforced by the violent controversy about its representation of the beginnings of Islam. This is understandable in those whose principal concern has been to attack or defend the integrity of Islam, but less so when it comes to readings which attempt to account for the novel as a whole. Whatever view is taken of the particular kinds of fictional strategy employed by Rushdie, it seems to have become unquestionable that *The Satanic Verses* is fundamentally about Islam, which is to say, about the history, values and violence of a culture projected as fundamentally other than the liberal, metropolitan, literary and English-speaking audience addressed by Rushdie. Stephanie Newell articulates this assumption when she writes that

> the novel represents Rushdie's own script-writing, and selection of actors to play out the problematic areas of Islam upon a fictional twentieth-century stage, to stimulate renewed debate within Islam and a questioning of the ahistorical purity and aura of sanctity surrounding the rules and laws within the *Koran*.
>
> (1992: 80–1)

This reading of the novel has to work quite hard against what is manifest in it, namely its interest in and depiction of the experience of the immigrant within British life; as hard, in fact, as the readings of Kazuo Ishiguro's novel which insist on seeing the concern with Englishness as a coded concern with the Other and which, by this act of translation, ship the novel safely abroad.

The Satanic Verses begins with fall, division and recombination. The two principal characters in the novel, the Bombay film actor Gibreel Farishta and the Anglicised Indian Saladin Chamcha, are seen falling through the air after the explosion of the hijacked aeroplane on which they have been passengers. The fall as it is described evokes a large number of other literary, mythical and theological falls: the fall of Icarus, Alice's fall down the rabbit hole, the fall of man, the fall of Satan from heaven, the fall of the tower of Babel and the fall or 'pftjschute' of the mythical Finnegan in

Joyce's *Finnegans Wake* (1939). Like the beginning of *The Satanic Verses*, this last is a compounding of many other falls, sunderings and epochal eruptions, in a language that imitates the annunciatory thunder of a new age and the mingling together of new and old: 'The fall (bababadalgharaghtakamminarronnkonnbronntonn- erronntuonnthunntrovarrhounawnskawntoohoohoordenenthurnuk!) of a once wallstrait oldparr is retaled early in bed and later in life down through all christian minstrelsy' (Joyce 1971: 3). Rushdie's novel asks us to accept that the two characters are kept alive by a kind of cooperation of opposites, and an exchange of attributes; the cosmopolitan, extravagantly pluricultural Gibreel begins to take on the sternly consistent self-definition of Saladin, the actor of many parts narrowing into the willed inhabitation of one identity only. As the novel develops, Gibreel becomes progressively possessed by the idea that he is an avenging angel come to wreak God's revenge upon the decadent city of London with his firethrowing trumpet of extermination, Azraeel. Saladin, by contrast, having been handed over by Gibreel to the immigration authorities after their miraculous landing on the beach at Dover, begins to abandon his neurotic dream of a true or ideally continuous self; magically transformed into a sulphur-breathing, horned devil, in obedience to the force of racist fantasies of the diabolical Other, Saladin founds his identity not on truth and adamantine persistence of identity but on mingling, mimicry and mutation. If Gibreel is angelic, it is by virtue of the fact that he 'has wished to remain, to a large degree, *continuous* – that is, joined to and arising from his past ... [to remain] at bottom an untranslated man' (Rushdie 1988: 427). What is satanic or diabolic about Saladin, on the other hand, is that he is 'a creature of *selected* discontinuities, a *willing* re-invention' (ibid.).

The central opposition between continuity and hybridity, the one and the many, truth and imitation, keys into a number of other important conflicts which the novel explores. The importance of the dream sequence which occupies the second section of the novel, in which Gibreel feels himself compelled into the role of the archangel Gabriel transmitting to Mahomet the divine revelation which is to inaugurate Islam, is that it links the question of continuity and adaptation to the relations between sacred and secular time. The revelation of Islam is shown as a violent, transfiguring cleavage of the historical world of changing human interests by the absolute truth of divine knowledge, which confronts the shifting impermanence of the commercial city of Jahilia, built on sand and vulnerable to the dissolving effects of water, with the terrifying intransigence of a faith that tolerates no admixture of error or impurity. As the beginning of the fourth section, entitled 'Ayesha,' makes clear, the world-historical force of Islam lies precisely in its identification of, and with, values and truths that lie outside history. In this section, Gibreel is summoned into his identification with the archangel by the brooding desire of the exiled Imam to exact exterminating revenge upon all of the feminine corruptions of error and the body that are associated with historical time:

> 'We will make a revolution,' the Imam proclaims . . . 'that is a revolt not only against a tyrant, but against history.' For there is an enemy beyond Ayesha, and it is History herself. History is the blood-wine that must no longer be drunk. History, the intoxicant, the creation and possession of the Devil, of the great Shaitan, the greatest of the lies – progress, science, rights – against which the Imam has set his face. History is a deviation from the Path, knowledge is a delusion, because the sum of knowledge was complete on the day Al-Lah finished his revelation to Mahound.
>
> (Rushdie 1988: 210)

Most emphatically in this section, in which Gibreel is drawn into the Imam's dream of the annihilation of history in the person of the goddess Al-lat, but elsewhere in more diffuse form in the novel, there seems to be a clear preference for the unpredictable and profuse energies of chance, change and commingling, which are associated with the historical, over the cold, nullifying satiety of absolute truth. *The Satanic Verses* thus appears to a certain degree to favour the position of the migrant – the creature of willing discontinuity – over that of the exile, whose longing for the return of the past freezes history, narrowing to nothing the gap between what has been lost and its undiminished return in the longed-for future. The novel appears equivalently to prefer the profane over the sacred, modernity against tradition, and secular over millennial or mythical time. Most particularly, it seems to underwrite the fallen word of ordinary language against the supreme authority of the religious Word. In Gibreel's dream, a scribe called Salman the Persian confesses that he has introduced his own variations into the word of God as dictated to him by Mahound, 'polluting the word of God with my own profane language' (367). Fleeing from the enraged Mahound, Salman tells Baal, a fellow writer, that he is sure to be killed, since 'It's his Word against mine' (368).

Given its promotion history, as encompassing growth, change and adaptive newness against timeless perfection, it would appear that of the detractors of *The Satanic Verses* are at least right to claim that the novel sets Western values against absolute Islamic values. Indeed, many defences of the novel, in the furore that followed the issuing of the *fatwa* or sentence of death by the Ayatollah Khomeini, relied upon just this characterisation of Islam as a grotesque survival of archaic time within but also outside the evolving, progressive, universal time of the West. To identify Islam as ahistorical, as lying outside or athwart the time of the West, is in part a repetition of that anthropological division, analysed by Johannes Fabian in his book *Time and the Other* (1983), between those 'primitive' societies who are held to be outside or prior to the beginnings of historical time and those 'civilised' societies who have entered history. We may leave aside the interesting irony that Islam was also accused by some of the defenders of *The Satanic Verses* of belonging too much to history, in being the most recently established of major world religions, with its roots too obviously in the documented doings of historical figures.

This irony takes another form in the fact that, in being read as it was by those Muslims who condemned and continue to condemn it, *The Satanic Verses* becomes vulnerable to the contingencies and 'satanic' perversions of history in just the same way as Mahound's words. One common defence of the novel has been to claim that, as a fictional text, it simply cannot and should not be read as any kind of literal truth. The problem with this defence is that it requires a distinction between the figural and the fictional on the one hand and the literal truth on the other, which is much stricter than the novel itself seems inclined to endorse. Thus it was widely alleged that *The Satanic Verses* represents the Prophet's twelve wives as prostitutes. No such episode or representation exists in the novel, though it is indeed possible that a certain skim-reading of the episode in which prostitutes in a Jahilia brothel pretend to be the Prophet's wives, followed and amplified by the unreliable trench-whispers of cultural transmission, might lead to such a distorted reading. But to defend the novel against this misreading is necessarily to repeat the authoritarian gesture of the Mahound who cannot tolerate the satanic deviations of history in his perfect text. Paradoxically, the doctrine offered by the novel of the necessary openness of all texts to historical rewritings, and misreadings, can only be maintained by protecting the novel against just this kind of historical process. Here, it is Islam that appears as the disruptive breaking in of history-as-difference to a closed, authoritarian universe of meaning. In a similar way, Rushdie as public figure (while he could still be a public figure, that is) was forced to take on a kind of authorial responsibility for his book, explaining, analysing, interpreting its meaning and his own intentions, in a way which seems to cut incongruously against the ironic undermining of the idea of the determining power of the author throughout the text, with the intermittent appearances in it of the author as shrunken, ineffectual and baffled god.

However, these are ironies to which *The Satanic Verses* is not wholly vulnerable, since it takes them partly as its subject. The point of Gibreel's long dream about the founding revelation of Islam is to reveal it as a transfiguring, revolutionary interruption of history, a sudden suspension or inversion of values, beliefs and ways of imagining which, whatever its growing antagonism to the impermanence of history, also enacts, in its arbitrary irruption into the world, the very uncontainable force of history itself. If Islam, in the person of the Imam, means the denial of history, then the troubled, miraculous beginning of Islam, as represented in Gibreel's dream, embodies the possibility of interruption that is the very essence of the historical. The ambivalence of Islam is borne out in the fact that it is at once hard ('*the cussed, bloody-minded, ramrod-backed type of damnfool notion that would rather break than sway with the breeze*'; 335) and possessed of the softening, dissolving effects of water – Mahound's new faith is the destructive watery element that is so dangerous to the dry city of sand that is Jahilia.

It is the power of this possibility that is transmitted to London, the centre of the Empire, the still point in the turning historical world. Saladin dreams of a perfect congruence between his assumed British identity and the city of London:

> He had been striving ... to be worthy of the challenge represented by the phrase *Civis Brittanicus sum*. Empire was no more, but still he knew 'all that was good and living within him' to have been 'made, shaped and quickened' by his

encounter with this islet of sensibility, surrounded by the cool sense of the sea. – Of material things, he had given his love to this city, London, preferring it to the city of his birth or to any other; had been creeping up on it, stealthily, with mounting excitement, freezing into a statue when it looked in his direction, dreaming of being the one to possess it and so, in a sense, *become* it.

(Rushdie 1988: 398)

But this congruence is a fitting or mirroring together of incongruities: 'London, its conglomerate nature mirroring his own' (ibid.). Gibreel, on the other hand, sees no possibility of correspondence between his nature and the growing sense of his redemptive, angelic mission on the one hand and the troubling confusion of forms and experiences that he finds in London on the other. His desire is for clarity of definition, a clarity that distinguishes in absolute terms the settler from the native, the outsider from the insider, the evil from the good:

He looked down upon the city and saw the English. The trouble with the English was that they were English: damn cold fish! – Living underwater most of the year, in days the colour of night! – Well: he was here now, the great Transformer, and this time there'd be some changes made – the laws of nature are the laws of its transformation, and he was the very person to utilize the same! Yes, indeed: this time, clarity.

(Rushdie 1988: 352–3)

Gibreel's desire is for a cleansing and absolute decolonisation which will at once evacuate the colonist from the mind of his colonial victim and round upon that colonist in revenge. The problem for Gibreel is that the very ferocity of the distinctions that he aims to reestablish and sustain keeps stimulating the troubling oscillation of antagonistic categories, whether political or metaphysical, and suggests the strange interdependence of adversary principles. His own adversary is Saladin, with his devilish apostasy from his true nature and his willed internalisation of Englishness, and Gibreel characterises in terms borrowed from the Algerian theorist of colonial identity, Frantz Fanon, as 'self-hating, constructing a false ego, auto-destructive'. Fanon again: 'In this way the individual' – the Fanonian *native* – 'accepts the disintegration ordained by God, bows down before the settler and his lot, and by a kind of interior restabilization acquires a stony calm' (353). But the interdependence of natures between coloniser and colonised suggested by Saladin's mingling of self and other – 'Native and settler, that old dispute, continuing now upon these soggy streets, with reversed categories' (ibid.) – slides into Gibreel's uneasy and recurrent sense of his own muddled, mimic nature, which is not to be wholly distinguished from that of Saladin: 'he was forever joined to the adversary, their arms locked around each other's bodies, mouth to mouth, head to tail, as when they fell to earth: when they *settled*' (ibid.). Not only are inside and outside not to be distinguished with the necessary clarity, but, given the fact that Gibreel and Saladin have each exchanged fixation for fluidity, the very distinction between distinction (Gibreel) and indistinction (Saladin) is compromised.

It is necessary to insist that *The Satanic Verses* makes this an issue that concerns and defines Englishness as well as the condition of the immigrant or outsider. If Gibreel represents the fixation of the Imam, the stopping of history, he also stands for history's interruptive, transformative force, which breaks in on 'the stony calm' of a Western chronology organised in terms of linear and orderly development, according to the single, governing movements that Jean-François Lyotard has famously characterised as 'metanarratives' (1984). The delusions of the angelic Gibreel serve as metaphorical solvents for the city of London. It is in thrall, like its mythical, materialistic shadow-city Jahilia, to a castrating, cannibalistic 'iron lady', the Grandee's wife Hind, whose 'refusals of time, of history, of age, which sang the city's undimmed magnificence and defied the garbage and decrepitude of the streets ... in which murder for small change was becoming commonplace, in which old women were being raped and ritually slaughtered' (361) caricature the jingoism attached to the Falklands campaign.

Self-inventing mutations such as Gibreel and Saladin threaten the idea of this kind of changeless or permanent self, whether at the level of the species, the race, the nation or the personality. Running through the novel are two associated arguments about the nature of change. Firstly, there are the alternatives set out in the work of Ovid and Lucretius, as explicated for Saladin's benefit by his host at the Shandaar café, Muhammad Sufyan. Where Ovid's *Metamorphoses* proposes the soul as an immortal essence undergoing superficial variations of form but remaining itself unchanged, Lucretius in *De Rerum Natura* argues for a more fundamental mutability of the self, such that, in Sufyan's translation, 'Whatever by its changing goes out of its frontiers . . . by doing so brings immediate death to its old self' (276). Secondly, there are the alternative accounts of evolution provided by Darwin and Lamarck. Where Darwin proposed that adaptations to environment could only come about through the preservation and transmission of successful forms of random mutation, Lamark believed that adaptive characteristics acquired in an animal's lifetime could also be transmitted and inherited. In a sense, therefore, Lamarck is to Darwin as Lucretius is to Ovid, since both pairs encode the contrast between a view of change as a steady, coherent development of a consistently existing entity and change as more catastrophic and unpredictable. The kind of mutation undergone by Saladin convinces him of the appropriateness of the Lamarckian–Lucretian model over the Darwinian–Ovidian one:

> Evolution theory had come a long way since Darwin. It was now being argued that major changes in species happened not in the stumbling, hit-and-miss manner first envisaged, but in great, radical leaps. The history of life was not the bumbling progress – the very English middle-class progress – Victorian thought had wanted it to be, but violent, a thing of dramatic, cumulative transformations: in the old formulation, more revolution than evolution.
>
> (Rushdie 1988: 418)

Saladin's successive mutations, first of all into the perfect counterfeit Englishman, then into the sulphurous devil of English racist imagination, and finally into something like the 'chimeran graft' he sees on *Gardener's World* – 'a chimera with roots, firmly planted in and growing vigorously out of a piece of English earth' (406), – are not just what happens on the periphery of Englishness; they have come to compose Englishness itself. Homi Bhabha, one of the few commentators to have discussed the embarrassment and transformation of Englishness by the reverse colonisation of characters such as Gibreel and Saladin, focuses on the episode early in the novel in which Gibreel Farishta is summoned into the role of Sir Henry Diamond, the deceased husband of Rosa Diamond who has given hospitality to the sky-fallen immigrants. Possessed by Rosa Diamond's fantasies of a lost colonial past and mirroring them back to her, Gibreel also interrupts them, suggesting the supplement of contradictory histories that these memories function to exclude, and must exclude to function. In his masquerade as Henry Diamond, writes Bhabha, Gibreel

> marginalizes and singularizes the totality of national culture. He is the history that happened elsewhere, overseas; his postcolonial, migrant presence . . . articulates the narrative of cultural difference which can never let the national history look at itself narcissistically in the eye.
> (Bhabha 1990a: 318)

There are signs elsewhere that London is less the centre of cultural continuity than a shifting maelstrom of impermanence. Images of hardness, petrified permanence and 'stony calm' are countered by images that suggest fluidity, imprecise distinctions and 'meltdown', the term used to described the bizarre, vengeful ceremony enacted upon wax effigies in the Hot Wax club. If the violence towards the wax figure of Margaret Thatcher is directed against her adamantine hardness, it also suggests the ways in which the values that she affirms, of resolve, clarity and unswerving self-identity, may be compounded with fluidity at their heart; when her effigy is strapped into the Hot Seat, it melts, significantly 'from the inside out' (Rushdie 1988: 293). It may be said of the reaffirmed values of British pride and identity out of and against which this novel is written, that the forms of exclusion and self-purification they practise ceaselessly disclose the very principles – of softness, darkness, otherness – they expel to the outside of themselves. Otherness – or the melting together of selfhood and otherness – is not on the outside of the self, or the nation, but on its inside.

This paradoxical exchange of what does and does not belong to the core of Englishness is played out in *The Satanic Verses* through the representation of London. The city that sees itself as the centre of an extended, far-flung circumference has been folded back in on itself, such that the topography of centre and edge is hard to discern. For Gibreel, London represents indeterminacy itself, the site, not of achieved and consummate national identity, but of 'England-induced ambiguities . . . Biblical–Satanic confusions' (353). It is the 'most slippery, most devilish of cities' (354). This is not exactly because it is corrupt, but because it allows no definitive judgement as to its soundness or corruption. Gibreel blames the soggy, equivocal British weather for this indeterminacy and imagines the changes that might come about were London suddenly to be, as he puts it, 'tropicalized', including 'development of vivid and expansive patterns of behaviour amongst the populace ... improved street life, outrageously-coloured flowers ... higher emphasis on ball-control among professional footballers' (355). But this imaginary turning of London inside out is in fact literalised later on in the novel, when riots erupt after the murder of a black community leader. London becomes the scene of a hellish conflagration that is no more clarifying or refining than the indeterminate climate that Gibreel so despises: 'How hot it is: steamy, close, intolerable. This is no Proper London: not this improper city. Airstrip One, Mahagonny, Alphaville. He wanders through a confusion of languages' (459).

In one sense, the indeterminacy of the city comes from the fact that it is the non-place of modern life, a kind of cultural thin air in which differences are compounded and annulled, histories flattened: the plane that is to take Saladin and Gibreel from Bombay to London travels

> from Indianness to Englishness, an immeasurable distance. Or, not very far at all, because they rose from one great city, fell to another. The distance between cities is always small; a villager, travelling a hundred miles to town, traverses emptier, darker, more terrifying space.
>
> (Rushdie 1988: 41)

In another sense, the city is so confusing and protean because it itself includes the frontier, or innumerable overlaid frontiers, between modernity and other kinds of life, other time-scales. The modern city, in the words of Otto Cone, the father of Gibreel's mountaineering lover Alleluiah Cone,

> is the locus classicus of incompatible realities. Lives that have no business mingling with one another sit side by side upon the omnibus. One universe, on a zebra crossing, is caught for an instant, blinking like a rabbit, in the headlamps of a motor-vehicle in which an entirely alien and contradictory continuum is to be found.
>
> (Rushdie 1988: 314)

Cone's terminology here oddly recalls that of Hal Valance, the racist producer of *The Aliens Show* in which Saladin once featured, who divides society into separate marketing 'universes' (the chocolate universe, the slimming universe), the better to safeguard his profits (264). The novel suggests that, for all their obvious differences, there are strange similarities too between the fervently patriotic, Thatcherite free-marketeer Valance, and the liberal, ironic, Jewish concentration camp survivor Otto Cone. The capitalist spirit which Valance sees as reviving the identity of Britain in fact is eroding it:

> 'I', Hal Valance announced, 'love this fucking country. That's why I'm going to sell it to the whole goddam world, Japan, America, fucking Argentina. I'm going to sell the arse off it. That's what I've been selling all my fucking life: the fucking nation. The *flag*.'
>
> (Rushdie 1988: 268)

Valance, like many of the immigrant characters in the novel, is 'a monster: pure, self-created image, a set of attributes plastered thickly over a body' (266).

Indeed, the arrival of mutants from outside only throws into relief the mutations being undergone within a city such as London, mutations which make it unclear where London itself begins and ends. London is doubled in Gibreel's dream, not just in the dry, hardened corruption of the city of Jahilia, but also in the very different landscape that forms the subject of the poetry of Baal, exiled behind the curtain in the Jahilia brothel: 'The landscape of his poetry was still the desert, the shifting dunes . . . Soft mountains, uncompleted journeys, the impermanence of tents. How did one map a country that blew into a new form every day?' (370).

In turning London inside out in this fashion, *The Satanic Verses* is at once inviting and declining comparison with novels such as Dickens's *Bleak House* (1853), which take London as a synecdoche for Englishness itself. In common with such novels, there is a close relationship between the form of the city and the form of the novel. In *Bleak House*, for example, the capacity of the city both to alienate and to connect is matched by the novel's multiplication and coordination of initially unrelated particulars. In such novels, the success or failure of the link between the physical space of the city, and the novelistic text, as conjoining imaginary space, ensures the degree of confidence in the capacity of the novel to effect a plausible and reconciling representation of the nation. But *The Satanic Verses* seems to disturb the mutually confirming relationship of text, city and nation. In this novel, the city is synecdochically 'English' only in so far as it enacts microcosmically the opening out of Englishness to its surroundings. Rather than offering any convergence of separate histories in a single narrative line, the London of *The Satanic Verses* is composed of overlapping but discontinuous narrative planes and an impossible mélange of actual and imaginary histories and chronologies. Nevertheless, if the terms of the triple equivalence between city, text and nation are altered in *The Satanic Verses*, it might be said that the equivalence itself remains a regular one, in that the complication and compounding of London and Englishness is matched by a complication and compounding of the form of the novel, which undergoes the same kinds of stylistic and organisational mutations as the city that is its subject. Like other novels considered in this chapter, *The Satanic Verses* seems to be intensely concerned with its own narrative nature and possibilities, and sees the question of identity as being closely implicated with the possibilities of fiction.

The novel hits a particularly rich seam of self-reflexivity in the episode in which Saladin meets Gibreel at Shepperton studios on the set of a musical production of Dickens's *Our Mutual Friend* (1865). There is both mockery and admiration in Rushdie's enjoyment of the vulgar travesty of the novel being brought about in this adaptation. As a literary novel, *The Satanic Verses* distances itself from the rank collapse of distinctions and flamboyant carelessness of the original text that is to be found on the film set; but as a novel that itself employs and closely affiliates to many of the devices and associative energies of film, the novel mirrors something of its own procedure in this episode. On the film set, the distorted, mirage-like London of *The Satanic Verses* is itself distorted and remade, with the alteration of the distances between and relative dispositions of different places, and the telescoping together of centres and margins:

> Here London has been altered – no, *condensed*, – according to the imperatives of film. – Why, here's the Stucconia of the Veneerings, those bran-new, spick and span new people, lying shockingly adjacent to Portman Square, and the shady angle containing various Podsnaps. – And worse: behold the dustman's mounds of Boffin's Bower, supposedly in the near vicinity of Holloway, looming in this abridged metropolis

over Fascination Fledgeby's rooms in the Albany, the West End's very heart!

(Rushdie 1988: 422)

If there is travesty here, however, it is of a particular kind. The film-set is not so much a distortion of an actually existing reality as a doubling of what is already a fabrication (and anyway the 'distorted' replication of the London of Dickens's *Our Mutual Friend* is curiously faithful to the sense of startling adjacency in the original). In a further sense, it might be suggested that the representation is actually a faithful rendering of the contemporary condition of London, or indeed any global metropolis, under the conditions of 'space–time compression' described by David Harvey (1989: 241–323). Harvey suggests that the years since the war have seen a huge acceleration in the capacities of travel and communications to shrink distances and therefore erase cultural differences. This produces not only a certain kind of cultural homogeneity – the unrelieved sameness of airports, restaurants, urban architecture, advertising and TV all over the world – but also the opposite effect, as the mutual encroachment of different cultural forms and time-scales, combined with the insatiable need to market difference and novelty, produces effects of eclecticism, hybridity and decentring.

We may press Harvey's analysis a little further to suggest that the years since the Second World War have seen a simultaneous intensification on the one hand, of globalism, in terms of multinational economic organisation, as well as political and military conflict and interdependence, and on the other hand, of localism, or the reassertion of smaller-scale kinds of cultural belonging and affiliation. The latter is both the opposite of the former and its secondary effect. As Harvey has argued, in an economy which is ever more centred around the production and circulation of images, representations and the equipment of cultural style, rather than around material goods of a more old-fashioned kind, cultural diversification is both a resistance to global processes of commodification and the very inner principle of those processes. In a more general fashion, the Islamic revolutions which swept across the Middle East during the 1970s and 1980s and the nationalist revolutions and revivals in Eastern Europe during 1989, the very year in which the conflict over Rushdie's novel was at its most intense, were in part a reaction against the vast, homogenising power of the USA and the USSR. At the same time, these revolutions have taken place on a global stage, and under economic conditions which forbid any kind of retreat into cultural or national specificity or self-sufficiency. The loosened, overlapping, dialogic space of international relationship is simultaneously what enables and limits the reassertion of national difference. Paradoxically, it is only in a globalised world that the new possibilities for the nation can arise.

Under such conditions, national identity and cultural difference are not annulled, but subject to continual reworking. The extremes of mutual visibility established by media such as film and advertising mean that the processes of forming and replicating cultural identity take place not as an endogenous process – the unfolding of Englishness from the inside outwards – but as an exogenous effect – the projection outwards for global consumption by the tourist and culture industries of an Englishness that is in some sense already derived from or dependent upon the images of self from the outside. Englishness comes to know itself in the process of emptying itself into self-display or selling itself off, with the likes of Hal Valance or the big-budget film of Dickens. Thus, the compression of urban place and space on the set of *Our Mutual Friend* also involves a kind of global folding inwards; Saladin sees clustered together on London Bridge 'a host of faces that would be recognized from Peru to Timbuctoo' (Rushdie 1988: 422–3), and the crowd of extras 'parts like the Red Sea before the children of Israel' (423). The London which Saladin hopes to possess and belong to is reflected back to him in the distorted image of a lustful actress who replays the chauvinistic routines of Mr Podsnap from *Our Mutual Friend*:

> Now, in Rex-Harrisonian speech-song, she addresses an invisible Foreigner. 'And How Do You Like London? – "Aynor-maymong rich?" – Enormously Rich, we say. Our English adverbs do Not terminate in Mong. – And Do You Find, Sir, Many Evidences of our British Constitution in the Streets of the World's Metropolis, London, Londres, London? – I would say,' she adds, still Podsnapping, 'that there is in the Englishman a combination of qualities, a modesty, an independence, a responsibility, a repose, which one would seek in vain among the Nations of the Earth.'
>
> (Rushdie 1988: 424)

There is multiple citation here, as the actress borrows for sexual purposes the speech of another actor in the play, which is part of a film reworking of a stage musical deriving from a Dickensian 'original' which is itself a certain kind of parody or empty display of Englishness on the part of the self-important, but vacuous Podsnap. All these baffle the claims for self-sufficiency, for 'modesty ... independence ... responsibility ... repose' of English identity. This structure of citation affects Rushdie's novel, too. Just as the nation is forced into unpredictable mutations and affiliations, so the novel whose structure has historically been so closely tied to the experience of national being and belonging begins to borrow from and mutate into the forms of its mass cultural 'others', in film, TV and advertising, in that interior redefinition of the nature of the novel that, as we saw in chapter 1, is an important part of its evolution during the years since the Second World War. Here it is important to note the ways in which *The Satanic Verses* takes to a certain ragged, vulgarly exuberant extreme the adaptation of the novel form which has been an important accompaniment to the investigation within the novel of the altering, assaulted conditions of England and Englishness since the Second World War. Ironically, one of the ways in which *The Satanic Verses* was defended against attacks from some Muslims was in terms of its genre: absurdly, it was claimed that the absence of the novel within Islamic tradition meant that Muslims did not know how to respond appropriately to fiction and its norms. To make this claim is in a sense to make the identification between the West and the form of the novel. Not the least of the ironies which radiate from the Rushdie affair is that the novel which stimulates this defensive association is in fact so permeated by other kinds of fictional style and purpose. These are derived from 'West' and 'East', tradition and modernity, alike, and include myths, fairy-tales, advertising jingles, films, fables, dreams, horror-stories, prayers, proverbs, chants and jokes. All of these strain the form of the novel to bursting point while also reaffirming the elasticity and permeability of form and language that is precisely its historical strength. The novel, the form which in its name has always promised news or novelty, is here caught in the process of refashioning which renders it able to show how, in Whisky Sisodia's words, 'newness enters the world' (272).

4

HISTORIES

No historical account of the novel, or account of the novel in history can afford to shelve for long the complex question of the relations between novels and history. This is to say that the perspective that takes novels as a resource for history – as a certain kind of historical evidence, for example – must always at some stage acknowledge the uneasy overlap between novels and history as forms of narrative. To study the meanings, functions and pleasures of the novel across different periods is always to be concerned at least in part with the ways in which those periods imagine and narrate their own histories and the histories of others. Novels are, undoubtedly, part of the history of social life; but they are so largely because they provide evidence of the ways in which others have themselves constructed history, or historical relations. Novels are therefore, in both senses, ways of making history; they belong to the history of events and they contribute to the historical narrative of those events.

Despite the claim seemingly made in the name of the form (the novel, surely, proposes the discovery of something new, rather than the recovery of what is old), the novel has never, in the course of its comparatively short history, been able wholly to abstain from historical aspiration. The attraction between the novel and history may in fact be unavoidable, given the close association between narrative and time. Though it is possible to imagine a narrative that did not have some form of temporal passage or series of events linked in time as its subject, a narrative that did not itself significantly occupy or lengthen itself through time is barely conceivable. The novel has a strongly developed sense of the regularly divided, progressive and irreversible time of the chronometer and the calendar. Such a division has much to do with the imperatives of a capitalism organising and rationalising its procedures, for which, increasingly, time is not just the background in which economic activity takes place, but is itself a vital element in the calculation and production of profit. This preoccupation is apparent even and especially in the novel's apparent concern with the opposite of chronological time, with Bergson's internal or subjective duration (1971), or the 'calendar of feelings' as Beckett called it (1965: 14), or the inward time of perception which was identified as the proper concern of the novel by Woolf, Richardson and others. The sense of inward time that is emphasised in modernist writing is unavoidably defined against the calendrical sense of time that is imprinted on the form of the novel. One might say, in fact, that what distinguishes the novel from other kinds of narrative – oral narrative, for example, or film or TV (at least until the advent of video technology) – is that it permits and promotes the establishment of relationships between calendrical and non-calendrical time; in other words, between the regularly divided and extended clock-time that must be occupied in reading the temporally extended events of the narrative, and the possibility of repetition, anticipation, rereading, variable rates of reading, and so on, which is superimposed upon this external structure by every individual reader and reading. The novel depends upon and is peculiarly defined by this mutual adjustment of private time and public time.

It is in this sense above all, perhaps, that the novel is always historical or has the potential to be so. What we tend to designate or recognise as history is in fact the recording and interpretation of the public events of the past. Despite recent enlargements in what counts as historical evidence, with the growing interest in journals, familiar documents and oral testimony, and all of the evidences of 'history from below' or unofficial history of all kinds, there is still a sense in which private lives and events are only historical once they attain a certain degree of typicality or exemplary significance. Although almost anything might in principle count as history for the historian, it is in fact hard to imagine either the historical uses of or significances of certain kinds of human experience or event; what would a history of dreams, fantasies or visions be like, for example? History begins to take account of such things only at the point when they have passed across into a public realm, which is usually to say into documentary form. History, as conventionally and institutionally construed, is not concerned with the intimate, the obscure and the idiomatic, but with the outward, the visible and the typical.

But, in saying that novels are always potentially historical, I want to resist the idea that there is a simple separation of spheres between the novel and history, as between private and public history. I mean also to call to mind by contrast Georg Lukács's famous claim (1962) that the historical novel is concerned with the presentation of particular characters and events in a way that gives them typifying force and reach. In constructing and developing the commensurability of individual narratives and the larger movements of history, the novel performs many of the same functions as official history. The difference between the novel and history lies not in any simple contrast between the public and the private, but rather in terms of the different stages in the process of translating private into public events. Official and institutional history concerns itself largely with events that are already credited with typical or general significance, with what has already merged into the solidity and definition of an event; history that is already History. Novels more often deal with events that are in the process of making this transition, where, indeed, they do not themselves constitute or bring about such a process. Novels, especially but not exclusively those that deal with the past, witness or inspect or assist the coming into being of events, the passage of history into History.

Most accounts of the relationship between history and the novel have concentrated on a rather different point of distinction between the two forms of representation, namely the question of truth. History, it is conventionally claimed, deals with things as they were; fiction with things as they might, or even should, have been. History, Michel de Certeau has suggested, sees itself as having a special relationship to the real because it maintains itself as the opposite of the falseness of fiction (1986: 201). The appropriate question to ask of an historical narrative is assumed therefore to be, 'is it true?'; the corresponding question to ask of a fictional narrative being 'is it good?' Much recent critical work has been devoted to complicating this simple, if resilient, contrast. On the historical side, the most important figure is Hayden White, who has maintained through a number of works the necessity for historians to acknowledge the literariness of their work, which is to say, its dependence upon rhetoric and narrative (1973, 1987, 1989). On the literary side, Linda Hutcheon has mounted in *A Poetics of Postmodernism* (1988) a strong and influential argument for the emergence of a new attitude towards history in a form of novel that she calls 'historiographic metafiction'. Such novels, she argues, combine a sceptical self-consciousness about the limiting, distorting or conditioning effects of language and its rhetorical forms with a continuing commitment to the representation of the past. Against those who have argued that the modern and postmodern novelist's concern with the form of the novel prohibits any serious engagement with historical reality, Hutcheon argues that

> both history and fiction are discourses ... [and] both constitute systems of signification by which we make sense of the past ... In other words, the meaning and shape [of history] are not *in the events* but *in the systems* which make those past 'events' into present historical 'facts'.
> (Hutcheon 1988: 89)

Hutcheon brings good news and bad news for the old-fashioned realist reader. The good news is that she refuses modernism's chilly exile from politics and history, restoring literary writing to the world and its interests, moral and political; the bad news is that the world and its interests are now revealed to be as thoroughly and inescapably 'textual' as the texts that mirror it. The literary text is returned to a relationship with an historical real that has in the meantime been refashioned in its image.

Hutcheon's work valuably alerts us to the fact that the self-conscious concern with the nature of language and representation which characterises much recent fiction in Britain and elsewhere does not prohibit, indeed may even stimulate, serious reflection on the relations between novels and history. Unfortunately, her work is limited by what seems to be too ready an acquiescence to the manner in which history and fiction have traditionally been contrasted, namely in terms of the degree of their respective truthfulness or capacity to refer accurately to the real. Although she disagrees markedly with those who would wish to maintain a clear distinction between history and fiction, she continues to assume the explanatory centrality of the question of truthfulness and referentiality on which such a distinction depends. One limiting effect of this is to produce the illusion that, prior to the emergence of the kind of postmodern fiction whose claims she is anxious to advance, novel writing either numbly accepted its relegation as false and unserious or, more alarmingly, maintained its dignity by borrowing the implausible claims of history itself to represent the real. The cramping effects of such a simple division between the unenlightened past and the canny present are dramatically apparent in remarks such as the following from Alison Lee, whose study of the uses of history in recent British fiction draws extensively from Hutcheon's characterisation of historiographic metafiction:

> The Realist aesthetic tended to distinguish between 'lying' literature and 'true', 'objective' history, and to ascribe a positive moral value to fact ... For the Realists, neither reference nor subjectivity were complicated issues. The Realists, as well as many of their critical and literary descendants, equated the presentation of the 'real' with the revelation of the 'true'. The transcription of the 'real' was *technically* unproblematic because language was perceived as transparent, and *ideologically* neutral because of a belief in a shared notion of what constituted both 'reality' and 'truth'.
>
> (Lee 1990: 29, 53–4)

It is hard to imagine a single text that would exemplify the breathtaking naivety alleged here, let alone the universal consensus that it claims (Lee habitually capitalises the term 'Realism', giving the impression that it is a whole school of thought, with its own manifesto and resident café). The flattening here may serve to illuminate certain uses and effects of historical writing in recent fiction, but it does so by blocking off awareness of the different ways in which novels may address historical material, be historical and act in history. The same objection may be mounted to the work of those who, on the other side of the argument, have espoused the cause of realism in historical fiction, along with the possibility of truth-telling that it seems to bring (Bergonzi 1979a; Swinden 1984; McEwan 1987); here, too, the exclusive emphasis on the truth-telling capacities of fiction prevents significant attention being paid to the other functions it performs. Such an approach to historical fiction also tends to relate novels only to other novels, rather than to the making and narrating of history more generally in social life, from gossip and personal diaries all the way through to official public history.

In the following discussions of such works produced since the Second World War, the hypothesis, as elsewhere in this book, will be that it is more interesting and profitable to ask what a novel *does*, intellectually, affectively, imaginatively, politically, with and in history than to ask merely what kind of truthfulness to history it displays or denies. It was suggested in chapter 1 that there were two contrasting forms of action or effect that could typically be brought about by narrative, which I described as consolidatory and transformative. There I suggested that narrative both extends and consolidates the sense of individual and collective identity and interrupts and transforms such identity. Narrative is one of the most important ways in which cultures name themselves and give themselves definition and extension in space and time, naming and defining the forms in which individual members of those cultures may be said to belong to them. But narrative can also deliberately expose cultures and their inhabitants to the accidents and conflicts of history, testifying to the need for sometimes painful forms of transformation, even revolution. Consolidation and transformation are contrasting, but not wholly antipathetic functions. Indeed, one, somewhat conservative view of the function of narrative might be that it exists to manage and mediate the shock of exposure to newness, contradiction and difficulty, to bind and transform transformation itself into a form of social consolidation.

Important to both functions of narrative is the question of agency. Narrative, it was suggested in chapter 1, is not just about actions and events in time, but also has as its function the installing of narrator and narratee as the authors and subjects of actions and events. Narrative is the form by which cultures make themselves subjects of history (in both active and passive senses, as the makers of history and those acted on by history). With the awareness of the multiple lines of consequence in the contemporary world has come the possibility of a plurality of forms of agency in or ways of being the subject of history. This chapter will suggest that, where the role of narrative might once have been to call its audiences into the position of the subject of history, narrative in the postwar world has been much more sceptically or modestly concerned to investigate the conditions of possibility under which history may be narratable at all.

Nevertheless, the importance of historical narrative – in many different forms alongside but also including the novel – in the period since the Second World War has been immense and various. As Jean-François Lyotard has influentially argued, it has been a period in which the horrors of mass conflict, combined with the mutual penetration of cultures in a globalised world, has produced a disaffection from long-range authoritative histories of all kinds and an awareness of all the local histories that are silenced in the name of such universal accounts (1984; 1988). Undoubtedly, novels have joined in the general suspicion of large-scale, long-range or universal history characteristic of this period. Margaret Scanlan points correctly to the deliberate circumspection of much historical fiction regarding the large events of history, or their representability. Historical fiction of the postwar period seems to lack, and only rarely to lament, the easy confidence in the capacity of fiction to encompass history, or plausibly to make that connection between small individual lives and the large tides of history which Lukács demanded of the historical novel. In the novels Scanlan discusses history is repeatedly decentred, which is to say, looked at askew, or experienced through the lives of characters detached from rather than significantly connected to history. History is not full, continuous and coherent, but a matter of gaps, absences and enigmas:

> History as presented in the contemporary British novel is neither glamorous nor consoling. It is too diffuse to offer lessons, too unfinished to constitute a space into which we can escape; and we ourselves, implicated in the failures of the past, cannot even enjoy its ironies comfortably ... What actuates these fictions is not, then, a confidence that the past will teach us how to behave, but a quieter conviction that it is better to know than to remain ignorant, even though what we learn is the enormous difficulty of understanding our lives historically.
>
> (Scanlan 1990: 16)

In terms of British experience since the Second World War, Scanlan is surely right to observe a certain collapse of confidence in the inherited narratives of the past. There seems a clear connection between the gradual but remorseless waning of British power, standing and self-esteem in the postwar years, with the falling away of the Empire and loss of military and economic power, and the growing scepticism about the shared myths of public history and their power to govern and organise ordinary life. Hence, as Margaret Scanlan observes, the tendency for postwar historical fiction ironically to revisit a well-known or public past, whether imperial or military, in order to focus on its hidden, inglorious underside (1990: 6). There is a moment from J. G. Farrell's *The Siege of Krishnapur* (1973), a historical novel set in India during the Mutiny of 1857, which seems to typify this move. Mr Hopkins, an official with the East India Company, has gathered around him a number of treasures and artefacts which act as a miniature of the Great Exhibition of 1851, in which Victorian

Britain had celebrated its confidence in itself as the leading edge of civilisation in its development through history. Among Hopkins's treasures, however, is a somewhat paradoxical exhibit, 'the model of a carriage which supplied its own railway, laying it down as it advanced and taking it up again after the wheels had passed over' (Farrell 1973: 97). The model is an image at once of sublime imperial confidence in the onward march of history, especially in India, where the penetration and organisation of the country by railways were the most emphatic evidence of British rule, and of a bizarre ignorance. Hopkins's belief in history as a self-sustaining perpetual motion apparatus is revealed both as the crankiest and most impossible of contraptions, and as a strangely apposite image of a history that must surreptitiously invent the authority and grounding it claims for itself.

However, if there has been a waning of confidence in the power of history, at the same time the prodigious explosion of means of representation and reproduction in this period has produced a surfeit of narrative effect and affect, with the multiplication of historical linkages, and chains of connection and causality, and an almost relentless narrativisation in the areas of economics, politics and science. The conditions of extreme cultural interfusion, with the meetings and conflicts of cultural traditions brought about by large-scale migrations as a result of war and post-colonial resettlements, have combined with the growth of an ever-more interdependent global economy to create a splintering of history in the postwar world, a loss of the vision of history as one and continuous. But these very same conditions of mutual impingement have acted to make it impossible to maintain any form of local or individual history in isolation from all the other histories, and in doing so have enlarged the scope of the conversation and collective memory that is constructed in the narration of histories. In a sense it has become impossible to reflect on one's condition other than historically.

On these points, at least, the postwar period has seen a huge expansion of history and history-making. Not the least important of these effects has been the narrativisation of the future, and especially the apocalyptic prospect held by that future, which is expressed not just as fantasy or moral–didactic instrument but terrifyingly in terms of day to day military and political planning. At no other period in history has the possibility of reaching narrative closure been so historically actual. But even in less lethal areas of social and political life, the practice of narrative prediction, and the drawing of the future into the economic calculations of the present, along with the general effects of accelerated reproduction of all kinds, have combined with the increasing availability and accessibility of different forms of historical evidence, and a corresponding tendency to encourage the tracing of lines of connection from imagined or narrated pasts into speculative futures. In a world in which narrative has become omnipresent, irresistible and inescapable, and yet also dangerous, suspect and oppressive, the function of narrative in the novel is certain to be complex. Thus, when the authority of history is exploded, the result is an explosion of histories and authorities.

One of the ways in which the novel has attempted both to accommodate to and protect against a world of expanding historicism has been by trying to assimilate the processes of historical duration in its own form. Thus, the years following the Second World War saw a remarkable revival of the novel-sequence (the uncertainty of this term, poised between the idea of a sequence of novels and the idea of a single novel lengthened and diversified into a sequence, is suggestive). The novel-sequence, which follows through the experiences of a range of characters, sometimes in one setting and period, sometimes in a wide variety of settings and periods, in a number of different, but interconnected novels, is an exercise in world-making. The world of the sequence has the self-sufficient density it supposes of the 'real' world. It is closed and complete in itself, a parallel universe or working simulacrum of the real not only in the encyclopaedic abundance of its narrative detail but also in its plethora of different possible perspectives; typically the novel-sequence will combine and juxtapose not only different experiences of different characters but also the same experiences revisited from different points of view. Often the sequence offers a concentrated or privatised version of public history, in the form of a family or generational romance, in an attempt to connect the realm of private extended time to the public time of history. There is a significant link here between the condition of England novel and the novel-sequence, in connected works such as John Braine's *Room at the Top* (1957) and *Life at the Top* (1962), or Margaret Drabble's more recent trilogy, *The Radiant Way* (1987), *A Natural Curiosity* (1989) and *The Gates of Ivory* (1991), or in even more loosely linked sequences such as David Lodge's *Changing Places* (1975), *Small World* (1984) and *Nice Work* (1988).

If sequences allow the production and renewal of a closed and self-consistent world, they also mimic the unpredictable looseness and contingency of lived historical time, in which the senses of process, interruption and discontinuity are as necessary a part as the principles of recurrence, resumption and repetition. The sequence novel can therefore be closed off from the historical real and also responsive to it; it has the packed inclusiveness of the historical novel and the porousness to its exterior of the chronicle. Most importantly of all, perhaps, the sequence calls for and perhaps even calls into being a particular kind of reading and reader. Novel-sequences such as C. P. Snow's *Strangers and Brothers* sequence (1940–70), Henry Williamson's *A Chronicle of Ancient Sunlight* (1951–69) or Anthony Powell's *A Dance to the Music of Time* (1951–75), the writing of which can encompass much of a writer's career, and thus of a reader's life, bring about in the sustained, renewed reading they require a kind of continuity which seems increasingly to be under threat in the postwar world. Nor is it necessary for the reader of these novels to have followed them through from beginning to end, since it is the fact of the sequence itself that summons the reader into participation in its alternative parallel chronology. This is reinforced by the fact that such novel-sequences seem to replicate and include the act of reading in their structure. In installing a temporal relationship to its own past – by suspending the forward flow of accretion and looping back in the sequence to fill out gaps, or provide 'prequels', for example – the novel-sequence reads itself and includes this reading of itself in its fabric and form. The long perspective promised by the novel-sequence, whose continuity is confirmed rather than threatened by its discontinuous syntax, made up as it is of breakings off and renewals, is the more impressive for being achieved against the grain of the conditions of publication, circulation and reading that are typical of the postwar fiction market, in which the high-pressure, short-turnover marketing of fiction seems increasingly designed to produce a kind of structural amnesia in the reading public. For all the cosiness that it can sometimes display, the novel-sequence is a heroic refusal of or compensation for this systematic loss of long-term memory, in the manner in which it draws the generalised and systematic threat of interruption in contemporary culture into a patterned syntax of resumptions. (See Connor 1996, forthcoming.)

Novel-sequences are not of course unique to or an innovation of the postwar period and this is in fact part of their significance.

HISTORIES

One may say that novel-sequences do not merely read and reread themselves, but also aim to read, recall and reconstitute previously created novelistic worlds and their forms of readership, in nineteenth-century versions such as the Barsetshire and Palliser novels of Trollope, the Rougon–Macquart cycle of Zola and the novels in Balzac's *Comédie Humaine* sequence, or in Edwardian versions such as John Galsworthy's *Forsyte Saga* (1906–21). The years following the Second World War saw the inaugurations of a large number of novel-sequences, such as C. P. Snow's *Strangers and Brothers* (though this had been begun with *George Passant* in 1940, the second volume, *The Light and the Dark*, did not appear until 1947); Anthony Powell's *A Dance to the Music of Time* (1951–75) and Henry Williamson's *A Chronicle of Ancient Sunlight* (1951–69); *Martha Quest*, the first volume of Doris Lessing's *Children of Violence* appeared in 1952, the same year as *Men at Arms*, the first volume of Evelyn Waugh's *Sword of Honour* trilogy; these were followed by Anthony Burgess's *Malayan Trilogy* (1956–9), Lawrence Durrell's *Alexandria Quartet* (1957–60), Olivia Manning's *Balkan Trilogy* (1960–5) and Paul Scott's *Raj Quartet* (1966–75).

The years of the War and its aftermath also saw a marked increase in the popularity of Trollope, the great nineteenth-century constructor of the autonomous world sustained and renewed across various novels. No doubt there is significance in this apparent return to nineteenth-century reading patterns in the middle of the twentieth century, immediately after the most destructive war in history and in the lengthening shadows of apprehension about the possibility of further, even more unthinkably annihilating conflict; and it seems plain that the popularity of novel-sequences expresses a desire for the stability and continuity that are attributed to the Victorian period. But identification is not identity, and the very desire to recall the nineteenth century is a mark of the unclosable gap between the conditions and potentialities of narrative between the nineteenth and twentieth centuries.

It is also important to remember that not all novel-sequences written in the period enact the desire for completed and coherent worlds. One of the most important and influential sequences, Beckett's *Trilogy*, written in French and then translated by the author into English, enacts a complex, repetitious, paradoxical time, in which the central narrator-characters, Molloy and Moran in *Molloy* (1950), Malone in *Malone Dies* (1951) and the unnamed narrator of *The Unnamable* (1952), persist, recur and are transformed in uncanny fashion across and between the individual novels. Just as interesting an exception to the rules of the novel-sequence is Doris Lessing's *Children of Violence* sequence. This follows through in five novels the development of Martha Quest from youth to middle age. The final novel in the sequence, *The Four-Gated City* (1969), centres on the defeat of Martha's rational political ideals. There is a tendency for the novel-sequence to turn sequence into cycle, by the mirroring of beginning and end, as in Anthony Powell's *A Dance to the Music of Time*, which ends with the image of the Poussin painting with which it began and which gives the sequence its title. *The Four-Gated City*, however, opens itself up to speculative history, incorporating an account of a nuclear apocalypse that destroys London and notes on the future that follows it. As Lorna Sage has observed, the defeat of Martha's political expectations and ideals is matched by the purposive failure of the novel form: '*Children of Violence* not only describes a crisis in progressive thinking but is itself an exemplary casualty – a deliberate disaster area' (1983: 66).

The problem posed and variously solved by nineteenth-century novel-sequences was how to bring together areas of human and social life that an increasingly rationalised and specialised world was splitting apart. The problem for a twentieth-century novel-sequence is rather different. In the postwar period it is no longer simply a question of the mutual alienation of the public and private, of the sphere of the 'human' and the force of impersonal process, whether historical, economic or political. In this period, the private is increasingly and irresistibly invaded by the public, in something of the manner conjured by Dennis Potter:

> Once upon a time, unless it was a fairy-tale . . . the human-made was more like a shell which we could leave and return to . . . It needed no simpler model than the streets of the city: real streets in the real city. We could walk among them, and, eventually, walk out of them, and shut the door on them.
>
> But now the streets of the city have electronically (and commercially and bureaucratically) extended themselves into every nook and cranny.
>
> (Potter 1984: 25)

Novel-sequences must deal with a condition in which the microscopic and the macrocosmic are both incompatible and oppressively, confusingly interdependent, their purpose being both to integrate the fragmented and to maintain dissolved distinctions. If they testify to the novel's continuing function of making history and extending the versatility of memory, they also bear witness to all the disruptions and complexities that attend the relationship of narrative and time during this period.

The novel-sequence is not the only form in which the novel has investigated and reimagined the forms of historical time and the relations between present and past in the postwar period. It has often been remarked that novels dealing with historical events and themes cannot avoid conscious or unconscious reflection on the relation between the narrated past and the present that narrates it. It is not quite a matter, as Neil McEwan suggests it is, of maintaining a judicious balance between truth to the past and truth to the needs of the present (1987: 1). Indeed, when one of the leading preoccupations of the present is precisely the necessity of being true to the past (to the degree that we respond to the pressure to be true to the past, the need for such truth becomes one of our own needs), there is no easy way to distinguish between the two competing principles. All novels, like all representations of the past, bear upon or read significantly the meaning of the past in the present. This is to say that all novels – and all histories – belong to their own historical moment. But it is also true and, oddly, for the same reasons, that every representation of the past is a historicising of the present, making it possible to inhabit or belong to one's present differently. In supplying the needs or confirming the values of the present, novels that deal with history make those needs visible and thus perhaps available for consideration and revaluation. All novels about the past to some degree construct and display their relation to the past that they seemingly retrieve. In terms of the functions of narrative distinguished above, they are habituations or attempts at self-possession carried out through certain sorts of self-distancing or transformation.

In many novels, these tensions are carried by the question of language. It is possible to suggest a distinction between two broadly different ways of narrating the past. The first employs the language and narrative style of the present to render the events of the past; the second attempts to simulate or construct a language and form of narration appropriate to the historical subject or period in question. There is a tendency for the former strategy to be employed in novels whose principal purpose appears to be the realistic rendering of the past; it is usual, for example, in popular historical fiction. There is a tendency by contrast for the latter kind of narration to be employed in novels that appear to bring into ironic visibility the distance between past and present. The former mode of historical narration assumes the possibility of translating the past into the customary and contemporary languages of the novel, while the latter seems to require the translation of the novel itself into other narrative forms and idioms.

On the one hand, there are novels such as Iris Murdoch's *The Red and the Green* (1965), which centres on characters involved in the Easter Uprising in Ireland in 1916, or J. G. Farrell's *The Siege of Krishnapur* (1973), or Peter Carey's *Oscar and Lucinda* (1988), in which a modern-day narrator reconstructs the story of his great-grandfather, the Reverend Oscar Hopkins, and his crazy dream of building a glass church in 1860s Australia. All of these render historical events, or narratives of events set at determinate moments in the past, in a twentieth-century language which may borrow from, or bend itself to, the usages of the historical moment being written about, but without any significant self-consciousness, or sense of ironic disjuncture. Related closely to this kind of historical fiction are novels which employ or incorporate quasi-historical material, in a way that allows an awareness of the contrast of present and past languages, but without suggesting that they are incompatible or opposed. An example here might be Marina Warner's *Indigo* (1992), which conjoins a narrative of the colonial settlement of a Caribbean island in the early seventeenth century with a contemporary narrative dealing with descendants of the original settlers; for the most part, the seventeenth-century portions of the narrative are rendered in twentieth-century novelistic language that makes no attempt to mimic the language of the seventeenth century, but this is diversified by the inclusion of certain pseudo-historical documents such as letters and proclamations. Another example is furnished by Timothy Mo's *An Insular Possession* (1986), which follows through the establishment of Hong Kong in the early nineteenth century in a mixture of authoritative impersonal narration and constructed contemporary letters and newspaper reports.

On the other hand, there are novels which seem to highlight and insist on the maladjustment or conflict between different languages and their originating historical moments. Examples here might include John Fowles's *The French Lieutenant's Woman* (1969) and *A Maggot* (1985), both of which involve long stretches of historical parody, of the styles of the nineteenth-century novel and of eighteenth-century formal writing respectively, but also include passages of narration which, rather than simply delivering the historical into the grasp of the present, reflect openly upon the differences between them. Another example might be Peter Ackroyd's *Hawksmoor* (1985), which layers together the first-person narrative of Nicholas Dyer, a seventeenth-century architect confessing a series of murders he has committed in the service of an esoteric pagan cult, and a third-person narrative concerning a present-day detective named Nicholas Hawksmoor (the name of the architect on whom the fictional Nicholas Dyer is obviously based) who is investigating a series of murders in the present which uncannily resemble the murders committed by Dyer.

The distinction between the two forms of historical writing would seem to be in terms of the degree of historical self-consciousness they imply and require from their readers. The first kind of historical fiction seems to assert in its form and language the capacity of the present to extend itself to encompass the past, either in a twentieth-century language which confidently assumes its adequacy to the task of historical representation, or in an ensemble of different historical languages which nevertheless speak in one voice, as it were, and thus enact the translatability of past and present each into the other. The second kind seems to highlight the difficulty of this translation, by displaying the lack of fit, or ironic incompatibility, between past and present viewpoints and languages. It might be possible to go further still, to suggest that the first kind of novel enacts the possibility of a knowable, narratable and continuous history, any one of whose points may be brought into communication with any other. Curiously, such a view of history often assumes, in its implicit claim that history has a form and a truth accessible to those who live within it, the privilege of escaping its limitations. As Christina Cosby has put it, such historical writing may express 'a longing for the past, a desire to overcome the separation of past and present, a wish to return, to make past and present coincide . . . [It is] a conceptualizing of history as home [which] is, of course, profoundly ahistorical' (1991: 75). The second kind of novel on the other hand suggests a discontinuous history, or the potential for many different, conflicting histories; unlike the first, it seems to disallow any perspective on history other than those contingently available within history, such that any kind of continuity established between histories and the languages that enact them will be provisional and constructed rather than essential and historically given. For these reasons it may be convenient to describe this as a distinction between *historical* and *historicised* fiction, between fiction about history and fiction about its own historically relative construction of history.

Such a distinction allows us to discern a general movement in postwar literature and culture generally, away from the first kind of history and the confident authority it assumes towards the more sceptical or relativised view of history exemplified in the second. However, the distinction itself also poses some problems. It is plain, for instance, that certain kinds of novel which seem to draw self-conscious attention to the limits of identification that are possible between different historical periods, sensibilities and languages may not necessarily relativise the sense of historical belonging. One such novel would be Ackroyd's *Hawksmoor*. Alison Lee, among others, has claimed this as an example of postmodern historical fiction, which uses its startling contrast between the vigorous and brilliantly sustained seventeenth-century narrative and the present-day narrative to induce a sense of the relativity or undecidability of historical truth (1990: 68–73); Linda Hutcheon sees the novel in a similar way as the enactment, as well as the theorisation, of 'the impossibility of final meaning' (1988: 15). The novel does indeed construct an elaborate series of coincidences and uncanny recurrences between the seventeenth and the twentieth centuries, which accumulate in a disturbing way to unsettle expectations of linear cause and effect and the coherent relations of past and present. Rather than being a given, external fact, time becomes subject to artifice and fictional patterning, and thus able to fold over itself, and to flow backwards as well as forwards. In this respect the novel seems steadily to build against the assumptions of the detective story which provides its rationale and structure, with its dependence upon the steady reconstruction of relations of cause and effect, and its inexorable movement forwards from the darkness of disconnection to the clarity and conclusion that come with understanding. In doing so, one might even say that it pulls against the temporal assumptions of the novel form itself, in so far as these are often related to the processes of thickening and then resolving enigma, or discovering the principles of connection underlying apparent disconnection. The gradual collapse of Hawksmoor's naive trust in the novelistic unfolding of the case ('we can proceed from the beginning until we reach our end . . . Think of it like a story: even if the beginning has not been understood, we have to go on reading it. Just to see what happens next'; Ackroyd 1988: 114,

126) is thus a challenge to the assumptions of novelistic narration and the historical sense that such narration underpins.

However, the view of history which *Hawksmoor* proposes needs to be distinguished from the account offered by Lee and Hutcheon. The novel sets recurrence against irreversibility, proposing against a developmental view of history a spatialised view which sees history as occurring all at once. In Nicholas Dyer's account of the designs for his church which surround him in his room, we are offered, in place of history as a novel, (history as) a novel as architecture:

> I have finished six Designes of my last Church, fastned with Pinns on the Walls of my Closet so that the Images surround me and I am once more at Peece. In the first I have the Detail of the Ground Plot, which is much like a Prologue in a Story; in the second there is all the Plan in a small form, like the disposition of Figures in a Narrative; the third Draught shews the Elevation, which is like the Symbol or Theme of a Narrative, and the fourth displays the Upright of the Front, which is like to the main part of the Story; in the fifth there are designed the many and irregular Doors, Stairways and Passages like so many ambiguous Expressions, Tropes, Dialogues and Metaphoricall speeches; in the sixth there is the Upright of the Portico and the Tower which will strike the Mind with Magnificence, as in the Conclusion of a Book.
>
> (Ackroyd 1988: 205)

In such a spatialised view of history, everything has both already happened and is yet to come, held in store for its inevitable repetition in a future that is only the ghostly reenactment of the past. But if such a view of history indeed dissolves the clear differentiations between past and present that conventional history requires, it equally neutralises the possibility of the conflict, productive or otherwise, between different or incommensurable historical realities or forms of understanding. Such a view substitutes for the coherence of a view of history founded upon continuous linear progress the coherence of history as a closed and echoing plenitude. Its final sentences seem to lift Hawksmoor into union with the Nicholas Dyer who is at once his other and his double. The historical chasm which has allowed the pattern of identification to be established between them is closed, in a way that seems to fulfil Dyer's prophecy that 'my own History is a Patern which others may follow in the far Side of Time' (205). The narrating 'I' which appears in the twentieth-century portion of the narrative for the first time at this point may be Hawksmoor's or Dyer's or Ackroyd's own voice, or an indifferent merger of them all. *Hawksmoor* thus challenges Western time by attempting to escape time as such.

Such a view of history may certainly be called postmodernist in one aspect, in its emphatic refusal of the sense of irreversible time that is so central to a modern conception of the world and history; *Hawksmoor* appears in this respect to diagnose and detach itself from the conjoined perspectives of the Royal Society and Sir Christopher Wren as they are represented in the novel in their commitment to the advance of science, as well as from Hawksmoor's confidence in the capacity for crimes to be solved by rational thought. In this sense, it recalls one of the most characteristic gestures of certain kinds of modernist historical fiction, which Avrom Fleishman describes as the attempt to suspend historical difference, 'to lift the contemplation of the past above both the present and the past, to see it in its universal character, freed of the urgency of historical engagement' (1971: 15). In this sense, at least, *Hawksmoor* seems more modernist than postmodernist.

The question of historical language in this novel involves more than just considerations of accuracy or plausibility. Such a sustained act of impersonation or historical identification embodies in miniature many of the functions and imaginative transactions at work within historical narrative in general. In one sense, the superb feat of impersonation represented by the narrative of Nicholas Dyer is an attempt to bring about a radical decentring of contemporary sensibilities, to force the novel into an estranging, but also enlarging mutation of form and language. At the same time, the very fact of seeming to make this historical language and consciousness so abundantly available to the contemporary reader risks confirming rather than disturbing that reader's historical confidence. The act of taking possession of the language of an historical Other, in a novel that appears to be about a reverse process, in which the present comes to an awareness of the ways in which it is 'possessed' by the past, enacts both of the principal functions of narrative at once: its apparent eviction or displacement of the contemporary reader in fact restores that reader whole to his or her sense of historical belonging. Speaking of the research he needed to undertake to write the seventeenth-century portion of *Hawksmoor*, Ackroyd remarked that he 'wanted to assimilate the voice of the time, to train myself so I could write in that style without self-consciousness' (Kolbert 1986: 3). It is in the completeness of the assimilation and the suppression of self-consciousness that this most historical of novels seems at once to raise and evade the difficulties of history.

Far from evading the difficulties of history, John Fowles's *A Maggot* appears to delight in them. The novel is a narrative accounting for the events leading to the birth of Ann Lee, the founder of the Puritan sect known as the Shakers. Most of it takes the form of an enquiry into the circumstances surrounding the disappearance of an unnamed Lord's son, who has travelled from London to the West Country in the company of two actors, a retarded manservant and a prostitute known as Rebecca Lee. Much of the novel is taken up by transcripts of the interrogations of a number of characters conducted by a lawyer named Ayscough, from which it appears to emerge that the Lord has been in contact with extraterrestrial creatures, who, having granted Rebecca Lee a vision of a paradisal future, have taken him away. Unlike *Hawksmoor*, which shows the interpenetration of past and present, Fowles insists on the fact of historical difference, breaking into the narrative to offer historical background and interpretation and making it clear that his own narrative is a fabrication – a 'maggot' in the eighteenth-century sense of a whim or caprice. The novel is interleaved with facsimile pages from the *Gentleman's Magazine* of 1736, the year in which the events of the novel are represented as having taken place, but the effect of these is not to naturalise the historical narrative, but to highlight its fabricated nature. The epilogue which Fowles provides breaks the fictional frame, in the manner of *The French Lieutenant's Woman*, to offer some reflections on the significance of the Shakers and their faith. Fowles makes it clear that, while he himself has no sympathy with any established religious belief, the novel was written out of an admiration for the revolutionary force and aspiration of the Shaker creed, and for the spirit of dissent in general, which Fowles defines as 'a refusal to believe what those in power would have us believe – what they would command and oblige us, in all ways from totalitarian tyranny and brutal force to media manipulation and cultural hegemony, to believe' (Fowles 1991: 459). The novel is therefore a historicising fiction in that it advertises and exploits the fact of historical disjuncture, the gap between pre-Romantic traditional societies and post-Romantic individualised modernity, and between their different narrative and linguistic forms, and does not seem to license any easy or simple continuity between the past and the present. But at the same time, the novel emphatically appropriates the past, supplying it with a meaning not available to it. In thus reading the meaning of the past, giving it a certain exemplary or allegorical status, if only in the whimsical, provisional way it does, *A Maggot* suggests after all the possibility of a continuity between past and present, between events and their matured significance. In this respect, *A Maggot* is rather less of an historicised narrative and rather more like *Hawksmoor* than might at first appear. Linda Hutcheon enthusiastically celebrates the novel's indeterminacy, and 'the challenging of certainty, the asking of questions, the revealing of fiction-making where we might have once accepted the existence of some absolute "truth"' (1988: 48), but does not recognise the ways in which the novel also takes historical possession of the past, offering to make available, albeit through the devices of fiction, a certain kind of truth, both about the eighteenth century and about its own.

Perhaps something similar might be said about the language of A. S. Byatt's *Possession: A Romance* (1990), the title of which signals openly the concern of the novel with the question of what it means to take possession of the past. The novel has a double historical plot that is rather similar to *Hawksmoor*, though it is carried through in a more comic fashion. The two central characters are Roland Michell and Maud Bailey, academic literary critics whose discovery of a collection of letters evidencing a previously unsuspected love affair between two imaginary nineteenth-century poets, Randolph Ash and Christabel LaMotte, brings about a parallel affection between them. The most remarkable feature of the novel is the fact that it puts its reader so amply in possession of the same documentary evidence as Roland and Maud have to work with, and much of the novel's considerable length is taken up with extremely accomplished parodies of nineteenth-century poetic and epistolary style. During the course of the novel, we are given not only the correspondence in full between Ash and LaMotte but also journal entries from other characters, such as Ellen Ash, Randolph's wife, and Blanche Glover, LaMotte's female companion, as well as, most remarkably of all, a large number of exemplary extracts from the alleged writings of Ash and LaMotte.

The novel turns on the modal ambiguity of the term 'possession' which forms its title. Like other characters in the book, Roland and Maud are 'possessed' by history, in the sense both that they have a ferocious curiosity about it and that, as a result, history seems to reenact itself through them. The plot solidifies neatly into a struggle for legal possession of the Ash–LaMotte letters, which is resolved when it is revealed that Maud Bailey is the direct descendant of the illegitimate child of the two nineteenth-century poets and under copyright law the owner of the letters. Indeed, the question asked throughout the novel is how far it is possible to distinguish the arrogant, proprietary desire of the historian for possession of the past from a more authentic openness to it on its own terms, a concern which is paralleled in the romantic relationship which we see growing simultaneously between Ash and LaMotte and Roland and Maud, in which the urgent desire for possession of a loved one is balanced by the need to retain self-possession and autonomy.

This thematic concern of the novel is also dramatised in its form. In one sense, the prodigious range and competence of the historical and literary inventions of the novel are testimony to the desire to give the past its own autonomy, bulk and dimension, unconstrained by the concerns of the present. The desire for the past is partly a desire for the past to be in some sense beyond the reach of the enfolding understanding of the present. But here, as in the plot of the novel, the willingness to be possessed by the past is inseparable from the more acquisitive desire to be possessed of it. The elaborately constructed simulations of nineteenth-century poetry are a testimony to a characteristically twentieth-century form of egocentricity, which confirms itself not by exclusion but by assimilation of what is other to it. The virtuous and attentive humility before the *thisness* of the past is here never absolutely to be distinguished from the virtuoso appropriation of it. One of the many interesting jokes that the novel plays is to attribute its ventriloquial speaking of the past to its own historical inventions: like Robert Browning, to whom he has many similarities, Randolph Ash attempts in his own poetry to mimic and assimilate the voices of other cultures and periods, a characteristic which leads one scholar in the novel, Mortimer Cropper, to entitle his biography of Ash *The Great Ventriloquist*. The novel's attention to this irony in its own structure is signalled by the quotation from Browning's 'Mr Sludge "The Medium"' which is employed as one of its epigraphs. Sludge, the fraudulent medium, defends his use of imposture and trickery, in which the spirits he summons up 'Participate in Sludgehood – nay grow mine/I veritably possess them', on the grounds that it resembles just the kind of fabrication of history which in poetry is conventionally approved:

> It's a History of the World, the Lizard Age,
> The Early Indians, the Old Country War,
> Jerome Napoleon, whatsoever you please.
> All as the author wants it. Such a scribe
> You pay and praise for putting life in stones,
> Fire into fog, making the past your world.
> (Browning 1970: 891, quoted in
> Byatt 1991: 507)

The novel seems to borrow Sludge's argument but in inverted form, for here fiction is justified on the grounds that it is a kind of conjuration, an authentic medium for allowing the past to speak.

Although the device of the parallel plot in *Possession* has some similarities to that of *Hawksmoor*, it differs from it too in the degree of its self-conscious attention to the difference and otherness of the past. In this, *Possession* is an interestingly hybrid case, suspended somewhere between the conditions of what I earlier distinguished as the historical novel and the historicised novel. The self-conscious romance structure moves the plot towards a redemption in the present of the love that was thwarted in the past. The relationship of Maud Bailey and Roland Michell makes good the past, giving the suspended or broken narrative of Ash and LaMotte its conclusion. The novel appears to assume the availability of the past to the narrating present, and the possibility of translating the past into the present. The structure of fulfilled romance functions a little like the elaborate structure of correspondences in *Hawksmoor*, for it closes together the past and the present in tight reciprocity; the collapse of boundaries between Maud and Roland, which is evoked in the description of their lovemaking ('Roland finally, to use an outdated phrase, entered and took possession of all her white coolness that grew warm against him, so that there seemed to be no boundaries'; 507), is simultaneously a collapse of boundaries between them and the past which is resumed and redeemed through them.

On the other hand, it is important to note that the expectations of romance are not wholly fulfilled in *Possession*: Roland and Maud end up in bed, but are going to have to maintain their subsequent relationship separated in different countries. More importantly, the book ends with a teasing fragment, an account of a meeting that may have taken place between Randolph Ash and his daughter, who is being brought up in ignorance of her parentage by Christabel LaMotte's sister. The deliberate exclusion of this episode from the design of the book (with which it cannot easily be integrated, since we are told that the letter in which Christabel tells Randolph of his daughter was never delivered to him, but buried with him by his widow) gives it the status of virtual history, which is neither hardened into the definiteness of document nor wholly invisible either. It is one of those things 'which happen and leave no discernible trace, are not spoken or written of, though it would be very wrong to say that subsequent events go on indifferently, all the same, as though such things had never been' (508). It is an outcrop from the book, whose very failure to be gathered into the design is to be read as a mark of its authenticity. If the completion of the past in the present is imaged as the final delivery of a letter, its solidification into an event achieved by its eventual arrival in the present, this final episode postulates a more indefinite kind of occurrence, which may never arrive in memory and narrative, or achieve the completeness of an event. Randolph makes his daughter a crown of flowers and asks her to deliver a message to Christabel, her aunt, but neither of these reaches its destination, since 'on the way home, she met her brothers, and there was a rough-and-tumble, and the lovely crown was broken, and she forgot the message, which was never delivered' (511). The book leaves unresolved the question of the status of this event, suspended as it is (like the book it concludes, but does not quite inhabit) between history and fiction. History, it is here suggested, may lie, not only in what achieves definition or arrives at its destination but also in what does not. The book both includes this episode and omits it, as though to keep open the loophole of difference in the relations between the past and the present; to dramatise the necessary incompleteness of fiction which itself inhabits history as well as taking it as its subject. If it is true, as Louise Yelin has skilfully argued (1992), that *Possession* is blind to its own repressions and partialities – for example in the promotion of the truth of love and art in its representation of nineteenth- and twentieth-century culture over the competing truths of politics and material circumstance – then this acknowledgement seems to indicate that the novel is not wholly blind to the possibility of such blindness.

The transition from historical to historicised fiction may also be observed in two of William Golding's novels, *The Spire* (1964) and *Rites of Passage* (1980). As we will see in a moment, *Rites of Passage* shares with *Possession* an interesting sense of the relations between history and narration as a kind of transmission or passage of meaning. *The Spire* is an imaginative reconstruction of the building of Salisbury Cathedral, which is attributed to the stubborn vision and self-deluding inspiration of one man, Dean Jocelin. The novel establishes an elaborate parallel between the raising of the spire on its dubious, shifting foundations, and Jocelin's increasingly intense and unstable determination to see his vision embodied. The central dynamic of the novel is Jocelin's fierce disavowal of all that belongs to what he sees as the corrupted underworld of sex, violence, nature and physicality, the sickening mutability of 'the renewing life of the world' (Golding 1964: 58). The novel follows through in dense and complex detail the return of everything that Jocelin represses in his lifting dream of the spire, in the revelation of his half-repressed awareness of the pressures of his own sexual desire, of the pagan practices and human sacrifice that have ensured that the spire continues to stand, and the steady encroachment of his own tuberculosis of the spine. The novel's climax counterposes the height and aspiration of the spiritual ideal with the unavoidable, necessary force of the body, as Jocelin, driving a chisel into a pillar, discovers it has been built full of rubble and is suddenly brought low by the angel of his illness who 'struck him from arse to the head with a whitehot flail' (188). Like much of Golding's work, the novel is a kind of metaphysical fable, which employs history only to abolish it, or to suggest the persistence of primordial truths and conflicts. Jocelin's struggles for awareness are rendered in a language which strains towards the visionary, but makes no attempt to imitate mediaeval English. Despite the fact that we are restricted to Jocelin's limited and self-deluding point of view throughout, the language of the novel renders this limitation and confusion with perfect self-command, enacting the same confidence in the translatability of Jocelin's spiritual distress and uncertainties as it has in the historical translatability of the mediaeval period into contemporary terms.

Rites of Passage, written some sixteen years later, returns to many of the same preoccupations as *The Spire*, and even recalls some of its imagery. The novel is written in the form of a journal kept by Edmund Talbot, during his long sea-voyage to Australia in the early part of the nineteenth century. More emphatically than *The Spire*, *Rites of Passage* concerns a process of change and development, as Edmund comes to confront various truths about his own limitations and responsibilities. The book explores Edmund's rite of passage as he learns of the humiliation effected upon Colley, a young clergyman who is a fellow-passenger, a humiliation that leaves the latter to die of shame; the narrative is oblique, but it becomes plain that, as part of the ceremony of crossing the Equator, Colley has been made drunk and induced into the public performance of homosexual acts with the sailors. Unlike *The Spire*, *Rites of Passage* is written in a language and with a range of reference that is a deliberate, highly skilful imitation of the spoken and written language of an early nineteenth-century aristocrat – or at least of contemporary literary representations of such a language. Most of the book is Talbot's own journal, though it also includes a journal kept by Colley which, in the manner of much eighteenth-century fiction, Talbot makes available to his reader.

Rites of Passage is organised in terms of various instances of 'crossing the line', sometimes in the sense of transgression, sometimes of progression. The ship is structured in socio-spatial divisions that are both horizontal and vertical: the former in the division between the officers and the passengers and the white line drawn on the deck which marks the division between the genteel passengers and the emigrants; and the latter in the division between the civilised world of the deck and the more enigmatic or menacing depths of the ship suggested by the stench from the ballast which assails the nostrils of the refined Talbot as he boards. This vertical imagery, which maps the contrast between the upper and lower body, the cerebral and sensual regions, on to social and spiritual distinctions, recalls the conflict between upper and lower in *The Spire*. The sense of the chasm between the airy height of the spire and the shifting nightmare of the pit in which its foundations are sunk returns in the narrative of Colley the clergyman, who is perplexed by the opacity of water as opposed to the clarity and perspective of the sky (1980: 196–7). These spatial boundaries are enforced and also regularly infringed through the narrative, which, like *The Spire*, seems to be concerned to display the essential complexity or hybridity of human and social life, despite all attempts to assert the powers of civilisation against what is intolerably or incomprehensibly other in itself. In Talbot's final judgement on the death of Colley, *Rites of Passage* seems to offer a fabular distillation of what Neil McEwan has called 'the permanent condition of man' (1987: 170), in terms of the relapse of the upper into the lower, or of historical life into some more essential and perennial darkness:

> A gill or two of the *fiery ichor* brought him from the heights of complacent austerity to what his sobering mind must have felt as the lowest hell of self-degradation. In the not too ample volume of man's knowledge of Man, let this sentence be inserted. Men can die of shame.
> ... With lack of sleep and too much understanding I grow a little crazy, I think, like all men at sea who live too close to each other and too close thereby to all that is monstrous under the sun and moon.
>
> (Golding 1980: 278)

Alan Sinfield, writing of Golding's *Lord of the Flies* (1954), has criticised the tendency in that novel and elsewhere in Golding's writing to treat 'man' as a metaphysical rather than historical subject, and the concomitant tendency to treat the essence of humanity as something that emerges only from the extremity of isolation or suffering (Sinfield 1989: 142, 147–8). It may well be that this criticism extends also to *The Inheritors* (1955) and *The Spire*, novels in which Golding turns to history to bring about this revealing extremity. But *Rites of Passage* can be accommodated to this view of Golding's writing only with considerable difficulty. Keyed closely into the structure of metaphysical oppositions between essential human characteristics are a number of other forms of contrast, crossing and transition, which give the novel a much more historical dimension and dynamic force. First of all, there is the question of the voyage itself, which takes the ship from London to Sydney, from the centres of civilised power to the edges or antipodes of all that is safely known. If the voyage is thought of spatially in terms of the reversibility of up and down, the 'above' of civilisation and the 'below' of savagery ('Do you but think that there the very stars will be unfamiliar and the moon stood on her head?' surmises Colley; 197), the voyage also has a mobility and a directionality which cut through this static symbolic deadlock. This sense of continued travel towards an intended but as yet unachieved destination is sufficient to nudge the rather self-satisfied lesson that the novel teaches itself about the essential nature of man ironically off balance.

Here the historical imposture involved in the language of the novel becomes crucial. In giving the final judgement of the novel to Talbot, Golding makes it possible to read it not only as an authorial statement about the nature of man but also as a display of premature, self-satisfied generalisation on the part of one who has yet much to learn. What we come to in the novel's final words is not 'man's knowledge of Man', but a representation of a particular, quasi-historical individual's judgement about the nature of 'Man'. What is displayed is not Truth, but the historical process of grasping at it. This does not wholly undercut the judgement offered, but it does not wholly endorse it either. It is not that Talbot is wrong or misguided in his judgement, but rather that his judgement is shown to be contingent, that is also historically situated; in this novel, that is also to say historically in *passage*. To read the final pages ironically is precisely to read it historically, and to wrench a static structure of symbolic opposites into a more dynamic horizontal movement.

Indeed, the novel has already displayed enough instances of the toppling of symbol into the mobility of history, in a number of other rites of passage. The book is structured not just around metaphorical alternation but also around more unpredictable interruptions, lopsided lurches of significance and transitions of meaning. There is first of all the question of history itself. The book is set at a period which allows Golding to dramatise the meeting and partial exchange of two worlds or historical sensibilities, in the elegant, self-conscious, somewhat posturing intelligence of Talbot, ored with epithet and allusion, and the more awkward, passionate energy of Colley's narrative. Plainly, Golding means to suggest something like the passage of Augustan into Romantic in the contrast between these two narratives, a contrast assisted by that between Mr Brocklebank, the drunken painter who quotes Coleridge's *Rime of the Ancient Mariner*, and Mr Prettiman, the dangerous radical free thinker, who is so disgusted by the superstition of Coleridge's poem that he spends much of the novel comically set on bringing down an albatross. The contrast between Augustan and Romantic is also unbalanced, since the representative of the Age of Reason, Mr Prettiman, is also a political radical of a kind very different from Talbot's unthinking conservatism. The historical passage from the eighteenth century to the nineteenth is underlined by the different literary allusions, to classical authors, to Shakespeare, Milton, Sterne and Richardson in Talbot's narrative, to Coleridge and other Romantic writers in Colley's journal. But this structure of allusion is complicated by the overlayering of a number of anachronistic literary parallels in other sea-narratives, from Melville's *Billy Budd* (left unfinished at his death in 1891 and not published until 1924), which also concerns a mysterious eruption of violence into the ordered life of a ship, to Conrad's *The Nigger of the 'Narcissus'* (1897), which concerns the withdrawal and unaccountable death of a member of a ship's crew.

If such jumping, syncopated time seems playfully disrespectful of history, this may only be from a perspective on historical time that this novel suggests may be unhelpfully simplified. The novel's commitment to the passage of history and meaning does not imply any reassuring view of history as linear and progressive. Talbot's own narrative quickly loses its sense of sequence, division and forward movement under the stress of seasickness and bewilderment and it begins to dart back and forth in search of coherence and understanding. Talbot becomes uncomfortably aware of the vexed transition between event and narrative, 'the distance between the disorder of real life in its multifarious action, partial exhibition, irritating concealments and the stage simulacra that I had once taken as a fair representation of it' (110). This sense of the difficulty of converting facts into intelligible representations connects with a more generalised concern with the possibilities of translation through the book. The idea of translation – etymologically a 'carrying across' or 'passage' – is itself carried across into other senses in the book. Talbot is embarrassed to be reminded of his earlier patronising attitude towards the social translation of Lieutenant Summers from seaman to officer, but tries to reassure him that 'Perfect translation from one language to another is possible and I could give you an example of it. So is perfect translation from class to class' (125). A few pages on in the same entry, Talbot returns to and elaborates his sense of Summers's easy commerce between different areas of the social life of the ship and its different languages:

> An odd fellow indeed! Truly as good a translation as yours, my lord! All those countless leagues from one end of a British ship to the other! To hear him give orders about the deck – and then to meet him over a glass – he can pass between one sentence and the next from all the jargoning of the Tarpaulin language to the plain exchanges which take place between gentlemen.
>
> (Golding 1980: 135–6)

Talbot's reference to the 'Tarpaulin' language of sailors reminds us that his own language is itself largely an affair of translation, in its transposition of this language into polite, educated diction. Despite Talbot's faith in 'the plain exchanges which take place between gentlemen', and his and Summers's capacity to pass from this kind of exchange to another, there are plenty of instances in the book of blocked or imperfect passage of meaning. Most notably, there is Colley, whom Talbot describes to Summers as 'one example among us where the translation is not a success', and as a man who 'has stepped out of his station without any merit to support the elevation' (125, 126). In fact, Talbot's protracted misunderstanding of the fatal humiliation undergone by Colley depends upon certain crucial opacities or failures of translation between seafaring jargon and polite language – most notably the sexual meanings of the 'badger bag' and 'getting a chew off a parson' (273). The idea of translation, social as well as linguistic, as active passage, rather than inert equivalence, connects with an ambivalence about the nature of the social microcosm mirrored in the passengers on board ship. If they are fixed in typified roles and relationships, according to the familiar allegorical disposition of representations of isolated societies, then, when Talbot congratulates himself that 'We were beginning to move in society' (45), it registers the intuition that this is a society itself in movement. Sometimes, as in the case of Summers's advancement, this movement can be seen as quite 'convulsive', to use a term that occurs on a number of occasions in Talbot's account. Summers announces, 'I have performed the naval operation known as "coming aft through the hawsehole". I was promoted from the lower deck' (51). The sexual hints of this phrase, anticipating the buggery of Colley, suggest the violent collapse of social and ethical distinctions embodied in that transgressive act.

The unreliable semantic passage of meaning enacted in translation is linked to the insecure fluctuation of mood or style in Talbot's account. 'It is a play,' he writes at one point. 'Is it a farce or a tragedy?' (104). Towards the end of his account he wonders quite what kind of narrative he has written:

> Wit? Acute observations? Entertainment? Why – it has become, perhaps, some kind of sea-story but a sea-story with never a tempest, no shipwreck, no sinking, no rescue at sea, no sight

nor sound of an enemy, no thundering broadsides, heroism, prizes, gallant defences and heroic attacks!

(Golding 1980: 277–8)

This instability of mode is enacted in several narrative episodes as well, most notably perhaps in the narrative of the seduction of the not-unwilling Zenobia Brocklebank which Talbot conducts in his cabin while the first of Colley's humiliations is occurring on deck. The manner and point of the episode is precisely to demonstrate the sudden passage from one frame of reference to another. The coupling with Zenobia is rendered in Popean mock-heroic terms as the boarding of an enemy vessel. The climax comes with the sound of a blunderbuss being discharged up on deck, which prompts a cry from Zenobia, and precipitates from Talbot an unintended discharge of his own:

She clutched me frantically.
'Mr Talbot,' she gasped, 'Edmund! The French! Save me!'
Was there ever anything more mistimed and ridiculous? Like most handsome and passionate women she is a fool; and the explosion (which I at once identified) put her, if not me, in the peril from which it had been my generous intention to protect her.

(Golding 1980: 87)

The squalid polish of this farcical account contrasts but also mingles grotesquely with the tragedy of what we come to know is happening on deck. The elaborate metaphorical correspondences set up between different regions of the life on board ship give way to a sudden metonymic slippage, as connections and disjunctures slide together. It is not clear which 'explosion' is which (the gun, the cry, the ejaculation), for example, since they combine and beget each other so instantaneously; while Zenobia's cry 'The French', which may refer primarily to her fear that the ship is under attack by the French, may also refer to the contraceptive device (the French letter) which is dangerously unavailable at this moment. It may also relate to many of the other associations which accrue to the idea of the 'French' through the narrative, for example, when Talbot later refers to the 'danger from *the French*', to mean the threat of pregnancy to Zenobia (94), or when he evokes the political instability and revolution that are 'the results of indiscipline among the Gallic race' (113). The narrative concentrates together at this moment a number of meanings that are in fact diffused through the reading of Talbot's narrative (including his own implicit and actual rereading of his narrative). In this, the narrative represents and undergoes a kind of temporal convulsion, for, while appearing on one level to rush precipitately to climax, at another it actually delays our understanding of the event taking place on deck. This is only assisted by the sly allusion to the beginning of Sterne's *Tristram Shandy* (1767), in which the narrator blames his insufficiency and impotence as a narrator on the sudden interruption to the flow of his father's animal spirits during his conception, an interruption caused by his mother's enquiry as to whether his father had remembered to wind the clock: Talbot's 'Was there ever anything more mistimed and ridiculous?' (87) corresponds nicely to Mr Shandy's cry of '*Did ever woman, since the creation of the world, interrupt a man with such a silly question?*' (Sterne 1985: 36). The lamination of sexuality, time and narrative establishes a more general connection between Golding's and Sterne's novels, since *Tristram Shandy* also builds into its very structure a kind of anachronism or failure temporally to coincide with itself: as is well known, Tristram Shandy spends a large proportion of his narrative just getting himself to the point where he can be born.

Semantic uncertainty in *Rites of Passage* is thus closely associated with temporal disjuncture, and the shifting of meaning with the uncertain passages and recursions of time. Perhaps the most important form which this takes in the novel is in its structure of address. Not only does the reader of this novel pass from one narrative (Talbot's) to another (Colley's), the reader is also made aware that the narratives, like the passengers on board ship, themselves have destinations, in their respective addressees. Indeed, once the fact becomes known that Talbot is keeping a journal for the benefit of his powerful, unnamed godfather, it loops round to become a material factor in the narrative itself, as Captain Anderson seeks to protect himself from blame or discredit by influencing Talbot's account (182, 258). The lines of intended and actual address of the narratives are complex. Talbot's narrative is addressed consistently to his godfather, though it also includes some passages of rhetorical self-address (183–4), and literally envelops Colley's manuscript, which is addressed to his sister. The addressive itinerary of Colley's narrative is particularly irregular. After the painfully precise solicitude of its beginnings, where Colley laboriously explains jokes and allusions for the benefit of his sister,

Colley's journal begins to be less certain of its ultimate reader, and his sister begins to yield place to a more remote addressee:

> My dear sister –
>   Yet this is strange. Already what I have written would be too painful for your – for her – eyes. It must be amended, altered, softened; and yet –
>   If not to my sister then to whom? To THEE? Can it be that like THY saints of old (particularly Saint Augustine) I am addressing THEE, OH MOST MERCIFUL SAVIOUR?
>
> (Golding 1980: 208)

In the end, of course, his journal is read not by his sister or his Saviour but by Talbot – though in Colley's fervent and romantic imagination Talbot is plainly identified with Christ (212). Talbot then transmits it to his godfather, deciding, as Colley seems to have decided, that it would not be right to convey it to its intended reader:

> I shall write a letter to Miss Colley. It will be lies from beginning to end. I shall describe my growing friendship with her brother ... A letter that contains everything but a shred of truth! How is that for a start to a career in the service of my King and Country?
>
> (Golding 1980: 277)

Don Crompton was, I think, the first to discuss the parallel here with Conrad's *Heart of Darkness* (1985: 134), which also ends with a withheld or distorted delivery of a message from a dead man to a woman; Conrad's Marlow is just as sickened by being unable to tell the fiancée of Kurtz the details of the horrifying moral collapse and death that he has witnessed as Talbot is by his knowledge that he will be unable to transmit the truth of Colley's degradation. The historical anticipation here redoubles this sense of deflected destination; Talbot's failure to deliver Colley's narrative is refracted through his report to his godfather, as our reading of that fact is bent anachronistically through Conrad's novel, reinforcing the sense of the necessary participation of historical delay in every communication, in the lapse of time that both breaks and makes the sense of the communication. Talbot's awareness of Captain Anderson's interest in his journal induces another kind of deflecting self-consciousness into it, as though the journal begins to be written partly for Anderson's benefit as well. In any case, the ultimate source of authority is itself never reached (the fact that the 'godfather' has the remoteness and silent inaccessibility of the godhead itself is a nice metaphysical tease in the novel), since our twentieth-century reading constitutes an interruption of this journal's transmission. This pattern of appropriations, overhearings and interceptions is of a piece with much of the communication that is imperfectly transmitted or construed in the novel. Perhaps the most surprising such incident occurs during the cruel festivities at Colley's expense during the ceremony to mark the crossing of the line, or the Equator. Colley has paraded out, determined to assert the dignity of his cloth, in what Talbot describes as 'a positive delirium of ecclesiastical finery' (105). Some hint of what is in train in the fo'castle, invisible to Talbot and the officers gathered on the quarterdeck, is given by the appearance of two figures who proceed across the deck, dressed in a parody of Colley's rig. One is wearing Colley's academic hood and walking 'with an exaggeratedly mincing parody of the female gait', while the other, conjoining the loose canvas garments of the common passengers with Colley's battered mortarboard, is pursuing the first. The passage of these two figures across the deck fixes and cruelly lampoons Colley's imperfect passage between classes and sexual identities. Talbot's narrative also emphasises the ironic conditions of the display:

> This play-acting was not directed only inwards towards the fo'castle. It was aimed *aft* at us! Have you not seen an actor consciously throw a soliloquy outwards and upwards to the gallery and even into one corner of it? These two figures that had paraded before us had cast their portrayal of human weakness and folly directly *aft* to where their betters were assembled!
>
> (Golding 1980: 112)

The complexities of display here match the complexities of address generally in *Rites of Passage*. The social coding of fo'castle (where the poorer passengers and emigrants are lodged) and quarterdeck (where the officers and richer passengers are standing) makes this theatricality political. The display is for the benefit of the quarterdeck, though it is enacted in full view of the fo'castle. What the fo'castle sees is therefore not just the display, but the fact of the quarterdeck seeing the display. The quarterdeck, too, sees itself being seen to observe the display. The ambivalence of visual address here, in which the lines of spectacle and display are intercepted and overlaid, is assisted by an inversion effected in Talbot's use of the theatrical metaphor. The two actors are in a sense 'playing to the gallery'; but in a theatre, the gallery is not where the richer clientele are seated, as the quarterdeck is on the ship, but where the cheaper seats are. In vulgarly 'acting up', the two figures are really acting down; the stalls and gallery, quarterdeck and fo'castle are unstably changing places.

A number of critics have pointed to the general theme of transition, spatial, psychological, social and, especially, historical in *Rites of Passage* (see Crompton 1985: 139). But the awareness it repeatedly instils of the transition of meaning, which is to say its historical condition of passage through time and between different times, makes it a novel that not only represents transition but itself inhabits that condition. The knowledge that *Rites of Passage* shows as being acquired is never brought together in the authority of the present moment, but is rather gained and sustained in the obscurity of the interim, in the time of transmission from one time to another. Talbot's narrative emphasises the unpredictable nature of comprehension which 'comes, when it comes, at a bound. In that semi-darkness between one wave and the next' (Golding 1980: 16). Knowledge that comes in the interim comes erratically, through jumps and dislocations, or what Talbot at one point calls 'convulsion of the understanding' (251) rather than by means of steady and regular working through: 'One's intelligence may march about and about a problem but the solution does not come gradually into view. One moment it is not. The next it is there' (85). The novel itself comes to rest in this intermediary position, its final revelation being out of place (it 'should have been fitted in much earlier', as Talbot confesses; 266), and the last entry of the journal being marked not with a number or even a letter but with an ampersand, conventional figure for the movement of linkage, without positive content of its own. The very title of the novel seems to represent a tension between form and force, the arresting of time into the fixed forms of ritual, and the drawing out of those forms into the uncertainties of history.

Rites of Passage was in fact followed by two further novels dealing with this voyage, *Close Quarters* (1987) and *Fire Down Below* (1989), to form a trilogy known as *To the Ends of the Earth*; in neither of the subsequent works, however, is the theme of passage represented and enacted with quite the same complexity. One may say that, where *Possession* attempts to rescue itself from being a 'historical' fiction, which yields up the past – or a version of the past – to the reader, by becoming a historicised fiction, which reminds us of what fiction cannot deliver to our possession of the past, Golding's *Rites of Passage* is worked upon by the other novels in the sequence in the opposite direction; where *Rites of Passage* stands as one of the postwar period's most interesting historicised fictions, in its dramatisation of the conditions of historical passage that affect all and every narration, the sea-trilogy rounds it into a completeness that is satisfying but less imaginatively demanding.

The postwar novel of history responds in various ways to the waning of a sense of 'continuous' history as it has been defined by Michel Foucault:

> Continuous history is the indispensable correlative of the founding function of the subject: the guarantee that everything that has eluded him may be restored to him; the certainty that time will disperse nothing without restoring it in a reconstituted unity; the promise that one day the subject – in the form of historical consciousness – will once again be able to appropriate, to bring back under its sway, all those things that are kept at a distance by difference, and to find in them what might be called his abode.
>
> (Foucault 1972: 12)

Continuous history assumes that history is unified, in the sense both that it is the steady unfolding of one story, rather than of many, and that those to whom history happens share an identity with those to whom history is addressed or transmitted in the form of that story. Foucault calls for a theoretical alternative to this sense of the necessary continuity of history, in order to open up awareness of everything that interrupts the smooth uniformity of consciousness and memory. Many of the actual conditions of postwar history have been propitious for creating the theoretical alternatives generated by Foucault and others following his example. This has been a period which has seen a steady waning of confidence in long-range, continuous narratives of all kinds – whether this be the history of Empire, the history of a nation, or the march of civilisation itself – and the continuous 'subjects' supposed and required by such histories. The disturbing reflux of the colonial 'outside' into the centres of imperial consciousness that we saw enacted in the condition of England novel is accompanied in many novels of history by the sense of the return of suppressed or heterogeneous histories and experiences, which do not restore the subject of history to itself.

On the other hand, it would be a mistake to assume that the interruption of long-range history has produced nothing more than the discrediting of truth, progress, and the possibility of attending to truth in history. The disturbed relation of the present to the past has also been an enrichment of that relation. In the period since the war, the erosion of confidence both in the certainties of history and in the belief that Britain belongs to history (that history happens in and to Britain), has produced a variety of responses, all of them attempts to make good or adjust to that decentring. As I suggested above, the period since the war has seen, not so much the discrediting of history, as the acceleration and diversification of its modes and meanings. The cruder attempts to restore continuous history – the intense, but unsustained flaring of national consciousness at the time of the Falklands War and the Gulf War, the call for a return to 'Victorian values' during the later years of the Thatcher administration during the 1980s, the generation of the 'heritage' industry – all take their meaning and impetus from a much more fundamental and generalised recognition of the breaking of those continuities. The Conservative party who have been in power since 1979 in Britain, and who are traditionally the party most committed to maintaining continuity with the past, have after all been driven by a free-market ideology which requires the sweeping away of the inherited forms and assumptions of the past.

Against this we may set the multiplication of different kinds of history – of women, of working-class culture, of ethnic cultures – and in a range of different forms. Here, film and television, which have been partially responsible for the accelerating amnesia of contemporary electronic culture, have also contributed very markedly to the making available of different kinds of history in different forms. The situation that has resulted from this is paradoxical; the sense of history has both evaporated and proliferated, the need for history has both shrunk and prodigiously enlarged. We have seen that one response to this disturbed sense of relation to the historical past is the attempt to define and assert the 'permanent condition' of man, in narratives that either claim to make the historical past wholly available or dissolve the distinctions between past and present. But another response is to imagine and particularise a relationship to the past that accepts the necessary discontinuity of history. The importance of *Rites of Passage* here seems to lie in its balancing, or passage, between these two modes of narrating the past. In it a narrative that strives to abstract the past into a frozen diagram of the essential dividedness of 'man' itself divides its own historical mode and narrative manner, to reveal how implicated in history any such apparently whole truth must be.

Most importantly, it is a novel that brings into the foreground the structure of address that is at the forefront of the novel of history. If there is no 'subject of history' in Foucault's sense, then it might seem as though the novel of history must give up any aspiration to address a collective audience, and either reconcile itself to a readership that is split and uncertain, or elaborately lament the lost possibility of constructing or communicating with such an audience. In fact, however, the very persistence of the problem of address in the postwar novel of history, in questions concerning who history is for, to whom it is addressed and belongs and who is entitled to speak of and for it, indicates that there remains in the form of the novel, if only in muted, utopian form, an aspiration to some inclusiveness of address. The importance of the novel lies in its capacity simultaneously to insist on the transformations and dislocations attendant upon the 'loss of history' and to offer a kind of habituation, or, in Foucault's terms, a form of 'abode' within history. The novel of history is the enactment of the continuing need to *inhabit* history, however discontinuous and enigmatic it may be. So the question of the truth of history, and the capacity or not of narrative to represent that truth, needs to be translated into slightly different terms. Historical narrative shows the continuing, renewing importance of constructing the links of transmissibility or passage between the present and the past. Historical narrative such as it is evidenced in the novel of history in the postwar period is not a matter of representing the truth of history but of constructing the terms of a conversation or structure of address between the past and the present. In such a structure of address, it is not necessary to assume the stability of the positions of addressor and addressee, not necessary to assume that there is already given a contemporary 'us' and a historical 'them', since it is the structure of address that largely constitutes this conversation. One of the most important functions of the novel of history is to maintain the kinds of conversation and communicative structure which will allow the formation of those identities, as it may be, in new and unprecedented ways. The contemporary narrative of history will not let us forget our decentring from the stage of history, but will not cease either to gather together provisional and historically mobile forms of collectivity in its structure of address.

5
ORIGINS AND REVERSIONS

We have seen in the last two chapters how the question of history works powerfully on the form of the postwar novel, compelling it to explore the relations between history as event and history as narration, as well as to test and transform the nature of its own authority. One particularly marked feature of postwar fiction, both in Britain and elsewhere, which establishes an important link between history and novelistic narrative is the practice of rewriting earlier works of fiction. Such novels are a particular effect of a more generalised sense of the eternal return that seems to characterise postwar fiction, both in Britain and elsewhere. In contemporary fiction, telling has become compulsorily belated, inextricably bound up with retelling, in all its idioms: reworking, translation, adaptation, displacement, imitation, forgery, plagiarism, parody, pastiche. This is evident in any of the following works: John Barth's rewritings of *Scheherezade*, Homer's *Odyssey* and Cervantes's *Don Quixote* in *Chimera* (1974) and *The Tidewater Tales* (1988); Robert Coover's skilful parodies of movie genres in *A Night at the Movies* (1991) and his extrapolation of the Pinocchio story in *Pinocchio in Venice* (1991); Alain Robbe-Grillet's reworking of the Oedipus story in *The Erasers* (1966); Gert Hoffman's literary transposition of Breughel's painting in *The Parable of the Blind* (1989); the obsessive auto-iterations of Samuel Beckett's work (see Connor 1988) and Paul Auster's rewriting of Beckett's Trilogy of novels in his *New York Trilogy* (1987); or, in British writing, D. M. Thomas's reworking of Freudian case-history in *The White Hotel* (1981); William Golding's parody of eighteenth-century narrative in his sea-trilogy, *To the Ends of the Earth* (1980–89), or his rewriting of R. M. Ballantyne's *Coral Island* (1857) in *Lord of the Flies* (1954), along with Marianne Wiggins's subsequent female rewriting of that rewriting in

John Dollar (1989; and see Connor 1994); Peter Ackroyd's literary replications in *The Last Testament of Oscar Wilde* (1983) and *Chatterton* (1987); Angela Carter's rewritings of fairy-tales in *The Bloody Chamber* (1979), and her vaudevillian travesty of Shakespeare in *Wise Children* (1991); the retellings of the Biblical story of the Flood in Jeanette Winterson's *Boating for Beginners* (1985) and Julian Barnes's *A History of the World in 10½ Chapters* (1989); parodies and impersonations of Victorian narrative forms, such as John Fowles's *The French Lieutenant's Woman* (1969), Susan Hill's *The Mist in the Mirror* (1992) and Alasdair Gray's *Poor Things* (1992); and feminist reappropriations in general of the genres of science fiction and the detective story.

The practice of fictionally rewriting well-known or culturally central texts can take different forms and have different effects, but a feature that allows it, at least provisionally, to be distinguished from other forms of cultural mimicry is that it consists of a particularised and conscientious attachment to a single textual precedent, such that its departures from its original must be measured in terms of its dependence upon it. I have in mind here such texts as Jean Rhys's reworking of *Jane Eyre* in her *Wide Sargasso Sea* (1966), to name what is probably the most well-known example, or Sue Roe's reworking of *Great Expectations* in *Estella: Her Expectations* (1982). In such rewritings, there is something different and more complex at work than the mere reduplication or replenishment of narratives. If rewriting of this kind compromises the cultural authority of the original text, then this never amounts to a simple denial of it; in its attention to its rewritten original, its fidelity-in-betrayal, the rewritten text must always submit to the authority of an imperative that is at once ethical and historical. In reflecting on the literary past, novels are often to be seen reflecting on the three-way relations between novels, other novels, and the history that connects and divides them. In engaging with their literary precedents, such novels engage with the history of beliefs and attitudes to which those originals have belonged and which they have helped to shape. In reworking their precedents, such novels both acknowledge the continuing force of the novelistic past in the present and investigate the capacity of novels to intervene in that present.

I want in this chapter to look closely at four recent instances of such rewriting: they are Brian Aldiss's reworking of Mary Shelley's *Frankenstein* (1818) in his *Frankenstein Unbound* (1973), Emma

ORIGINS AND REVERSIONS

Tennant's rewriting of Stevenson's *The Strange Case of Dr Jekyll and Mr Hyde* (1886) in her *Two Women of London: The Strange Case of Ms Jekyll and Mrs Hyde* (1989), J. M. Coetzee's rewriting of Defoe's *Robinson Crusoe* (1719) in his *Foe* (1987) and Marina Warner's rewriting of Shakespeare's *The Tempest* (1613) in *Indigo: Or, Mapping the Waters* (1992). In each case, the rewriting is of a well-known and canonical text; in this kind of rewriting, there would hardly be any point in taking as one's object a text that were not thus well known. The cultural centrality of these target texts has to do with the fact that they are all in different ways myths of origin and/or reversion. I want to suggest that, in all four cases, the action of rewriting involves intensifying or restoring the awareness of everything that the idea of an origin must put aside or suppress in social and historical life. In *Robinson Crusoe* and *Dr Jekyll and Mr Hyde*, a certain form of extreme experience produces a reversion to origins. The stranded Robinson Crusoe is forced to invent himself from nothing on his island, building from the ground up his self, his culture, his history, and spelling out in the process, as many have noted, a powerful Puritan lesson of individual self-making. *Dr Jekyll and Mr Hyde* does not depend upon isolation from society in order to produce its condition of extremity and its action takes place, not on an island, but in London. But *Dr Jekyll and Mr Hyde* does indeed involve extremity, in the form of that Romantic Faustianism in which a single inspired scientist is impelled to reach beyond the limits of conventional knowledge and morality. Dr Jekyll's 'transcendental medicine' is the metaphorical equivalent of the shipwreck, which separates him from ordinary life, by revealing to him a certain truth about man's primitive nature. Henry Jekyll actually uses the metaphor of the shipwreck to describe his own history: 'I thus drew steadily nearer to that truth by whose partial discovery I have been doomed to such a terrible shipwreck: that man is not truly one, but truly two' (Stevenson 1979: 82). In this isolation from society, and in his attempt to surpass social and moral norms, Jekyll resembles Victor Frankenstein. In creating life, Frankenstein not only establishes himself blasphemously in the position of divine creativity but also, like Robinson Crusoe and Henry Jekyll, makes a claim to have originated himself. The enchanted isle of *The Tempest* similarly allows a myth of original self-making to flourish by erasing the history of other inhabitants of the island, crystallising the complex encounter of histories between coloniser and colonised into the brittle simplicity of magic and fable.

When such texts are subject to rewriting, the question of origin is interestingly redoubled. If all four 'original' texts concern the establishment of or reversion to different sorts of origin, then the return to such texts for the purposes of rewriting may be seen as a reversion of a similar kind. Indeed, a striking feature of many literary rewritings is their interest in trying to narrate the conditions of emergence of the original: very often, rewriting involves 'prewriting'. In the cases I will be looking at in this chapter, the originality of the original cultural myth of origin is doubled and divided by the act of the rewriting, which runs together in its 'reversioning' the processes of revision, reversal and reversion. But there is one further crucial feature of these three rewritings, which is the question of gender in them. In *Two Women of London*, a female author rewrites a myth of male origin. Although J. M. Coetzee is not a female author, the whole purpose of *Foe* is nevertheless to postulate a female narrative alongside, or in place of, the male narrative of Daniel Defoe; as we will see, the novel attempts to write the narrative which the male narrative must have displaced in order to represent itself as original. In *Indigo*, the novel's rescue of the history of a colonised people takes place largely through the restoration of the narrative of the 'witch' Sycorax which is obscured by Prospero's account. In these rewritings, the substitution or insertion of a female narrative draws attention to the remarkable absence of the female in the originals, revealing the ways in which myths of extremity and origin, literary and otherwise, have often been bound up with a male myth of parthenogenetic self-authoring.

In Aldiss's *Frankenstein Unbound*, by contrast, a text originally written by a woman is undone by a male narrative, which both repeats and subverts the original's gesture of self-origination. The novel adopts the device of a 'timeslip' – the result of disturbances to the fabric of space and time caused by conflict and pollution in the twenty-first century – to install its narrator, the ex-presidential advisor Joe Bodenland, in early nineteenth-century Switzerland. There he encounters the literary circle consisting of the young Mary Godwin, soon to be Shelley, her lover Percy Bysshe Shelley, Lord Byron, his sister Claire Claremont and Polidori as well as, existing happily alongside them in the same ontological frame, Victor Frankenstein, the obsessive, remorseful scientist who is the subject of the very novel Mary Shelley is engaged at that moment in writing. On first arriving back in the nineteenth century,

Bodenland attempts to rescue the servant girl Justine Moritz who, as in Mary Shelley's *Frankenstein*, has been falsely accused of murdering Frankenstein's younger brother. Failing in this, he encounters the Shelley circle and, after a brief affair with Mary Shelley herself, sets out in pursuit of Frankenstein, but is himself imprisoned on suspicion of having murdered his quarry. He is released by a sudden cataclysmic flood, caused by the same convulsion in the space–time continuum which opened up the timeslip to bring him to the nineteenth century in the first place, and tracks Frankenstein to his lair. He is a horrified witness to the creation of a female mate for the monster and kills Frankenstein. From this point until the novel's close, he becomes more and more closely identified with his victim. Rather than pursuing the monster to the Arctic, as Frankenstein does in Mary Shelley's novel, Bodenland follows him through the 'frigid lands' which have appeared in the neighbourhood of Geneva as a result of another timeslip. The novel ends with Bodenland killing both monsters, and himself heading off towards a strange domed city which looms up out of the landscape.

Although this novel is very crude and skill-less in many respects – in its awkward lurches of plot, its wearisome passages of banal philosophising, its spasms of melodrama and sentimentality ('Our gaze met and became an eternal thing'; Aldiss 1991: 161) – it nevertheless deals with the same closely-looped knot of concerns as are apparent in many other rewritings or prewritings, and in particular with the relationship between authorship and the origination of narrative on the one hand, and biological and sexual origination on the other. The myth of Frankenstein is a kind of creation myth, marking, as Bodenland insists, both the beginning of the scientific imagination and the beginning of the genre of science fiction which shares and examines this imagination ('the first novel of the Scientific Revolution and ... the first novel of science fiction'; 67). Aldiss himself has written in similar terms of the inaugural force of *Frankenstein* for science fiction in an essay significantly entitled 'The Origin of the Species' (1973). According to the allegorical reading with which Bodenland (relentlessly) supplies his readers, *Frankenstein* is a novel about an act of illicit authorship, an act of hubristic origination which spins horrifyingly out of control. The novel has retained its importance, Bodenland informs us, 'because Frankenstein was the archetype of the scientist whose research, pursued in the sacred name of increasing knowledge, takes on a life of its own and causes untold misery before being brought under control' (67). And again, as Bodenland explains the allegory to Mary Shelley: 'Man has the power to invent, but not to control' (107).

In *Frankenstein* it is the very desire for control, the desire to know and govern nature, which produces ungovernable monstrosity. In Aldiss's rewriting, the issue of control is shifted from the plot of *Frankenstein* to its form. What Mary Shelley's novel seems to allegorise as an issue of control over nature, Aldiss displaces into a concern with the control over narrative itself. In doing this, and despite his embarrassingly inept swipes at feminism and his romanticisation of Mary Shelley, which would be insulting if they were not so risible, Aldiss actually anticipates the concerns of some of the most perceptive feminist readings of *Frankenstein* during the 1970s and 1980s (Moers 1979; Poovey 1980; Johnson 1982; Hodges 1983). Aldiss's novel establishes an exact parallel between the monster, which in Mary Shelley's novel 'takes on a life of its own' (Aldiss 1991: 67), and the novel as a whole which, once begun, also spirals out of the intentional control of its author. The parallel is made quite plain when Joe Bodenland declares that 'I had accepted the equal reality of Mary Shelley and her creature, Victor Frankenstein, just as I had accepted the equal reality of Victor and his monster' (94).

In the face of this, Bodenland decides to intervene in history, in order to put a stop to what he comes to regard as Frankenstein's blasphemous interference with natural process, an interference which in the end is to result in the very space–time disturbances which have put Bodenland in a position to intervene at all. The problem here is that Bodenland cannot help but reproduce the very form of the story that he is attempting to quell at its inception. Bodenland's will-to-power, as he turns his impressively annihilating twentieth-century weapons against the monster, is the very creature of the Promethean spirit of scientific modernity that it aims to abort – as indeed the monster appears to make clear in his dying address:

> This I will tell you, and through you all men, if you are deemed fit to rejoin your kind: that my death will weigh more heavily upon you than my life. No fury I might possess could be a match for yours. Moreover, though you seek to bury me, yet will you continuously [*sic*] resurrect me! Once I am unbound, I am unbounded!
>
> (Aldiss 1991: 215)

Bodenland is both the creature of *Frankenstein* and its aspiring creator. Initially, the effect of discovering himself to be both *beside* and *inside* the novel that Mary Shelley is engaged in writing is to dissolve his sense of authority and identity. His initial attempts to track down the monster require him to try to remember or, given his hazy memory of the book *Frankenstein*, to reconstruct the developments of the plot. He demands of Mary Shelley that she tell him what is to happen in her as yet unfinished book.

> She bit her lip. 'Why, it is the history of the world. The creature naturally wants a soul-mate. Frankenstein . . . agrees to make one, a female . . . Frankenstein has to go away to make it . . . He has to make a journey, as we must.'
>
> (Aldiss 1991: 108)

It is not surprising that Bodenland is a little puzzled about this hint, for in Mary Shelley's completed novel Victor Frankenstein repents his promise to make a female mate for his monster. But, in *Frankenstein Unbound*, Frankenstein does make such a mate. Aldiss thus rewrites Mary Shelley's novel to actualise the narrative possibility that she deliberately revokes, in a move that both gives her novel back to her and dispossesses her of it, realising and thwarting her intentions at once. In rewriting her novel to allow the possibility of a female creature (an idea developed in a number of film versions of the book, of course), Aldiss seems to be allowing for the possibility of female propagation that in Mary Shelley's novel is so intolerable, the possibility of further progeny being the reason that Victor Frankenstein brings his work on a female creature to an end (Shelley 1985: 435). However, the female monster assembled by Aldiss's Victor Frankenstein is a grotesquely masculinised one, with hugely powerful thighs, and a kind of penis for excretion of urine (161–5), as though the very female principle were being revoked in the moment of allowing it. What is more, Aldiss's rewriting of Mary Shelley's novel in this respect is only temporary, since he ends up obliterating the female creature with his incendiary bullets just as effectively as Mary Shelley's Frankenstein obliterates the possibility of making her by destroying his work and instruments.

This connects with a more general alternation between respect and rivalry in Aldiss's *Frankenstein Unbound*. While seeming to give Mary Shelley credit for inaugurating the scientific imagination and the genre of science fiction that both celebrates and interrogates such imagination, the book also attempts to deprive her of responsibility for her novel. There are two ways in which this is done: by suggesting that her novel is a mere replication of existing male precedents, and by suggesting that it is in any case a product of unconscious or spontaneous imaginative process rather than conscious artistic design. Mary Shelley is made to provide an account of the origins of her novel which nervously effaces her own inaugural part in it. In the preface to the 1831 edition of *Frankenstein*, Mary Shelley describes its origins in a challenge issued to each other by members of the Shelley–Byron group to write a ghost story (Shelley 1985: 53–6). Her version of this famous Gothic competition in *Frankenstein Unbound* emphasises how much she owes to the soaring Promethean fancies of Byron and Shelley, in a way that is itself presented as a passive replication of a former act of helpless listening; Mary remembers hiding behind her father's sofa to listen to Coleridge reciting *The Rime of the Ancient Mariner* (Aldiss 1991: 105–6). When she subsequently dreams her horrifying dream and begins to write it out, it is all on the basis of male writerly precedent, as she sets herself to write, 'as Horace Walpole did with his dream of Otranto' (ibid.) and to infuse into the story 'some of my illustrious father's principles of conduct' (ibid.). Even the slimmest claim for her own creature's originality of conception is turned into evidence of daughterly obedience:

> My poor creature, you see, is not like all the other grim shades who have preceded him. He has an inner life, and his most telling statement of his ills is embodied in a Godwinian phrase, 'I am malicious because I am miserable'.
>
> (Aldiss 1991: 106)

In implying that it is the meeting with Bodenland which will give her the impetus to finish her novel, *Frankenstein Unbound* adds Bodenland himself to the list of fecundating male influences. It is true that Mary Shelley is careful in her own 1831 Preface to avoid the immodest dreams of parthenogenetic originality that her story warns against, emphasising that

> Every thing must have a beginning, to speak in Sanchean phrase; and that beginning must be linked to something that went before ... Invention, it must be humbly admitted, does not consist in creating out of void, but out of chaos.
>
> (Shelley 1985: 54)

But in Bodenland's narration, Mary's story is something over which she has no control at all: 'When I invent I scarcely know what I am inventing. The story seems to possess me, and that is why I have put the manuscript by for some days' (Aldiss 1991: 106). Later, Bodenland asserts that she 'received Frankenstein's story from the thin air as far as I could determine' (162).

Where one strategy discredits Mary Shelley's work by suggesting that it has no originality, the other does so by suggesting that her work is illegitimately without precedent. In either case, the possibility of an inaugural female imagination is discounted, or seen as monstrous, because Mary Shelley's writing of her novel parallels the act of creation it narrates, as well as the very condition of the monster created in that novel. On the one hand, the monster, too, has no authentic life of his own, being made up of second-hand parts of others' bodies, as well as out of his own reading, and rewriting of texts such as Milton's *Paradise Lost*. On the other hand, his existence, like that of the novel he inhabits, is illegitimate precisely to the degree that it has no precedents; it is an origination without legitimate origins, though he insists in his dying words to Bodenland that this is in fact a general human condition: 'As for our births – when I first opened my eyes, I knew I existed – as did you. But who I was, or where, or from what cause, I knew not – no more did you!' (215).

It is not surprising, therefore, that Bodenland comes to repeat the confusion between the monster and his creator for which he reproaches popular tradition. To kill the monster means also to kill its maker, lest he make a second monster: 'What would Frankenstein do then? Would he make a second creature? Should I also anticipate that it was my duty to eradicate, not only the monster, but the author of monsters?' (94). Here, Bodenland seems to enact that further slide that connects Frankenstein's hubristic creation with Mary Shelley's invention of him. In killing off the actual monster and its creator as conjured up by Mary Shelley's novel, Bodenland is also apparently killing off the novel itself. When Bodenland calls Mary's work in progress her 'Diseased Creation myth' (167), the uncertain attachment of the adjective creates an interesting semantic shimmer between the idea that Mary Shelley's novel is a myth about diseased creation and the idea that it is itself a diseased creation. The paradox encountered by Aldiss's novel is that, in rooting out at its birth the diseased myth of creation, it is also discrediting the premonitory diagnosis of diseased creation that the novel contains. Once again, it repeats the act of irresponsible and illegitimate self-origination against which the novel warns.

As the novel progresses, Bodenland's narration of his adventures both prewrites and rewrites its ending, his pursuit of the united male and female monsters supplying in advance an ending to supplant the ending which was in fact written. But in his pursuit Bodenland becomes more and more closely identified with the Frankenstein he has killed:

> Frankenstein had gone. One thing remained for me. I had now to take on his role of monster-killer. Imperfectly though I recalled Mary's novel, I knew that her Frankenstein had embarked on a pursuit of his creature which had taken them both into those gloomy and ice-bound regions which held so strong a lure for the Romantic imagination.
>
> (Aldiss 1991: 194–5)

Bodenland's description of the landscape embodies the sense of uncanny repetition, in which every attempt to escape from the pull of the story winds back into a reenactment of it:

> The road winds and winds to reach one end of a giant recession into the mountains; then it winds in an opposite direction to reach a point but a short distance from the first as the crow flies. Then the same procedure must be repeated ... a hundred times, two hundred, three.
>
> (Aldiss 1991: 205)

At the end of the novel, as described earlier (see p. 171 above), Aldiss also engineers an interesting confrontation between the (male) monster and his killer, in which the dying monster describes his extermination as the beginning rather than the end of his allegorical power. This identifies as monstrous, not the original transgression of the borderline between life and death, but the very act of destruction which ought to restore their orderly contrast. Thus it draws tight the paradox that this novel manages, almost despite itself, to dramatise – that there are no other means to destroy the monstrosity that is technological and scientific modernity other than those derived from modernity itself and that, in seeking to rewrite the catastrophic story of technological modernity, Bodenland cannot but reaffirm it. Aldiss ends up recapitulating the central moral shape of *Frankenstein*, in which the destruction of the monster is both a redemption and an intensification of guilt, an undoing and a compounding of the transgressive violence that initiates the novel. Here again, there is an interesting interference between the acts of origination and destruction practised in Mary Shelley's narrative and the acts of origination and destruction practised on it by Bodenland's narrative. As the narration of Bodenland's unwriting of Mary Shelley's *Frankenstein*, Aldiss's *Frankenstein Unbound* is a kind of rebuke to her unleashing of the monstrosity of modern science, and seems to accuse Mary Shelley of a crime of narrative unbounding which is equivalent to the decoupling of science from imagination and morality that it represents and to a degree repudiates in the actions of Frankenstein. As such, the rewriting of the story is a kind of expropriation, an attempt to commandeer and control an illegitimate narrative. In this sense *Frankenstein Unbound* attempts to unbind the links between Mary Shelley and her own creation. But, in doing so, Bodenland is forced to bind himself ever more tightly within the structures of paradox that are already at work within the novel over which he seeks control. Bodenland attempts to take Mary Shelley's novel from her, by providing an explanation, interpretation and emphatic conclusion to a novel that otherwise seems to remain troublingly open-ended in its implications. But in doing so, he cannot but reassert the unbounded, uncontainable force of the monster and the monstrous narration that originates him.

Frankenstein Unbound dramatises this uneasiness in its failure to provide the full narrative closure that its mode of address implies and logically requires. Bodenland's narrative is in the form of a tape-recording, dictated at intervals during the action, which is addressed to his wife in his own time. But since his account leaves him stranded in a temporal no-man's-land, uncertain whether he is at the beginning or the ending of the story of self-destructive modernity, it is unclear whether or not his narrative is ever to have been heard by its intended addressee. In unbinding the story of Frankenstein from Mary Shelley's ownership and control, Aldiss ends up actually restoring it to her, since he is so conspicuously unable to bind his own narrative into finality; for this is to repeat the troubling unboundedness of the Frankenstein myth, the exorbitant tendency towards reworking, repeating and travestying that is so much a feature of the text's afterlife. This exorbitance is itself a repetition of the gesture of unleashing or unbinding which is intrinsic to the novel itself, which is readable in part as a narrative about the unleashing of narrative. The form of *Frankenstein Unbound* seems, in short, to reveal that its original is a novel which it is impossible to rewrite, since it already consists of a process of unbounded rewriting. The monstrosity of rewriting the novel consists precisely in the fact of this repetition.

Interestingly, Aldiss has recently attempted to rewrite his own rewriting, in a sequel to *Frankenstein Unbound* which appeared in 1992. Although *Dracula Unbound* is in many ways a more accomplished novel – there are fewer embarrassments in the writing, and the plot is more elaborately contrived than in the former rewriting – there is nevertheless a disappointing flatness about it. In this novel, Joe Bodenland, having returned in some unexplained fashion from the desolate intertemporal waste land in which he had been abandoned at the end of *Frankenstein Unbound,* is the inventor of a primitive form of time travel. The plot is set in motion by the discovery in prehistoric graves of what appear to be the remains of human beings whose manner of death (silver bullets and stakes through the heart) indicate to every reader (but of course to no single one of the characters) that they are vampires. A ghost train rushing through the site attracts Joe Bodenland's curious attention and he naturally contrives a way to board it. The elaborate plot sweeps us forward in time to a point many centuries hence at which human beings have become slaves to a race of prehistoric vampire mutations who parasitically drain the energy of the sun in order to power the time train that transports them back in time on raids for human prey and slave labour from earlier periods. Joe Bodenland arrives back in London in 1896 and makes the acquaintance of Bram Stoker who is at work on his *Dracula*; Bodenland recruits Stoker for some derring-do struggles against the vampires and their master Dracula, which end with the former's borrowing a fusion bomb from the future in order to obliterate the prehistoric ancestors of the vampires. Despite its increased narrative complexity and sophistication (much play is made of the paradoxes attendant upon trying to alter the past and great advantage is derived from the recent popularisation of fractal and chaos theory), the novel is actually a much simpler and less interesting act of rewriting than its predecessor. This has a great deal to do with the much reduced rivalry between Bodenland and the author whom he is displacing. Here, Bodenland is not drawn into any attempts to rewrite or reimagine Stoker's novel. Stoker himself is turned into a bluff man of action who joins willingly in Bodenland's energetic cross-temporal heroics. There is no sense of the uncanny mirroring of form and content that makes the rewriting of the action of

Frankenstein so odd a recapitulation of Mary Shelley's act of writing the novel; as a result, though the novel is concerned with many of the same questions as *Frankenstein Unbound* – the nature of origins, the relation between science, religion and power – these are not questions that are relayed through the question of the writing of the novel itself. *Dracula Unbound* is much more sure of its bearings, much more adequate to the limited generic ambitions of science fiction fantasy, than Aldiss's first rewriting, which, as we have seen, so intriguingly fails to keep a grip on itself and its narrative ambitions.

Emma Tennant's *Two Women of London* is probably the closest and most faithful rewriting of the four at which I am looking, for it follows with deliberation most of the stages of the narrative of *Dr Jekyll and Mr Hyde*. Indeed, Emma Tennant has made the rewriting of male narrative, or of male narrative of female lives, something of a speciality in recent years, with subsequent rewritings of the Faust story in her *Faustine* (1992) and Hardy's *Tess of the D'Urbervilles* in her *Tess* (1993). She has also published a continuation of Jane Austen's *Pride and Prejudice* in her *Pemberley* (1993). The difference is that, where Stevenson's tale has a male narrator and a cast of characters who are exclusively male, the narrator and characters of *Two Women of London* are female. Dr Jekyll has become the beautiful, cultured and affluent Eliza Jekyll, whose opulent apartment backs on to the miserable rooms where dwells the slatternly and violent Mrs Hyde. The narrative takes the form of an elaborate reconstruction of the case of Ms Jekyll and Mrs Hyde by an unnamed editor–narrator, who stitches together video footage, taped interviews, letters and other forms of testimony from a number of middle-class women inhabiting Nightingale Crescent in West London. During the period dealt with by the narrative, the area has been tyrannised by a serial rapist. The crucial event in the narrative is the killing of a man thought to be the rapist by Mrs Hyde, a man who turns out to be the innocent local businessman and magistrate, the Hon. Jeremy Toller – an event corresponding to the motiveless killing of the MP Sir Danvers Carew by Mr Hyde in Stevenson's story. Just as in Stevenson's original, the story ends with the testimony of the Jekyll-figure. This reveals the single most important difference between the first and the second versions. Henry Jekyll is driven initially by the desire to confront his other, to separate out the good and evil constituents fused together so painfully and incongruously in a single human nature. Having released the figure of Mr Hyde from his psychic confinement, Jekyll then finds it more and more difficult to return to his 'true' self. In *Two Women of London*, it is Mrs Hyde who finds that the fortuitous combination of a tranquilliser and the drug Ecstasy can transform her into her idealised self-image, Ms Eliza Jekyll. In Stevenson's story, the singular, but compounded ego attempts to give birth to its not-self. In Tennant's version of this story, it is the disintegrating ego, the suffering and atrophied not-self that Mrs Hyde has become, who craves the drug as means to restored self-possession. Here, self-possession is a derived rather than an original effect, and the transformation wrought is not a reversion but a reinvention.

In feminising Stevenson's version of the male split self, Tennant actually compels attention to the ways in which the apparently absent female is in fact present in the original story. Although there are no leading female characters in Stevenson's story, women are important to its structural scheme. There are three females who feature in it briefly. The first such figure is the little girl who is trampled underfoot by Hyde in the opening episode of the story (Stevenson 1979: 31). The second is the maidservant who witnesses Hyde's murder of Sir Danvers Carew (46–7). The one is the victim of Hyde's motiveless violence, the other is the helpless spectator of it, and both of these stand for a pure, mute innocence, the exact and abstracted antithesis to the evil represented by Hyde. There is something extraordinarily deliberated in Stevenson's account of the foolish and childish innocence of the maidservant:

> Never (she used to say with streaming tears, when she narrated that experience), never had she felt more at peace with all men or thought more kindly of the world. And as she so sat, she became aware of an aged and beautiful gentleman with white hair drawing near along the lane; and advancing to meet him, another and very small gentleman, to whom at first she paid less attention.
> (Stevenson 1979: 46)

Here woman is on the side of goodness and of self-identity, but only because her identity is a pure abstraction, part of that neurotic separation of the male and female spheres and values in Victorian ideology. Here the female is not only defined according to ideological and psychic processes of distinction, but she seems to guarantee distinctiveness as such, the boundary between the inside and the outside, law and criminality, virtue and licence.

But, according to a well-documented psycho-cultural process, woman can also stand for loss of identity, and the reversion to indistinction. The third female who features in *Dr Jekyll and Mr Hyde* is Hyde's housekeeper, who mirrors the indefiniteness of her master: she is 'ivory-faced and silvery-haired', but with 'an evil face, smoothed by hypocrisy' (49). This figure connects in a complicated way with the theme of appearance in Stevenson's story. The woman resembles Hyde not so much in her appearance of being evil as in the fact that her face is 'smoothed by hypocrisy'. Although Jekyll thinks that Hyde's face 'seemed more express and single, than the imperfect and divided countenance I had been hitherto accustomed to call mine', and attributes this to the fact that Hyde is 'pure evil' (84–5), the people who meet Hyde are perplexed by being unable to give a name to their feelings of disgust for him. This means that the evil of Hyde consists as much in his uncertainty of definition as in the more comfortable doctrine that he is pure evil. This contradiction perhaps arises from a psychic economy in which evil is characterised precisely as the not-self, the indefinite, the impure (the female); an economy which makes it impossible to maintain consistently the notion of 'pure' evil.

There are one or two occasions when Mr Hyde is characterised in Stevenson's story not only as a kind of evolutionary throwback (he is said on several occasions to be 'apelike') but also as female. The cultural connections between women and ideas of degeneracy in the late nineteenth century have been well established, for example in the work of Bram Dijkstra (1986) and Lyn Pykett (1995). Dr Lanyon writes of Edward Hyde that 'he paused, and put his hand to his throat, and I could see, in spite of his collected manner, that he was wrestling against the approaches of the hysteria' (78). In a passage towards the end of Henry Jekyll's deposition, Hyde is characterised as between life and death, as the embodiment of a Sartrean vision of the female *visqueuse*: 'This was the shocking thing: that the slime of the pit seemed to utter cries and voices; that the amorphous dust gesticulated and sinned; that what was dead, and had no shape, should usurp the offices of life' (95). Jekyll then suddenly genders this terrifying liminality: 'And this again, that this insurgent horror was knit to him closer than a wife' (95). It is the female that here must name the indistinct union of self and not-self, the joining of joining and dissolution.

By making the doubling take place between the two versions of woman offered by Stevenson – the degraded and the idealised –

rather than within the single person of the man, Emma Tennant makes manifest the latent anxieties about gender that are encoded within *Dr Jekyll and Mr Hyde*. At the same time, she substitutes for the series of male narrators (Mr Enfield, Mr Utterson, Dr Lanyon, Dr Jekyll) a network of female narrators, though they are marshalled together by a single, authoritative and unnamed narrator. The substitution of network for series means that Tennant's rewriting designedly sacrifices the sense of development towards closure. In particular, the dispersal of the narrative of Mrs Hyde among a number of witnesses and narrators prevents that final authoritative act of self-immolation with which Henry Jekyll closes his – and Stevenson's – account of his life: 'Here, then, as I lay down the pen, and proceed to seal up my confession, I bring the life of that unhappy Henry Jekyll to an end' (96). In Emma Tennant's version, Jekyll/Hyde does not die, but escapes, perhaps to the continent, nor does Jekyll have the final word. Although the narrator surmises that 'perhaps she has at last been able to find herself' (Tennant 1989: 129), the final words of the book are the narrator's describing the lawyer Jean Hastie's determination to keep the wholesome and the murderous separate, by protecting Mrs Hyde's children from knowledge of their mother:

> I'll make sure they don't find the other side of this tragic victim of our new Victorian values: the word, scrawled across the pad under a list of household essentials –
> Ajax
> fishfingers
> ketchup
> Mother's Pride
> KILL
>
> (Tennant 1989: 121)

But Jean Hastie's conviction that some irreducible and, it seems, metaphysical evil lies within Jekyll/Hyde represents a partial retraction of the critique which Tennant has made throughout the novel of Stevenson's ethical determinism. Jean Hastie is the author of an academic work on the Gnostic Gospels which aims radically to revise the Augustinian doctrine of Original Sin, arguing that 'The message of the story of Adam and Eve in the Garden of Eden is that we are responsible for the choices we freely make, good or evil, just as Adam was' (73). This doctrine of ethical self-determination and self-authorship stands against the demonising impulses both of Stevenson's story, which denies women's self-determination by identifying the female merely as the inhibiting or corrupting materiality from which the freely self-determining male must extricate himself, and of the women in *Two Women of London* who demonise men in something of the same way. But in refusing the determining force of Stevenson's myth of self-determination, Tennant also reproduces it. Stevenson's fear of reversion *into* the female resurfaces as a fear of reversion *in the female* into pure and unrepresentable 'evil'. As in *Frankenstein Unbound*, in reversing her predecessor's premises, Tennant reverts to them.

Of the four rewritings with which I am concerned here, J. M. Coetzee's *Foe* pays the most explicit attention to the interrelations of subjectivity, origination and narrative. The novel is centred around Susan Barton, a woman who is shipwrecked on an island with Robinson Cruso and his slave Friday, and her attempts to get their, or, more properly, her story written by one Daniel Foe. (Coetzee distinguishes 'his' castaway from Defoe's by calling him 'Cruso' rather than 'Crusoe', and distinguishes his author by calling him by his original name of 'Foe' rather than the 'Defoe' which he took later. I will maintain this orthographical distinction between the two castaways and the two authors wherever possible.) Indeed, although it is a rewriting of *Robinson Crusoe*, *Foe* must also be seen as a 'prequel', whose main concern is not with the events which have taken place on the island, but with the struggles over the narrative of those events. On the island, it is Susan who urges Cruso to think of the future, to extend himself beyond his sterile dominion over his kingdom, and she who urges him to keep some record of his stay on the island; but, once returned to England, Cruso having died on the journey, Susan becomes marginal to her own narrative:

> When I reflect on my story I seem to exist only as the one who came, the one who witnessed, the one who longed to be gone: a being without substance, a ghost beside the true body of Cruso. Is that the fate of all storytellers?
>
> (Coetzee 1987: 51)

Her urgent desire to repeat the truth about her stay on the island with Cruso is what gives Foe the narrative material which enables him to construct the myth of Cruso's self-construction. If *Robinson Crusoe* is a cultural myth of the birth of social life in male individuality, then Coetzee's narrative shows the necessary (non)participation of the female in, and as, the sacrifice that enables this supplementary, revisionist myth of origin to be generated. In one episode in the narrative, Susan travels to Bristol with Friday, in order to get him a passage on a ship back to Africa. Her shabby appearance and unconventional companion mean that she is mistaken for a gipsy, making her wonder, indeed, 'Am I become a gipsy unknown to myself?' (109). Here, her condition seems the exact reverse of Crusoe's; where, in Defoe's account, he creates social life out of his own resourceful solitude, Susan discovers her solitude and marginality in the very midst of social life.

Temporarily abandoned by Foe when, like his historical original, he flees London to escape his creditors, Susan tries to take possession of her own life by writing her story, declaring 'I am a free woman who asserts her freedom by telling her story according to her own desire' (131). In so doing, Susan is attempting to rewrite the story of male self-origination of which *Robinson Crusoe* is the archetype, even sitting at Foe's desk and supplanting him as controlling author:

> I have your table to sit at, your window to gaze through. I write with your pen on your paper, and when the sheets are completed they go into your chest. So your life continues to be lived, though you are gone.
>
> (Coetzee 1987: 65)

Endeavouring, as she puts it, 'to be father to my story', Susan must also resist the deceitful fatherhood of Foe, who sends to her a young girl whom he has primed with the plausible story that she is her long-lost daughter, also named Susan Barton. Susan tells her:

> I do not know who told you that your father was a brewer from Deptford who fled to the Low Countries, but the story is false. Your father is a man named Daniel Foe . . . I will vouch he is the author of the story of the brewer.
>
> (Coetzee 1987: 90–1)

But, in resisting the false paternity of Foe, Susan also deprives the girl of her maternal origin, ironically confirming the sacrifice of the female which she is attempting to resist: 'You are father-born. You have no mother. The pain you feel is the pain of lack, not the pain of loss' (ibid.).

In fact, Susan increasingly risks falling into the same desire for authoritative self-possession as that apparently guaranteed in

Robinson Crusoe. 'I was intended not to be the mother of my story, but to beget it', she says to Foe, reversing their genders. 'It is not I who am the intended, but you' (126). But the acknowledgement of the joint parentage of her narrative brings her slowly to recognise the ghostly indeterminacy of its issue. Dedicating her life to the telling of her story, but compelled to deliver that story through another, story and life become interchangeable and interchangeably indefinite:

> In the beginning I thought I would tell you the story of the island and, being done with that, return to my former life. But now all my life grows to be story and there is nothing of my own left to me. I thought I was myself and this girl a creature from another order speaking words you made up for her. But now I am full of doubt. Nothing is left to me but doubt itself. Who is speaking me?
>
> (Coetzee 1987: 133)

The transferential effect of narrating, of speaking for oneself as another, or speaking for another as oneself, means that the responsibility of narration can never be one's own alone; narration can never be self-authorship, or pure paternal self-begetting. It is for this reason that Susan Barton's narrative, or the narrative of how her narrative comes to be silenced, joins with another, even more profound loss of voice – that of the tongueless Friday, whom she takes with her from the island to England. Foe is confident that he and Susan can decipher the nonspeech of Friday, can penetrate to his heart. In this, of course, Coetzee is meditating on the unending responsibility of those who tell stories to speak on behalf of those who have had no voice, or no words that can be heard. To rewrite the narratives of the past is to allow and foster the remission of that 'eternal and inhuman wakefulness' of self-present consciousness, to allow those blinks of the eye, 'the cracks and chinks through which another voice, other voices speak in our lives' (30). But such rewriting must also beware of the danger that it admit the voice of the other only in the terms of the dominating self: the image for this in *Foe* is the document that Susan writes and hangs around Friday's neck to say that he is free, the very linguistic form of the manumission signalling Friday's continuing exclusion from its terms. For Coetzee, to hear or to speak the voice of the other may only be possible in artfully contrived, ethically sustained disruption of the self-possession of narrative. It may only be possible, therefore, in the ethical interval of transference, as narrative passes from author to author, rather than in the proprietary self-begetting of narrative. Either to speak the self or to speak the other in the self's terms is to do violence to the transferential ethics of narrative, which always expel the self from centrality.

Coetzee offers an image of this commitment to the other in the final episodes of *Foe*. In these episodes an 'I', who may be Foe, or Defoe, or Coetzee himself, or some compound of them all, begins to rewrite the rewritten narrative which Susan Barton has already provided. The dreamlike quest of this 'I' is for the speech of Friday, a speech which is below or before the speech that always drowns his speech. It takes the 'I' deep in dream or vision, first to Foe's room, where it lies with Susan, Friday asleep at their feet, and then into the waters off Cruso's island, where Susan Barton and her captain lie drowned, along with Friday. Somehow, an unimaginable utterance passes from Friday through his interlocutor and out into history, an urgent, ceaseless, speechless speech:

> His mouth opens. From inside him comes a slow stream, without breath, without interruption. It flows up through his body and out upon me; it passes through the cabin, through the wreck; washing the cliffs and shores of the island, it runs northward and southward to the ends of the earth. Soft and cold, dark and unending, it beats against my eyelids, against the skin of my face.
>
> (Coetzee 1987: 157)

To make the voice of Friday articulate would be to betray it sentimentally into self-present intelligibility, for the comfort of the guilty self; but not to articulate its silencing would be an even worse treachery. In attempting to speak with, or give a voice to, one who would speak from the condition of linguistic sacrifice, Coetzee's novel attempts to resist the reversion to sacrificial myths of origin which characterises Aldiss's *Frankenstein Unbound* and Tennant's *Two Women of London*. The voice with which the novel speaks at the end belongs to no one; it consists in, or occupies the space of, its giving, the sacrifice of itself. In a sense, the decision not to offer a wholly new or other narrative in a wholly new and self-possessed voice is what confirms *Foe*'s radical novelty. We need to specify the originality of *Foe*'s apparent sacrifice of self-possession carefully. Is it not possible to judge *Foe*'s combination of the gift of voice to the other and the refusal to credit that other as anything but a negativity as being a certain curbing of the gift, a donation which reverts to the credit of the self that is seemingly dispossessed? As we have already seen, Coetzee's novel itself provides an image of just such a recursive structure, in Susan's document of manumission which is hung like a yoke round the neck of Friday. The gift of freedom is given in a language the exclusion from which marks the very impossibility of freedom for Friday, making him 'the helpless captive of my desire to have our story told' (150). Such acknowledgement, however, of the difficulty of giving freedom unconditionally on the part of Susan and Coetzee guarantees no immunity for the novel itself against the dangers of reversion to the mentality of the slave-owner, the colonist, the self-originator.

But perhaps there is no such immunity. If it is impossible to begin again, to write entirely anew the false story of the parthenogenetic origin of man, culture, and language, then this is because narrative begins and prevails in a process of transference and contamination which is the very impossibility of such ethical immunity. What is rewritten in these three narratives is precisely the wrong of the issueless insulation of the self from the other. No revision can entirely avoid reversion; no attempt to rework the myths of self-possessed beginning can entirely avoid becoming possessed by the desire for self-possession on which it lays hands. It is only by taking the risk of reversion that it may be possible to imagine, diversely, collectively, intermittently, myths of founding and finding which are instituted otherwise than on sacrifice and silence.

The three novels so far considered are distinguished by the closeness and continuousness of their rewriting. In each case, the revisionary purpose is so strong that it enjoins that, from beginning to end, faithful attention must be paid to the original text from which the rewriting watchfully defects. But this is not the only mode of rewriting to flourish in contemporary fiction. Marina Warner's *Indigo* (1992) is an example of a novel whose rewriting of a particular text – Shakespeare's *The Tempest* – carries it significantly out of the orbit of the original. *Indigo* is more of an improvisation upon its original than an attempt to translate it. Although the engagement between original and rewriting is much less close and sustained than in other cases, it is nevertheless highly impressive and provocative.

Marina Warner's rewriting of *The Tempest* reflects a change of attitude towards a play that, as Marguerite Alexander has noted (1990: 167–85), has been an alluring model for a number of novelists, including John Fowles in *The Magus* (1967, 1977), Iris Murdoch in *The Sea, The Sea* (1978) and John Banville in *Ghosts* (1993). For many in the postwar period, the importance of *The Tempest* has lain in its exploration of the relations between art and magic, and emphasis has fallen accordingly on the figure of Prospero the enchanter and on the self-reflexive meditations upon art to be found in the play. A story such as Robert Coover's 'The Magic Poker' (1970) establishes a continuous parallel between the idea of the enchanted isle of *The Tempest* and the enchantments and deceits of art, and a film such as Peter Greenaway's *Prospero's Books* continues to exemplify this form of attention to the play. *Indigo*, on the other hand, is evidence of the tendency which grew through the 1980s to read the play less allegorically, paying attention to the relations of power that subsist between Prospero and the other inhabitants of the island who have preceded him, but over whom he now has dominion. In this way of reading the novel, Caliban and Ariel are viewed not just as allegorical appendages to the artist-like Prospero but as colonised subjects and the values of art and magic are unintelligible apart from the facts of history and imperial power.

The novel is set in two separate times: the early decades of the seventeenth century and the period from 1948 to the 1980s. The seventeenth-century portion of the plot deals with the life of Sycorax, a local wise woman on the Caribbean island of Liamuiga, who is expert in herbal medicine and in the ways of preparing indigo dye. One day a group of African bodies is washed ashore on the island, after having been thrown overboard from a slaving ship; Sycorax delivers a male child from the womb of one of the dead women, whom she names Dulé. She also takes custody of a foundling Arawak girl called Ariel, brought by European settlers from the Surinam mainland. The island is invaded by Kit Everard, a colonist bent on making his fortune, who captures Sycorax and Ariel and holds them hostage to secure his safety. In captivity Ariel bears his child and Sycorax dies of the crippling wounds she receives when she is burned out of her tree-house by Everard and the invading Europeans. Dulé warns Ariel of an impending uprising; Ariel, attempting to kill Everard, unwittingly gives him advance warning of the uprising which is brutally put down. Dulé is captured and mockingly renamed Caliban. The twentieth-century portion of the narrative follows the twinned fortunes of Miranda, the granddaughter of Sir Anthony Everard, descendant of the seventeenth-century founder of Liamuiga and national sporting hero, and Xanthe, his daughter by a late marriage. Some of the events of three centuries earlier are repeated in the lives of Miranda and Xanthe, not least in their involvement in a renewed invasion of the islands, this time by means of the establishment of a tourist hotel, and in a political coup that leaves Xanthe drowned. The novel ends a little stagily with Miranda reunited with a politically radical black actor, whom she sees playing the part of Caliban in a production of *The Tempest*.

In this text, as in the others considered in this chapter, the return to and revision of a textual original replicates a thematic concern in the novel with the relations between origins, narrative and history. The island in *The Tempest* figures for Gonzago, one of the courtiers shipwrecked on it by the storm, as an Eden, or as a site where Eden might be restored:

> Had I plantation of this isle, my lord . . .
> And were the king on't, what would I do? . . .
> I' th' commonwealth I would by contraries
> Execute all things; for no kind of traffic
> Would I admit; no name of magistrate;
> Letters should not be known; riches, poverty
> And use of service, none; contract, succession,
> Bourn, bound of land, tilth, vineyard, none;
> No use of metal, corn, or wine, or oil;
> No occupation; all men idle, all;
> And women too, but innocent and pure;
> No sovereignty . . .
> All things in common nature should produce
> Without sweat or endeavour. Treason, felony,
> Sword, pike, knife, gun, or need of any engine,
> Would I not have; but nature should bring forth,
> Of its own kind, all foison, all abundance,
> To feed my innocent people.
> (Shakespeare 1987: II:i, 142–62)

Gonzago believes that, in its self-renewing plenitude, his paradise will 'excel the golden age' (II:i, 166), but his vision is strikingly defined almost wholly through 'contraries', by which, as it turns out, he means negations. It is possible to imagine the concord and prosperity of a time before history and politics only from the vantage point of history. Like all visions of absolute natural origin,

Gonzago's is tainted with afterthought, and belongs entirely to the set of mind it aims to transcend. Indeed, Sebastian and Antonio, who are less impressed by the beauties of the isle on which they have landed, interrupt in Gonzago's speech to remind him of just this contradiction. Prompted by Gonzago's mention of 'no sovereignty', Sebastian comments, 'Yet he would be king on't' and Antonio observes that 'The latter end of his commonwealth forgets the beginning' (II:i, 155–7). Gonzago sees his golden age as a spontaneous return to a natural beginning, before the eruption of power and conflict into the world, but this end can be brought about only by continuous enforcement.

The strategy of *Indigo* is to enlarge and renew the self-consciousness already displayed here in Shakespeare's play. Kit Everard's sailors think of the island they inhabit as a paradise like that imagined by Gonzago:

> We don't have to live by the sweat of our brow. Others may be obliged to. Not us. We can stand by and watch the crops ripen and grow. Sunshine by day, sweet dew by night, the soft wind. I tell you, this is the original garden God forgot to close.
> (Warner 1993: 180)

Nevertheless, Kit Everard is troubled by the inconvenient fact, with which most colonists have to deal, that the island is not an uninhabited paradise, free of the complexity of conflict, force and responsibility. He is forced to make an uneasy compromise with the inhabitants of the island and finds himself to his shame sexually involved with Ariel.

> There'll never be such a place without people in it already, he groaned. His troubles also gave him a longing to escape, to try again, with Mistress Rebecca noble and pure at his side: a fresh start, without the muddles he had already made.
> (Warner 1993: 179)

Indigo reacts to such fantasies by showing the inescapable force and complexity of history that lies behind every myth of absolute beginning, and acknowledging the prior inhabitation of every paradisal garden. The myth of the colonised land as a tabula rasa, an empty field of possibility, where men may start anew, like the sailors on Alonso's ship in Shakespeare's play, with their clothes freshened and not corrupted by the sea-water, is sustained by the erasure of the history that is always already in place in the colonised land. This is often an erasure of the fact of violence; though the erasure is always an act of violence in itself. Part of the purpose of *Indigo*'s rewriting, like that of the other rewritings of myths of origin looked at in this chapter, is to secularise the mythical, to insist on what is already *there* before the creation of myth, or the myth of creation. The island on which Kit Everard and his band of adventurers land is inhabited by a well-established community, with a developed agricultural economy, trade relations with other islands, as well as with other colonists, and a complex religious and social structure. It is true that the novel projects the island of Liamuiga as a place of beauty and exotic abundance, but these are presented as the fruit of labour and experience: Sycorax's knowledge and power come from observation and experiments with plants and foodstuffs, to which the novel gives exact and detailed attention.

In the account given by Prospero in *The Tempest*, Sycorax is said to have been marooned on the island for 'mischiefs manifold, and sorceries terrible' (I:ii, 264) and there to have given birth to the monstrous Caliban. In *Indigo*, by contrast, Sycorax is no witch, or fearsome 'blue-eyed hag' (I:ii, 269), but a woman respected, if also a little feared, for her knowledge. Prospero's narrative manages both to represent Caliban as an ignorant savage, so distant from civilisation and nurture as scarcely to be touched by its influences, and to discredit his claims to ownership of the island ('I am all the subjects that you have,/Which first was mine own king' says Caliban; I:ii, 341–2). Shakespeare's Caliban both belongs to the island and yet has no dominion over it. Some recent interpretations of *The Tempest* tend to identify Caliban as the figure of the dispossessed native, but *Indigo* resists this simple and in some ways wish-fulfilling inversion. In *Indigo*, the Caliban figure is Dulé, delivered from the womb of a drowned African slave by Sycorax. Sycorax names Dulé with a word that signifies 'sorrow' in her language, and 'doulos' means 'slave' in Greek; the name perhaps also derives partly from a condensation of Gonzago's references to 'dolour' early in *The Tempest* ('When every grief is entertained that's offered,/Comes to the entertainer . . . /Dolour' (II:i, 17–20) and Prospero's reference to Caliban as the 'Dull thing . . . he, that Caliban/Whom now I keep in service' (I:ii, 285–6). Dulé is thus no earthy elemental. *Indigo* stresses his split, uprooted condition, aware that he is in a kind of exile on the island in which he was born and brought up. 'Dulé apprehended that he was born in a place that the ocean never brought back to lay at his feet, even in fragments, a shell here, a pebble there: something lay far, far beneath him, and he could not dive deep enough to retrieve it' (95).

Dulé, has in fact entered the same temporal world as the European adventurers bring with them, a world of linear progress which makes possible ambition, attainment and transcendence, but which also, because it is irreversible, links the experience of time to the condition of loss. By contrast, Sycorax's experience of time, and that of the natives of the island, is as a recurring plenitude, in which no loss can be permanent, since 'the past abided, rolling into the present, and ocean swelling and falling back, then returning again' (95). Two images concentrate these opposed conceptions of time. For Sycorax, time is a churn,

> in which substances and essences were tumbled and mixed, always returning, now emerging into personal form, now submerged into the mass in the continuous present tense of existence, as in one of the vats in which Sycorax brewed the indigo.
>
> (Warner 1993: 122)

For Dulé, history is imaged in the free-standing ladder he teaches himself to climb and balance on, as a ritual enactment of his sense of loss and yearning for unity with the lost past:

> 'I'll throw a ladder between . . .' Dulé paused, laughed, 'you wouldn't understand.'
>
> 'She said, 'Yes, I do.' But it saddened her that he could not allow himself to belong wholly to her place, her present.
>
> He went on, a slight mockery turning up the corners of his lips, 'Between earth and sky, of course!'
>
> She knew he had meant something different, some other link.
>
> 'Between the time now and the time I can't remember.'
>
> (Warner 1993: 96)

The ladder is both an image of graduated, linear time, and the impossible dream of its transcendence. It establishes imaginary lines of connection between past, present and future, 'spanning one isolated phenomenon of space–time to another' (121–2) and yet it also severs Dulé's connection with his immediate time: 'It was as if he put himself out of her reach, in the same way as he chalked a circle round the foot of the ladder on which he balanced high up in the air' (110). The ladder also images the desire to constitute one's own beginnings autonomously; rejecting Sycorax's motherhood, Dulé acts out a myth of return that is also a kind of self-origination. In this respect, too, he is close to the colonist and pioneers, with their ideology of the new world and the return to primal innocence. Dulé/Caliban is thus made a creature of air, as opposed to his lowly, earthly embodiment in *The Tempest*: the swift, ethereal Ariel, by contrast, is held in Warner's version much closer to the ground; as she watches the magical acrobatics of Dulé, 'Ariel ... wished that she too could defy the bonds that tied her to the earth, and her blood leapt with Dulé's ascent' (160).

To rewrite the figure of Caliban in this way is to historicise the mythical, in establishing a plausible, complex prehistory for a character who seems to be shrunk and mutilated to the condition of fabular monstrosity in *The Tempest* and its cultural aftermath. In *The Tempest*, Prospero says that Caliban is punished for attempting to rape Miranda. In *Indigo*, Dulé leads the ill-fated uprising against Kit Everard's rule and is taken prisoner, has his hamstrings slit and is humbled to the condition of Everard's slave. The last we see of him is in a letter of Everard's from the year 1620, in which he is well on the way to becoming identified as a picturesque figure of myth (though all of the events imagined in this novel in fact postdate the writing of *The Tempest*, which received its first performance in 1613):

> The aforesaid captain I shall endeavour to keep beside me as my bondsman; hobbled, and under my eye, he cannot do me injury. He has a mordant wit, 'tis plain, and it diverts me to teach him our language as he serves me. He has already learned how to curse.
>
> Some of our men call him 'cannibal', seeking to undo the power of his monstrousness by naming it, like to conjuring. 'Tis to my mind a false notion, and I prefer the lisping usage of the children, Caliban.
>
> (Warner 1993: 201)

There are a number of other significant rewritings of the *Tempest* original in *Indigo*. Perhaps the most remarkable is the change of Ariel from a male spirit to a female child. In *The Tempest*, Ariel is forced to serve Prospero as payment for having been released from the cloven pine in which he has been immured by Sycorax. In *Indigo*, Ariel, like Dulé, has her origins elsewhere than on the island, in common with the general preference through the novel for complex and uncertain origins over simple and obvious ones. She is captured by Kit Everard, along with her foster-mother Sycorax, who has been crippled in the fire Everard uses to force her out of her tree-house. From this point on the novel follows the tense intimacy between Ariel and Everard and the growing hostility of Sycorax to them both. If the early part of *Indigo* is an exercise in rehabilitation, rescuing Sycorax from the discredit of Prospero's account of her, in these later portions she becomes a more ambivalent and even sinister figure. Her growing malice and bitterness towards Ariel creates a metaphorical prison which reproduces rather than revises the details of the confinement of Shakespeare's Ariel: 'She did confine thee,/By help of her more potent ministers,/And in her most unmitigable rage,/Into a cloven pine; within which rift/Imprisoned thou didst painfully remain' (I:ii, 274–8). Sycorax curses the child that Ariel has conceived with Everard, and, although she secures the escape of both Ariel and the child from the stockade at the cost of her own life, the constraining force of Sycorax's curse continues beyond her death.

And then Sycorax is forced herself to undergo the confinement that she imposes upon Ariel in *The Tempest*. Buried upright beneath the saman tree in which she had her house, she and the tree become the object of a cult. She is the channel of continuity between the seventeenth and the twentieth century portions of the novel, for her 'long death' is imagined as continuing unabated and uncompleted. Like the figure of the drowned Friday at the end of Coetzee's *Foe*, hers becomes the very voice of negativity, absence and loss, of history erased and yet somehow preserved in imagination or potential narration, as suggested in the fragment from Paul Celan's poem 'Psalm' which Warner quotes as the epigraph to this section of the book. Sycorax's long afterlife, poised between dying and living, is patterned on the play of reversal enacted in this poem, in which a negative 'no one' is converted into a substantive by the agency of the poem itself, in its memorialising of the Jews of the holocaust:

> No one moulds us again out of earth and clay,
> No one conjures our dust.
> No one.
>
> Praise be your name, no one.
> For your sake
> we shall flower.
> Towards
> you.
> (Celan 1990: 175, quoted in Warner 1993: 75)

If the novel keeps alive the memory of Sycorax and the female history that lies behind male myths of cultural self-origination, then Sycorax's long unconcluded death is also seen as a kind of deathly constriction of the present. Sycorax, confined within the tree just as she confines Ariel in Prospero's narrative (and is herself in a sense incarcerated within that narrative), seeks to arrest the unfolding complexity of history, as she apprehends the beginnings of the long nightmare of slavery in her islands:

> Over and over she utters her lament:
> – Oh airs and winds ... HEAR ME NOW, now that I only hear groans and Dulé hobbles on slit ankles as he rails and Ariel is captive again and croons over Roukoubé and does not speak. Turn back your currents in their course, the stiff breeze and the gentle wind, pull back the tide and send the sun, the moon, and the stars spinning in the churn of the heavens – so that we can return to the time before this time.
>
> (Warner 1993: 212)

Here Sycorax borrows Prospero's gesture of renunciation, his determination that 'this rough magic I here abjure' (V:i, 50–1) echoed in her resolve that 'once back in those days before everything changed... I would abjure my art then and there' (212). But, just as the origins of power and identity are made uncertain in *Indigo*'s rewriting of *The Tempest*, so too are endings. Sycorax is denied the self-defining consummation of Prospero's gesture, for, identified as she has become with the island's history, she finds that 'she cannot set limits on her powers, neither then nor now... She cannot abjure, give up, control the force by which she is possessed. On her own, she cannot stop the churn from tumbling round and round' (212–13). If the events of *The Tempest* are all in a sense produced and directed by the waking dream of Prospero's magic, then the events of *Indigo* appear to emanate involuntarily from the long nightmare of Sycorax's life-in-death.

The rest of the novel from this point on is given over to the twentieth century narrative. It seems designed to show that history can neither be wished away nor allowed to confine the present. Here the parallels with *The Tempest*, which are already uneven and unsustained in the seventeenth-century portions of the narrative, grow even more distant and diffuse, as the characters and details of the setting are distributed and recombined almost unrecognisably. This loosening, as Warner deliberately allows her novel to develop new combinations and preoccupations in excess of its originating model, may indeed be part of the point of the rewriting, in its desire to escape the repetition-compulsions of literature and of history. Most notable is the way in which the theme of magic is separated from any single Prospero figure. Magic in fact becomes a generalised metaphor in *Indigo* for power. Serafine, the black nurse and storyteller to the young Miranda and Xanthe, has some of Sycorax's wisdom and poetic power; and the charisma and prestige of Sir Anthony Everard, along with his miraculous prowess or *sangay*, at Flinders, the imperial game Warner has invented for this novel, give him some of Prospero's powers as an enchanter. More sinisterly, Sir Anthony seems to be as possessive of his young daughter Xanthe as Prospero is of Miranda: 'You know, Poppa would have liked to marry me himself if he could', Xanthe tells Miranda, as they bathe in the natural springs where Sycorax had dispensed potions and spells centuries before. 'I'm telling you. Under lock and key, lock and key, in the tower for ever' (329). Magic is associated in the person of Xanthe with the power of sexuality, though Xanthe has to wait until her death by drowning at the end of the novel to gain an insight into the value of love. Magical power is diffused also into the theme of gambling. Sir Anthony Everard is famed for his courage and triumphant bidding in the game of Flinders, while his son, who also, like his seventeenth-century ancestor, bears the name of Kit, is an inveterate gambler in the casino rather than the sports field. Prospero's magical power to subordinate is translated into the power of speculative capital over the island, as represented by the tourist hotel set up by Xanthe and her husband, Sy Nybris.

The second half of *Indigo* also has a political dimension that fills out and redeems the violently curtailed history of Caliban and his resistance in the first. The island undergoes an attempted coup by an extremist organisation called the Shining Purity of the One God Liberation Movement, led by a religious zealot called Jimmy Dunn, who has changed his name to Abdul Malik, the latter not far from being an anagram of the combined letters of Caliban and Dulé. This uprising fails just as the earlier raid led by Dulé had, but this time it appears that it may lead to some more permanent liberation. This political redemption is matched, a little sentimentally perhaps, by the emotional redemption of Xanthe. The theme of transformation that is articulated in Ariel's song in *The Tempest* –

> Full fathom five thy father lies;
> Of his bones are coral made;
> Those are pearls that were his eyes;
> Nothing of him that doth fade,
> But doth suffer a sea-change
> Into something rich and strange.
> (Shakespeare 1987: I:ii, 397–402)

– is climactically confirmed in *Indigo* in the purification of Xanthe's humanity with her last, redemptive opening to the vulnerability of love:

> In the soft, walled chamber of her marine host, she was mantled in pearl, layer upon layer spun about her foreign body until, mummified at the mineral heart of a pale rainbow, she became forever smooth and sheeny and hard.
> (Warner 1993: 376)

This pearly purification is similarly to be found in the hardened will and vision of the politician Atala Seacole, whose speech is overlaid with Xanthe's.

This redemption is also enacted in *Indigo*'s refashioning of the romantic relationship between Ferdinand and Miranda that carries so much of the sense of promise for the future in *The Tempest*. The novel ends with Miranda's rediscovery of another Caliban figure, George Felix, a politically radical black actor with whom she has had an affair some years before. The association is secured by the fact that Miranda sees her lover playing the part of Caliban in a production of *The Tempest*. Her renewed love for him is the sign of a loosening of the historical traps of enmity and fantasy that have persisted through the history of colonialism and its aftermath, and is an acceptance of both the necessary changeability of history, and the ineliminable otherness of the other. The famous scene of Ferdinand and Miranda playing chess in Act V scene i of *The Tempest* becomes an image of a more significant coupling of historical antagonists, Miranda and Caliban; while the image of mapping which has recurred throughout the novel here modulates into an image of reciprocity:

> They had begun play. Their openings were well-tried, unadventurous. But these same familiar moves would take them in deep: face to face and piece by piece they would engage with each other so raptly that for a time they would never even

notice anyone else outside looking in on the work they were
absorbed in, crossing the lines, crossing the squares, far out
on the board in the other's sea.

(Warner 1993: 395)

However, the fact that the novel has warned us against the easy
closure that this image suggests ought to make us read it with
appropriate caution: Miranda thinks to herself that 'she wasn't
living inside one of Shakespeare's sweet-tempered comedies, nor
in one of his late plays with their magical reconciliations, their
truces and appeasements and surcease of pain' (391). The novel
ends with a return to the figure of Sycorax, whose long, lingering
undying seems to be coming to an end. However, Sycorax herself
seems to have learned the lesson that time cannot be suspended in
the cloven pine of desire. The fulfilment of Sycorax occurs not by
a return of history to its origin but by an acceptance of the
uncertain and shifting nature of identity in history. If this novel sets
out to restore the voices that are suppressed by *The Tempest*, to make
audible once again those mysterious sounds which Caliban describes
in his enraptured speech beginning 'The isle is full of noises' (III:ii,
133–41), this is not to suggest any final or permanent settling of
accounts. Rather, it is to open up narrative to the many voices that
continue to resound through history:

> There are many noises in her head these befuddled days of
> her old age; they whisper news to her of this island and that,
> of people scattered here and there, from the past and from
> the present. Some are on the run still; but some have settled,
> they have ceased wandering, their maroon state is changing
> sound and shape. She's often too tired nowadays to un-
> scramble the noises, but she's happy hearing them, to change
> into stories another time.
>
> (Warner 1993: 402)

These four rewritings all attempt, in different ways and with
differing degrees of success, to break into history, in that they lay
hands upon and rework texts whose centrality to the cultural life
of the West, and especially of English-speaking cultures, has been
great, and whose historical persistence has been an important part
of the self-definition of those cultures. By reaching back imaginatively to the points of origin of these texts, all themselves myths of
a certain sort of origin, these rewritings both interrupt history and

restore something of its suppressed fullness. They show how every myth of origin is itself a kind of violence, in what it narrows, excludes or denies. In all four cases, this violence against cultural memory is relayed through a violence against the female. Despite their reparative intent, the assault mounted upon the myths of origin that are variously sedimented in *Robinson Crusoe*, *Frankenstein*, *Dr Jekyll and Mr Hyde* and *The Tempest* cannot help reduplicating some of the violence of those originals, for the very gesture of refashioning such texts is just such a violence against history conceived as progression and continuity, as the story of the founding of an origin or the reversion to an origin. What has been left out of history can only be restored to it by a calculated break with the false continuities of history. But in accepting this necessary violence of reparation, of rewriting wrong, contemporary novel-rewritings attest both to the historical complicity of the novel form itself in maintaining certain kinds of exclusion, and to the continuing power of the form to reflect on itself and its powers.

6

ENDINGS AND LIVING ON

We have seen in the last two chapters that the postwar novel of history attempts to understand and represent the vexed and uncertain relationship of the present to its past or its many possible pasts. In looking backwards, such novels inspect their own increasingly complex times, keeping alive the capacity for the kinds of collective address and shared exchange of memory necessary for historical consciousness. The novel of history, I have said, is in part the investigation of its own possibility, the possibility of conferring sequence, direction and narratability upon the past and on the present in relation to that past.

As we have seen, the imagination of history has become particularly urgent at a time when history has become enigmatic, broken and in a certain sense resistant to being imagined. The experience of the Second World War and its aftermath provided a particular, historically unprecedented set of fears and misgivings with regard to history. The effect of the discoveries of the concentration camps in which the Nazis had pursued their systematic programmes of extermination, combined with the knowledge of the huge power of the atomic bombs dropped on Hiroshima and Nagasaki, rapidly produced a sense that the unimaginable had taken up residence in history. With the beginning of the Cold War and the rapid development of huge arsenals of nuclear weapons by both sides, the world began to face the possibility, for the first time within history, of its own ending as a datable, historical event. If one form of the novel of history is concerned with investigating the new relations to the past required by the dramatic changes of the late twentieth century, another form is concerned with the possibility of narrating a future, and with the assailed potential of narrative as such in a world in which absolute finality and closure, which had hitherto been available to human life only through narratives, now threatened to bring to an end the narrative of human history. In the period since the Second World War, the novel is forced to try to imagine the paradoxical inhabitation of history by this possibility of absolute, apocalyptic ending.

If narrative is orientated towards ending, habituating us to a mode of living-towards-ending, and offering more absolute and definitive endings than are otherwise available to us, then this is partly because it also characteristically offers a transcendence of endings. Every conventional, and maybe every unconventional narrative in fact ends twice. First it comes to an end, arrives at the point at which narrative ceases and then, actually or metaphorically, it takes a step beyond its end to designate its ceasing as a completion. A narrative that merely comes to a halt – a narrative left unfinished by its author's death, for example – does not strike us as having ended, precisely because of the fact that it lacks such recognition and avowal by the narrative itself that its latest instalment is in fact its last; lacks, so to speak, the actual or implicit appendix on which ending depends. Sometimes this effect can be supplied in a movement of retrospection, in which the narrative explicitly doubles back to consider itself as a whole, weighing different possibilities for ending. But such a redoubling is always there implicitly in any narrative which seems to supply the sense of an ending; the ending of event cannot itself be completed until it can be seen as the event of ending.

In recent years, the movement of apocalypse from the realm of eschatology into the grasp of the actual has produced some interesting and important disturbances of the narrative economy of ending. The fact that our century has been brought closer and closer to the possibility of absolute ending occurring within the timespan of an individual life has provided a certain challenge to narrative as well as significant kinds of contortion within narrative structure. The challenge of absolute ending for narrative lies in the fact that it both discloses and perturbs the ordinary expectations of ending; namely the satisfaction of completeness within continuation. Absolute ending seems to offer the terrifying prospect of an ending without appendix, without the possibility of resumption or transcendence, or of the smallest sliver of aftermath in which the ending might be known as such.

Absolute ending puts a limit to narrative's craving to reach beyond itself, to redouble its limits. Narrative may be said characteristically to reach beyond and gather to itself whatever seems to escape it of time. Gillian Beer has shown how the stretching backwards of the origin of human or earthly history through the nineteenth century produced an anxiety about the inaccessibility or forgetfulness of origins and a corresponding desire to strain the narrative imagination back to encompass such origins (1989). In contrast to the painful recession of origins, the planned or unplanned imminence of nuclear catastrophe, along with the entry of other forms of potential apocalypse, such as the ecological, into measurable historical time, produces an effect of agonising proximity. Instead of an unconscionable stretching of time, we experience an intolerable contraction. Here, the event of ending seems to deny the possibility of narrative consolidation, interrupting the very continuity or prolongation of the personal and social imaginary beyond its own cessation. In breaking into our sense of self and historical belonging, the contemporary apocalyptic narrative may provide, in terms of the contrast between narrative functions proposed in chapter 1 (see above pp. 4–6), the ultimate narrative of transformation, though it is a transformation of which we could never hope to have the benefit. In its seeming refusal of the consolations of consolidation and self-extension, it is nevertheless always a provocation to live and narrate beyond the ending, to encompass within narrative the annihilation of all narrative possibility.

This makes for a particular kind of imaginative problem alongside the ethical problem of potential apocalypse, since apocalypse is as much a challenge to our capacities to conceive, represent and narrate it, as it is to our will to avert it. Indeed, we must say that the ethical and imaginative challenges are so closely involved with each other as to be indistinguishable. This is partly because averting the unthinkable seems to require us imaginatively to entertain it, and thus precisely to make it a subject that we can represent to ourselves. The preclusion of apocalypse seems to require as a terrifying preliminary a disavowal of that very disavowal that puts its possibility aside as 'unthinkable'. The unthinkable must first be thought in order to preserve its unthinkability, must be made actual in imagination in order to remain purely potential in fact. Where narrative has traditionally articulated and territorialised certain kinds of extreme or barely representable experience, the narrative of apocalypse has as its purpose the deterrence rather than the cultural substantiation of its subject.

At the same time, this may give rise to a kind of superstitious dread that, by representing the unthinkable, one makes it more rather than less likely to happen. In this respect, the representing of nuclear apocalypse can begin to seem uncomfortably like planning for it, and the narrative of absolute finality a sinister shadowing of that systematic modelling and strategic narration which characterised the hottest years of the Cold War. Seen in this way, there might be a kind of blasphemy involved in attempting to represent the event of annihilation, even in allowing it to have the status of an event. There is an equivalence here between the potential annihilation of nuclear disaster and the actual entry of mass extermination into history, in the Jewish Holocaust of the Second World War, an equivalence signalled in the shared word 'holocaust'. In both cases, there exists a compulsion to shelter the event from representation, to maintain it in a condition of sacred virtuality. It is almost as though, having once become historical, the horror of mass annihilation must nevertheless be kept out of history, lest it become habituated as a repeatable event or idea. Of course, this necessity only arises because the event has in fact taken place, and the possibility of planning for it and doing it again has entered history.

On the one hand, then, there is the ethical demand to imagine and narrate the unimaginable and the unspeakable; on the other, there is the opposite demand (though in the same ethical interests) to hold off from imagining and narrating. Hence the excruciating paradox attaching not only to the Holocaust of the Second World War but also to the as yet unrealised total annihilation of nuclear holocaust, that one must bear witness to that which nevertheless remains barred from witnessing and report, must continue to think a form of unthinkability which is subject simultaneously to interdiction and incitement.

The intensity of this paradox is sharpened by Jacques Derrida's observation that there is in fact no choice about whether or not to narrate the possibility of nuclear apocalypse. This is because nuclear apocalypse is 'a phenomenon whose essential feature is that of being *fabulously textual*, through and through', there being no other mode in which to represent it other than fable and fiction (Derrida 1984: 23). The nature of the event of absolute annihilation or absolute termination will be to have destroyed all possibilities of memorial or history, everything that would enable it to persist, or come to being as an event, which means that it can only be known in advance, in projections, predictions, and premonitory narratives. The paradox here is that an event or terminal eventuality which stands outside the continuum of history and narrative, in so far as it signals the obliteration of history and narrative as such, can in fact only ever be signalled by and within narrative itself. The intimate proximity of the end of the world which has characterised life since the Second World War, making this period of history qualitatively different from that of any other period in human history, means the habituation of a double-bind in which we simultaneously must and must not narrate a kind of absolute ending that we anyway both cannot and cannot not narrate.

Not the least pervasive of the effects of this awareness of the possibility of the pseudo-event of absolute ending is a newly paradoxical inhabitation of history. Our closeness to an event that could never belong to history, could only bring it to an end, infects us with something of its unreality, barring us too from belonging fully to a history whose nature has been not to be certain of its ending, not to be able to measure its likely posterity. The sense is of living in a ghostly aftermath, as though history were somehow already finished, in a cultural magnification of that predicament imagined in novels such as Samuel Beckett's *Malone Dies* (1951), or Maurice Blanchot's *Arrêt de Mort* (1948), translated as *Death Sentence* (1978). In a sense, the persistence and proximity of the *not yet* introduces the end of history into history itself, turning it into an *always already*. The unavailability henceforth of any notion of cultural culmination other than the negative culmination of extermination makes our cultural condition one of indefinite survival, a strange, repeatedly remortgaged condition of debt to the future, in which we defer what has not happened yet but, by taking account of it so thoroughly in our present, nevertheless seem somehow to have projected ourselves beyond it. Despite, perhaps even because of, the fantastic acceleration of the present into the future, our present life can come to seem an insubstantial lingering or marking time. We live in a present that can neither emerge meaningfully from a past nor open meaningfully on to a future, but can only ever be temporarily renewed. It is the time of living evoked by Samuel Beckett's Molloy, when he says 'My life is over and yet it goes on and what tense is there for that' (1959: 36), or in Derrida's account of the condition he describes as 'living on' in Blanchot's *Arrêt de Mort* (Derrida 1980).

These predicaments have called for and elicited powerful narrative embodiments, not just because they are hugely pressing and painful issues, but also because they concern and enact questions of narrative itself. The question of how we are to live in and out of history is answerable only in some form of narrative, since the question of history – of what kind of history or relation to history is now and henceforth possible – is itself a question of narrative.

I think it is possible to make a broad distinction between two ways of dealing with apocalyptic ending, which correspond roughly to the theoretical distinctions I have been drawing so far. On the one hand, there is the narrative of survival. This kind of narrative borrows the force of absolute ending, by assuming it as a given or a starting point. In narratives of survival such as Russell Hoban's *Riddley Walker* (1980) or Bernard Malamud's *God's Grace* (1982), the 'fabulously textual' (non)event of nuclear annihilation is given the strategic solidity of an event by being turned from an ending into a starting point. Narratives of survival project us beyond the ending and, by so doing, allow us to place that ending as an event within a chain of consequence. Thus, they seem to solve a number of problems. To make an ending a principle of narrative generation is to digest it back within the history whose exterior it had hitherto constituted; it is to resume the possibility of a history the evaporation of which is presumed in apocalypse. For the ending of event to turn out to be, after all, just one more event, in one sense dissipates its force, because if there is memory, representation, survival of apocalypse, then it has not been apocalypse at all. But in another sense it gives this ending a force to punctuate and order history, gives it precisely the explanatory function of a kind of revelation that a pure or 'absolute' ending, an ending without residue or resumption, can oddly never have. Not surprisingly, it is very hard to offer any narrative rendering of absolute ending that is not in fact predicated upon some sort of narrative survival, or survival of narrative; does not depend, so to speak, upon the annulment of annihilation into narrative. Peter Schwenger has observed that the representation of nuclear annihilation 'baffles conventional narrative structures' to the degree that such structures depend on the orientation towards a kind of ultimate revelation which is systematically refused in the narrative of absolute ending. This seems to mean that, in fact, all narratives are apocalyptic in their aspiration towards the consummation of meaning attainable in death, *except for* the narratives of actual apocalypse which systematically refuse such consumption (Schwenger 1986: 41–2). On the other hand, such narratives might seem to be open to the charge of having transgressed the ethical requirement to disbar apocalypse from history, speech and narrative representation, in their tendency to naturalise the possibility of absolute ending.

However, another kind of apocalyptic narrative rigorously eschews the consolation of extrapolation, austerely denying the idea that there might be any kind of point of view on, or experience of absolute ending, any kind of language in which to narrate it, or audience to address the narration to. Peter Schwenger suggests that such narratives attempt to render holocaust in the narrative present, rather than placing it as an assumed narrative past, though this does not take enough account of the strange contortions in the very idea of past, present and future that are induced by the attempt to represent an atemporal or antitemporal event within a temporal continuum (ibid., 44). In one sense, this category of narrative is purely virtual or theoretical, since it is in fact impossible to represent the fact of nuclear holocaust otherwise than as an event, which is to say, by offering a certain imaginative or narrative survival of it. The most developed and challenging literary example of this mode of representing apocalypse I know is Maggie Gee's *The Burning Book* (1983), which I discuss later on in this chapter. This kind of narrative simultaneously transgresses and maintains the taboo on representing apocalypse, demanding that we think the possibility of apocalypse, but maintaining its inaccessibility to thought or representation.

But there is a third possibility for apocalyptic narrative, which combines or mediates between these alternatives and may in fact be latent within each of them. In this kind of narrative, the emphasis is neither exclusively post-apocalyptic, using annihilation as an event to generate narrative (my first category), nor pre-apocalyptic, seeing annihilation as the other or death of narrative (my second category), but is on the temporal contortions introduced by the very notion of representing the end of representation. The emphasis, we might say, is neither on 'living on' after the event of apocalypse nor on 'living out' the time remaining before apocalypse, but is on living through the paradoxes attendant upon the changes in our historical sense that are produced by the possibility of nuclear or other forms of annihilation. The experience of imminent or possible nuclear catastrophe, especially when this is seen as the repetition of an event, the Shoah or Jewish Holocaust, which has already errupted into history, fundamentally changes the experience of history, and the relations between presentness and futurity. For this reason, a number of the most interesting narratives of the ending of history produced since the Second World War have focused on an experience which is simultaneously pre-apocalyptic and post-apocalyptic, in which the not yet and the already agitate and exchange places in perturbing fashion. If such fiction does not allow itself clearly to distinguish the stages of anticipated ending, the event of ending, and the aftermath of ending, it is because it attends to and itself enacts the paradoxical convulsions induced within the temporal continuum by the very experience of waiting for such an absolute ending. The ethical force of such fiction, or fiction operating in such a manner, is meta-ethical, for it is not to be measured simply in terms of its fulfilment or nonfulfilment of the condition that we do or do not speak of the absolute end. Such fiction reflects on, or creates the cognitive and imaginative conditions for reflecting on, the nature and force of such ethical requirements.

One of the earliest novels to imagine the possibility of the absolute ending of history and thus of narrative does not centre on nuclear apocalypse, although nuclear conflict plays a part in it. The terrible power of *Nineteen Eighty-Four* (1949) lies in its vision of a world closed in on itself, and enduring for ever in the circuit of violence and repression which is summoned up by O'Brien during his interrogation of Winston Smith: 'a world of victory after victory, triumph after triumph after triumph: and endless pressing, pressing, pressing upon the nerve of power' (Orwell 1981: 216). If *Nineteen Eighty-Four* is concerned with the understanding of power, it is also concerned with the fate of narrative under such conditions. Although Orwell is not usually thought of as a self-reflexive novelist, who uses fiction to explore its own condition, *Nineteen Eighty-Four* does have a marked and sustained preoccupation with the question of writing and of narrative writing in particular.

Writing is a political and a subversive act in *Nineteen Eighty-Four* principally because writing presupposes the fact that individuals are different, but in communicable ways. This is why Winston Smith addresses his diary to a time '*when men are different from one another and do not live alone*' (26). The form of writing that we recognise as narrative also belongs to history. Any narrative, in so far as it is a narrative, necessarily encompasses and represents the facts of time and change. Narrative therefore provides a way of living in time and history, a model which allows us to register the difference between the past, the present and the future at the same time as we recognise what holds them together.

Obviously, *Nineteen Eighty-Four*, taken as a whole, is one such narrative, a projection forwards into an imagined future from a particular point in the present. Orwell's choice of 1984 as a date for his novel is therefore not completely accidental, since it inverts the date of 1948, the year in which he completed the novel; this should serve always to remind us that this novel embodies a vision of '1984-as-seen-from-1948'. But Orwell's vision of the future has been one of the most powerful and widely-diffused narratives of our own, Western culture since the Second World War, and this is surely because it ties together the past, the present and the future in a singularly compelling relationship.

In the light of this, what is striking about the world which is depicted in the novel is the fact that it has abolished narrative. At first sight, the opposite may seem to be the case, for it is true that the society of Oceania devotes enormous amounts of time and energy to the production of fictions of all kinds, from pornography to propaganda, intended to keep the past up to date with the political requirements of the present. We should remember that both of the central characters in the novel are involved in the production of these narratives, Julia because she works in the Fiction Department, and Winston Smith because he works as a writer for *The Times*; indeed he derives considerable satisfaction from his work, as is evident in the story he fabricates about the life of the model citizen, Comrade Ogilvy (41–2). But none of this can be said to constitute narrative in the essential sense, because it does not involve any kind of change or progression from the past to the present to the future; in the world of *Nineteen Eighty-Four*, the past does not change into the present, since the past is endlessly changed by the present, in a process that, for all the feverish reinvention of history that it involves, is actually designed to disguise and deny the fact of change. As Winston explains to Julia:

> Every record has been destroyed or falsified, every book has been rewritten, every picture has been repainted, every statue and street and building has been renamed, every date has been altered. And that process is continuing day by day and

minute by minute. History has stopped. Nothing exists except an endless present, in which the Party is always right.

(Orwell 1981: 127)

The denial of change is directed towards the future as well as towards the past. O'Brien points out to Winston Smith that what distinguishes this regime from other totalitarian dictatorships is that it makes no attempt to justify itself by telling the story of a transition towards any kind of paradise or ideal social state. In other words, there is no narrative extension into the future in the practice of the Party, but only the infinite reproduction of the present. O'Brien therefore offers no justification of the Party other than in a series of numbing tautologies, whose repetitions mime the endless repetition of the world of Oceania: 'The object of persecution is persecution. The object of torture is torture. The object of power is power' (212).

Against this, Winston Smith's struggle in *Nineteen Eighty-Four* is to put together a coherent narrative, not only of the recent history of Britain, but also of his own life. The book is punctuated by puzzling passages of reminiscence, fragmentary dreams and memories which rise up into Winston's consciousness unbidden and cannot easily be made sense of, or put into narrative sequence: these include his dream of his mother and sister drowning, his memory of an air-raid, his recurrent vision of the landscape he calls the Golden Country and his memory of stealing the chocolate from his mother followed by her disappearance. When he tries to find out from an old man what life was like before the Revolution, he is driven to despair by the realisation that for him too there are only atomised details which can no longer be pulled together to form a narrative. The few scattered survivors from the world before the Revolution, he reflects,

> remembered a million useless things, a quarrel with a workmate, a hunt for a lost bicycle pump, the expression on a long-dead sister's face, the swirls of dust on a windy morning seventy years ago: but all the relevant facts were outside the range of their vision. They were like the ant, which can see small objects but not large ones.
>
> (Orwell 1981: 78)

Winston Smith tries, by contrast, to remember, and to tell coherent stories. This is actually embodied in Orwell's method of telling the story of *Nineteen Eighty-Four*, which is not to focus from the outside on events or experiences but to see everything from Winston's point of view, following his thoughts as he ranges backwards and forwards among his memories, experiences and speculations. In this respect, the first part of the novel seems to do the thing which Winston himself sets out to do in his diary, which is 'to transfer to paper the interminable restless monologue that had been running inside his head, literally for years' (10). Winston uses his diary to remember and to speculate about the public and personal past; at one point he copies out a passage from an official Party history of the twentieth century, at another, he painfully tells the story of his encounter with an aged prostitute. Most importantly, he directs his diary at the future, or at least to a time when things will be (or even once were) different from now. His diary will be the guarantee of continuity through change, the bridge between the world of *Nineteen Eighty-Four* and a world that might supersede it:

> We shall meet in the place where there is no darkness,' O'Brien had said to him. He knew what it meant, or thought he knew. The place where there is no darkness was the imagined future, which one would never see, but which, by foreknowledge, one could mystically share in.
> (Orwell 1981: 86)

This projection into the future is a positive version of that anguished ghostliness which Winston usually experiences when writing; it is a way of absenting oneself from the oppressively self-identical present, which refuses to allow the possibility of any alternative versions of life. But this orientation towards the future is repeatedly denied through the book. When Winston finally joins, or believes he joins, the conspiratorial Brotherhood via O'Brien, he is warned that he will be part of a movement that has no definition, no structure and no presence. In other words, the Brotherhood offers in actuality none of the guarantees of movement towards some alternative future, of a narrative of redemption, that it seems to. O'Brien tells Winston that

> there is no possibility that any perceptible change will happen within our own lifetime. We are the dead. Our only true life is in the future. We shall take part in it as handfuls of dust and splinters of bone.
> (Orwell 1981: 144)

Like other novels that we have examined, the anxiety about history in *Nineteen Eighty-Four* is also an anxiety about address. Beginning his subversive diary, Winston Smith is suddenly paralysed by the sense that he can have no conceivable reader. 'How could you communicate with the future?' he wonders. 'It was of its nature impossible. Either the future would resemble the present, in which case it would not listen to him: or it would be different from it, and his predicament would be meaningless' (10). Writing, under these circumstances, is deeply paradoxical. On the one hand, it is the most defiantly individualistic of activities in the world of Oceania, in its scandalous assertion of the existence of a private self. But, at the same time, to write without any conceivable audience is a constant reminder of the tenuousness and eliminability of the self: 'How could you make appeal to the future when not a trace of you, not even an anonymous word scribbled on a piece of paper, could possibly survive?' (26). It is this fact about his writing that turns Winston Smith into 'a lonely ghost' (27).

This articulates the sensation that Winston has throughout the novel that his life is in fact already over. The first time this sensation assails him is actually at the moment when he begins to write, when he becomes aware that, whether or not he commits himself to paper, he will always already have committed the one inescapable crime – Thoughtcrime. Thoughtcrime includes many different things in *Nineteen Eighty-Four*, but among them are the possession of memory, the desire for records and the creation of connections between the past and the present – that is to say, the illicit desire for narrative. It might therefore be said that Winston Smith's crime begins at precisely the point when he tries to tell the story of his own life, or begins to imagine what such a story might be like. In Oceania to tell the story of one's own life is ultimately to lose it.

The novel keeps demonstrating that this attempt to imagine or project a narrative forwards or backwards is precisely what guarantees in advance the necessary outcome of Winston's death.

> What was happening was only the working-out of a process that had started years ago. The first step had been a secret, involuntary thought, the second had been the opening of the diary. He had moved from thoughts to words, and now from words to actions. The last step was something that would happen in the Ministry of Love. He had accepted it. The end was contained in the beginning.
>
> (Orwell 1981: 131)

Here, as is usual in the novel, the story is being told from Winston's viewpoint, and in his characteristic way – that is to say, in terms of logical steps and sequences ('he had moved from thoughts to words, and now from words to actions'). But if, as the novel seems to show, 'the end was contained in the beginning', then this contradicts the very idea of sequence. In fact, the most terrifying thing about *Nineteen Eighty-Four* is not so much the fact that Winston's rebellion is detected and defeated, as that his rebellion is shown to have been hopeless, perhaps even to have been predicted and controlled, from the very beginning. The motif of dust which recurs in the novel as an image of Winston Smith's inevitable annihilation also furnishes an example of the way in which Winston's actions have all been cancelled out in advance; Winston remembers the tiny pinch of dust that he uses to mark his diary and detect spying eyes and realises that the Thought Police must carefully have replaced it. As O'Brien painstakingly explains, the power of the Party is so encompassing because it includes *in advance* every opposition to it. Indeed, the most coherent and powerful critique of the political system of Oceania turns out to have been written by O'Brien himself; the most powerful intellectual weapon against the Party, the analytic narrative of its rise to power, is in fact its subtlest defence against opposition. The power of this political system comes not from its intolerance of dissent but from its deployment and the assimilation of the fact of dissent in its own endless reassertion of power: 'The face will always be there to be stamped upon. The heretic, the enemy of society, will always be there, so that he can be defeated and humiliated over again' (215).

In fact, so pressing is this sense of being closed between the jaws of the beginning and the inevitable end of his story that Winston comes increasingly to think of his life not as forming a narrative order but as a refusal of such order. His love for Julia therefore comes to seem simply an 'interval' of time snatched out of time, its beauty and significance, like that of the coral in the glass paperweight which he buys, being echoed in his vision of himself and Julia 'fixed in a sort of eternity at the heart of the crystal' (121). Where Winston has earlier despaired of the old man's incapacity to articulate isolated details into a narrative whole, by this point he comes to see the power and promise of the proles' vitality as lying precisely in their capacity to resist the large narratives of history and to hold to the immediate details of physical life.

The collapse of the possibility of narrative for Winston Smith also has implications for the reader of *Nineteen Eighty-Four*. For the reader as well as the character, the second half of the book, far from providing any climax or resolution to the narrative of the first half, seems simply to cancel or negate it. One might almost say that the first part of the book is subjected to the same kind of rewriting that the Party inflicts on all events that it finds unacceptable. If Winston Smith becomes – or is shortly to become – an '*unperson*', then, according to the logic of *Nineteen Eighty-Four*, the very narrative which brings us to this point makes of itself an *unbook*. The power of Orwell's achievement and warning lies in the way that this self-undoing is engineered, to suggest that, for all the intensity of incident and reflection in which the reader has participated, nothing has in fact taken place. If Winston Smith has truly been monitored and controlled throughout the novel in the way that has been suggested, then, in a sense, he cannot even be said to have rebelled and been defeated, since his challenge to the Party has involuntarily been the very form of his obedience to their wishes. Many readers have reported their sense that narrative has run down by the end of *Nineteen Eighty-Four*, especially with the inclusion of the lengthy extracts from Emmanuel Goldstein's 'Theory and Practice of Oligarchical Collectivism' and the appendix on the Principles of Newspeak. But it seems to me to be mistaken simply to lament this dissipation of narrative impetus, since it is precisely in conformity with Orwell's structural design. Orwell uses the vehicle of a traditional realist narrative, with all its conventions not only of character, setting and plot but also, most importantly, of a past tense, with all the expectations of narrative resolution that it brings with it; but he uses this vehicle to project us into a world where narrative of this kind has come to an end.

If, as I believe, this was Orwell's intention, then we might ask why he did not write a novel which abandoned traditional narrative form altogether. (Orwell had in fact experimented with the abandonment of realistic narrative in an earlier novel, *A Clergyman's Daughter*, [1935], parts of which are written in the form of a dramatic script.) In fact Orwell's stubborn cleaving to the norms of realistic storytelling serves to remind his contemporary readers of the necessity and human value of storytelling. The fact that we read the narrative of *Nineteen Eighty-Four*, partaking of its energy, its invention, its cohering and explanatory force, is the most potent resistance that the book offers to the horrifying denial of narrative that it depicts. One of the great ironies of the book's career is that scarcely five years after the arrival of the date chosen to represent the ending of history in totalitarianism came the sudden disintegration of totalitarianism itself in Europe, with the collapse of the USSR, followed by a wave of revolutions across Eastern Europe. But the book has not simply been contradicted or rendered a historical curiosity by this development. It continues to warn and protest about any attempt to proclaim and enforce the end of history, which is to say, any explanation of history that subsumes the irregularity and unpredictability of human lives in the enforced coherence of a single narrative. The absolute continuity forced upon history by the assumption that everything up to this point has been leading towards the benign dominion of global capitalism is itself a kind of shutting down of history, and the kind of narcissistic reinvention of the past in the image of the present against which *Nineteen Eighty-Four* protests.

Anthony Burgess's *The End of the World News* (1982) attempts, like Orwell's *Nineteen Eighty-Four* and Angus Wilson's *The Old Men at the Zoo* (1961), to put the condition of the ending of history at the disposal of narrative. It is a survival narrative; a book about the diminished but continuing possibilities of narrative beyond the ending of history. Like a number of other such narratives, it is written from a perspective so far distant in the future as to be practically posthuman, or no longer recognisably human. The book is unusual in at least two respects. Firstly, it attributes the end of the world to a natural cataclysm rather than one engineered by human beings, and secondly, it splices together with its apocalyptic narrative two other narratives – the story of Freud's later years and the story of the visit of Trotsky to New York in 1917. The first of these is rendered largely through retrospect, as Freud remembers stages in the history of his own life and that of psychoanalysis, and the second in the form of a Hollywood musical, complete with songs and lyrics. The annihilation of the earth is narrated in a science-fiction narrative concerning the catastrophic collision between the earth and an asteroid named Lynx, and the escape from the disaster effected by the building of a spaceship, the *America*. The three stories are not given in chronological order, but cut together in short sequences. The effect of this intercutting is to mitigate the finality of the end of history, by presenting it as part of a historical continuum. This suggests the possibility both of a gathering together of history from the vantage point of its end, and of the assimilation of the end itself into the continuum of history. The end of the world in this novel is repeatedly renewed; and the radical exteriority or transcendence of history represented by the end of the world is reduced not only by the device of the narrative that survives it as a chronicle of the final years of the earth but also by the network of prefigurations and retrospections that links it to other points earlier in history in which history seemed to be suspended and renewed.

The end of the world in this novel is therefore contained as an event within history – presented as an immanent principle rather than an imminent possibility. The novel focuses two concerns alongside the question of ending: the desire for power and the strength of story. All three of the narratives in the book contain a version of the powerful leader and all present versions of the attempt to take hold of and control the fact of ending. In the Trotsky and Freud sections, an old world is giving way to a new. In each case, the originator of the new, and parricidal slayer of the old (capitalism, neurosis), struggles to maintain his hold over the history that reasserts itself in the face of his authority. In the science-fiction portion of the narrative, the continuation of the world is guaranteed only by the fascist domination of Bartlett, the leader of the spaceship project who actually threatens to extinguish all the virtues of civilisation it is the purpose of the mission to preserve. In all three narratives, there is the desire in the inaugurator of the new world to be both first and last, to break into and definitively break with the past in an act of self-naming and self-origination – 'There's only one ambition worth having, Carl,' says Freud to Jung, 'and that is *to be first*' (Burgess 1983: 208) – and then to hold to this pure freedom in the face of a history that threatens to fall back into imperfection, contingency and consequence. The effect of plaiting together a future narrative of the end of the world with historical narratives that concern the epochal coming to an end of earlier ways of thinking and being, is to point, in the end optimistically, to the reversibility of beginnings and ends, to meditate on the equivalence between the beginning of finality and the finality of every new beginning.

All these concerns in the novel are bound up tightly with the question of representation. If science in this novel appears to be on the side of absolute and self-creating newness, art, especially the art of narrative, is on the side of the bodily, the contingent and the residual – in other words, the historical. The latter qualities are imaged in the person of Val Brodie, university teacher and failed writer of science fiction, who is married incongruously to the scientist Vanessa Frame, a physical and intellectual paragon, and in the Falstaffian actor Willett, with whom Brodie takes up and shares much of the final days of the earth, before eventually finding his place on the spaceship as archivist and chronicler of those last days. One of the most significant ironies of the book concerns Val Brodie's first novel, which itself is actually about the end of the world and serves as a blueprint for the escape project. But its story, which Brodie discusses in a science-fiction seminar early in the novel, is unusual in that it refuses to allow its reader the satisfaction of closure, revealing only that 'the end of the world came in a form that nobody had expected' (29). The definitive end of the world is demonstrated in the final pages of Burgess's book, which reveal that all the foregoing has just been narrated to a group of children some generations into the journey of the spaceship *America*. Val Brodie has discovered that the only records he has been able to salvage from earth are tapes of the Freud memoir and the Trotsky musical, and determines that these will have to be abandoned, like all other evidence of the past, in the pursuit of a new culture, fitting the new conditions of humanity. The children who have listened to the story we have just read are unconvinced and indifferent. For them, history has no force, and their present state is all there is: 'Your generation talks about a journey,' declares one of them. 'Our generation knows we're just *here*. We've always been here, right back to what they call the mists of myth' (388). Another agrees, adding, 'We'll always be here . . . It stands to reason. We've always been here, we always will' (ibid.). The novel is balanced here between despair and comic resignation. If, in one sense, the world has come to an end in this flattening of history into the simultaneity of myth, in another sense it survives and develops in the very conditions of forgetfulness on board the ship, in which the mythical distortions of narrative are evidence of the possibility of newness; Val Brodie's descendant, Maria Brodie, speaks about 'The one about the bad man called Fred Fraud who kept people strapped to a couch and the good one called Trot Sky who wanted people to do what he did and run through space' (ibid.).

The irony here is that, by taking us out beyond the end of the world and the end of historical narrative, Burgess appears also, as Margaret Scanlan has argued, to be demonstrating the dangers of the historical forgetfulness of the present, and in particular the 'spatialising' of time in what Scanlan calls the 'continuous topicality of television' (1990: 191) and the reading of human history as the repetition of timeless patterns which characterises certain modern currents of thought (certain styles of Freudianism and Marxism among them). In his prologue to the book, its fictionalised editor, John B. Wilson B. A., records a note allegedly found among the effects of the author whose novel, the one we are about to read, he is preparing for publication:

> Saw photograph of late President Carter and wife in White House late at night eating hamburgers and watching television. Note well – they were watching three screens simultaneously . . . But – this must be future viewing pattern. True visual counterpoint. Is this also possible future for the novel?
> (Burgess 1983: ix)

In one sense, the flattening of history induced by the incessant shuttling between images of different pasts indicates that the postmodern world may already have projected itself beyond history. The contemporary world resembles the space-ship *America* not in being emptied of history but in having so much history simultaneously and indifferently available for consumption and recombination. In a certain sense, *The End of the World News* seems to argue, our very capacity to read this novel indicates that the end of history has already taken place in contemporary culture.

But the novel tries to balance this with a sense of the continuing openness and contingency of history. The prologue to the book explains that it has been reconstructed from a manuscript found packed into a shopping bag. As opposed to the homogenised histories represented in the novel, the structure of the novel itself is presented as a puzzling enigma:

> Perusal of this typescript by myself, and by others on whom I called in the hope of enlightenment, my own powers of literary or sub-literary judgment being only moderately developed, was a process fraught with dubiety and puzzlement. There seemed, despite a double unity – that of the typeface (Olivetti STUDIO 45) and that of the typing paper (Gevafax 701) – and the fact of willed collocation, to be not one work here but three. Another possible factor of unification, that of the sub-literary nature of the style, was the only internal indication that this was intended as a single work, though the heterogeneity of the contents militated against that supposition.
> (Burgess 1983: viii)

The pretence of the novel to be a thing of scraps and fragments has a serious purpose, in pointing to the principles of survival and renewal in the lowly and disorganised energies of dissociation associated with contemporary culture. If the multiple, simultaneous culture of the contemporary world works to flatten and homogenise history, then it is also suggested that its scrappiness and heterogeneity allows newness to emerge and survive. The contemporary culture of adaptation, which threatens to dissolve the singleness and autonomy of every form – including and especially that of the literary novel – also offers the possibility of imaginative resistance to every attempt to bring change and renewal to an end in the name of the whole truth of finality. History comes to an end when difference is annulled into equivalence, when everything, science fiction, politics, psychoanalysis, literature, can be translated into everything else. But the very translatability of these terms also discloses and intensifies the awareness of difference between them. Translatability need not stand for homogeneity; it can also serve the musical principle of 'counterpoint' which Wilson informs us was so important to his author (vii).

The End of the World News is poised in subject and manner between these two possibilities, the end of the world in indifference, vacuity and forgetfulness and the survival and revival of history in aggregation, invention and narrative. The title of the novel seems to enact these two possibilities. Wilson explains that the title is borrowed from the formula used by BBC World Service newsreaders: 'That is the end of the World News'. If the novel concerns the end of the world, it also gives us *news* about it, thereby offering the possibility of some surviving principle of newness in the world. The end of the world is compounded with the idea of the ending of narrative (I have already had occasion in this book to note the etymological association between news and the novel); but the novel that narrates the end of the world and of its narratives necessarily and optimistically contradicts itself. Burgess is one of a number of novelists who have dramatised the end of the world by a return to history, to reveal the ways in which the principles of apocalypse and annihilation of the past, which have become so terrifyingly actual through the twentieth century, are themselves generative principles; Burgess narrates the survival of the ending, and the survival of narrative, by showing the ways in which history is made up of endings.

Another remarkable novel which uses the idea of survival beyond nuclear apocalypse to explore the relations between narrative, endings and history is Russell Hoban's *Riddley Walker* (1980). This novel is set some 2,500 years in the future in the aftermath of nuclear war. Human life has been reduced to an Iron Age condition, though the inhabitants of this civilisation have preserved the memory of the more developed civilisation whose destruction has led to their own condition, in the myth of Eusa, a strange amalgam of the story of St Eustace and a fabular account of the events leading to the splitting of the atom and use of the nuclear bomb by the USA. In a sense, therefore, *Riddley Walker* solves the problem of how to narrate the unnarratable fact of ending by simply evading it, setting its narrative at a point when human life has been resumed, and the apocalyptic ending of that life returned to history. Here, annihilation is again annulled by narration. Nevertheless, the question of ending retains its force and mystery in the novel, since the inhabitants of this civilisation and especially Riddley Walker, the narrator of the novel, spend their time struggling to reconstitute the events of the holocaust and, more alarmingly, the scientific knowledge and power that have led to it. There is thus a strange parallel between Riddley Walker's civilisation and our own, in that both derive their sense of historical identity from the presence and force of something that lies outside knowledge and history, an explanatory principle that both inheres in and is unavailable to the history it organises: the absolute ending that lies unavoidably but unthinkably in front of our present and the absolute beginning that lies inaccessibly behind Riddley Walker's civilisation. Peter Schwenger has written persuasively about this parallel; both our culture and that of *Riddley Walker* are organised around a principle that cannot be clearly represented or brought to consciousness. The genre of writing that Schwenger calls 'nuclear fiction' attempts, as does Riddley Walker's narrative from the other end of history, to 'write the unthinkable', an enterprise which 'must always raise questions about what structure is adequate to this project, on what the structure grounds itself, and in what ways the writing moves' (Schwenger 1991: 254). The riddle of origin is persistent but opaque throughout Riddley Walker's narration, which is forced to begin and gather itself *in medias res*: 'I dont think it makes no diffrents where you start the telling of a thing. You never know where it begun realy. No moren you know where you begun your oan self', says Riddley early in the book (Hoban 1982: 8), while later on a charcoal-burner called Granser tells him, 'you wont never fynd no beginning its long gone and far pas. What ever youre after youwl never fynd the beginning of it thats why youwl all ways be too late' (147). To be in search of knowledge in this culture is always to be, in the felicitous phrase Hoban gives to Granser, 'after it'.

Riddley Walker's narration is convergent with the act of interpretation, with unriddling the various signs, emblems and evidences of the lost knowledge. Hoban puts the reader in an equivalent position by giving his future world an impenetrably degenerated language, formed out of the mutations, contaminations and scorched stumps of twentieth-century language, in which scientific terms – 'chemistery and fizzics', 'teckernogical progers', 'Puter Leat' (computer elite), 'pirntow' (printout), 'datter' (data) – jostle with children's rhymes, proverbs and decayed Kentish dialect, all rendered in a phonetic language that testifies to the volatile relationship between speech and writing in a civilisation in which, after having been forgotten for centuries, the art of writing has only recently been regenerated. It is a language characterised, as Jeffrey Porter has noticed, both by fission and fusion, the splitting apart of words and their grafting together (Porter 1990: 450). The twentieth-century reader comes gradually to understand the conditions of this new civilisation in step with the process by which it, in the person of Riddley, comes to rediscover its own history.

Riddley's narrative understanding, and that of his culture, consists primarily of making connections between the surviving and decayed elements of what, in a kind of hermeneutic explosion matching the physical explosion of the nuclear bomb, the holocaust has scattered. The guiding sacred text for this culture is the 'Eusa Story'. This story centres on a mythically transformed account of the splitting of the atom, which becomes a prototype for division as such:

> Eusa wuz angre he wuz in rayj & he kep pulin on the Littl Man the Addoms owt strecht arms. The Littl Man the Addom he begun tu cum a part he cryd, I wan tu go I wan tu stay. Eusa sed, Tel mor. The Addom sed, I wan tu dark I wan tu lyt I wan tu day I wan tu nyt. Eusa sed, Tel mor. The Addom sed, I wan tu woman I wan tu man. Eusa sed, Tel mor. The Addom sed, I wan tu plus I wan tu minus I wan tu big I wan tu little I wan tu aul I wan tu nuthing.
>
> (Hoban 1982: 30)

Riddley Walker himself becomes a 'connexion man', for his group, his function being to offer interpretations of various signs, omens and events as well as of the Eusa Story itself on the occasions when it is reenacted by Goodparley and Orfing, who are the agents of the Ram, the name for the governing powers of the area. 'Connexion' means being able to perceive the unity of what appears as scattered, disjunct and meaningless to Riddley. Riddley imagines that what separates his civilisation from its pre-holocaust past is the loss of unifying sensibility:

> Becaws it com to me what it wer wed los. It come to me what it wer as made them peopl time back way back bettern us. It were knowing how to put ther selfs with the Power of the wood be come stoan.
>
> (Hoban 1982: 156)

In such a world, appearance and significance are puzzlingly bifurcated, as Goodparley tries to explain to Riddley: 'Its about some thing else. Which every thing is innit. Every thing is about every thing. And what evers in 2 wl be come 1' (136).

The question of connection is related to the two models of time found in two rival interpretations of the Eusa Story. That story ends with a conversation between Eusa and the 'Littl Shyning Man'. Eusa has unleashed the destruction of the 'Bad Time' on the world, but now wants only 'tu liv qwyet' (34). He is told by the Littl Shyning Man, however, that he must undergo a kind of renewing purgation, in a series of 'Master Chaynjis', which may lead him to knowledge about his identity or 'the idear uv yu'. There is no given starting point, or clearly identifiable destination in this process:

> Eusa sed . . . Woan yu pleas tel me how menne Chaynjis thayr ar? The Littl Man sed, As menne as reqwyrd. Eusa sed, Reqwyrd by wut? The Littl Man sed, Reqwyrd by the idear uv yu. Eusa sed, Wut is the idear uv me? The Littl Man sed, That we doan no til yuv gon thru aul yur Chaynjis.
>
> (Hoban 1982: 34)

This story is interpreted by most people in Riddley Walker's world as the proof of their condition of inexpiable guilt, in which humanity is endlessly suspended between existence and identity, appearance and truth, the present and the past. Orfing articulates this sense of the impossibility of transcending the present condition of bafflement and confusion, when he insists that

> What the Littl Shyning Man is hes jus what ever cant never be put to gether. There aint no moren that to it nor you cant

make it be mor. Any thing as *can* be put to gether aint the
Littl Shyning Man its some thing else.

(Hoban 1982: 39)

But there is also the desire among various agents of the Ram,
especially Orfing's associate, Goodparley, for the reactivation of
linear historical time, conceived as a progress to an end:

> You can say what you like Im saying wewl get it put to gether
> weve got it all in front of us and going to make it happen.
> Youre looking sideways but Im looking frontways and going
> to get every body moving that way.
>
> (ibid.)

This contrast between recurrent and progressive time is dramatised at different points in the novel, most strikingly after Riddley Walker's visit to what he thinks of as the 'woom' of 'Cambry', the remains of Canterbury Cathedral which has been 'ground zero', or the point of impact of a nuclear bomb. There he has discovered a wooden puppet head, with 'wide open grean eyes staring up at me wylst the vines and leaves growit out of his mouf' (163), a figure that he names 'Greanvine'. As he walks away from Cambry, he improvises an exchange between this figure and the figure of Punch which he has dug out of the ground earlier in the narrative:

> Greanvine said, 'Wel air is the short sky innit but earf is the long 1.'
> Punch said, 'Balls my boy. Thats what you aint got a nuff of.'
> Greanvine said, 'It dont matter how much balls youve got its all the same in the end.'
> Punch said, 'No it aint the same its diffrent if youve got balls a nuff.'
> Greanvine said, 'Hows it diffrent?'
> Punch said, 'Its diffrent right the way up to the end and thats why the end is diffrent. If the way is diffrent the end is diffrent. Becaws the end aint nothing only part of the way its jus that part of the way where you come to a stop. The end cud be any part of the way its in every step of the way thats why you bes go ballsy.'
>
> (Hoban 1982: 167)

Punch here articulates the desire for progress and the transcendence of nature in the will-to-power and the will-to-knowledge. The interchange dramatises the contrast and complicity between the passive knowledge of nature's secret essence in the recurrent references to the 'hart of the wood' and the desire to know that essence, which Riddley re-spells as 'the hart of the wud . . . the hart of the wanting to be' (160). In the cyclical inhabitation of nature represented by Greanvine, ends and beginnings are reversible and equivalent. Punch represents the desire to activate the open, unpredictable itineraries and ends of progressive historical time; what Goodparley, speaking through Eusa, refers to as 'Good Time which I mean every thing good and every body happy and teckernogical progers moving every thing frontways farther and farther all the time' (46).

The alternatives of recurrent ('sideways') and progressive ('frontways') time are linked to the question of power. Despite himself, Riddley Walker is drawn into the quest to rediscover or reconstitute the lost knowledge of the past. Arriving at Cambry, the centre of what he calls the 'Power Ring', a circumference of towns round ground zero, Riddley Walker is suddenly possessed by the craving for onward movement articulated by Goodparley and Punch: 'Power wantit you to come to it with Power. Power wantit what ever cud happen to happen. Power wantit every thing moving frontways' (150). In Goodparley's address to Orfing, power, will and progress are also associated with the desire for connection, the reintegration of what has been lost from human knowledge: 'wewl get it put to gether weve got it all in front of us' (39). For Riddley, the principle represented by the Littl Shyning Man is similarly that of the drive towards integration: it is 'jus and very what *wantit* to put its self to gether and trying its bes to do it' (144), against the '2ness of everything' (ibid.), the inertial tendency of things to fall into division and difference.

David Cowart, in the course of an interesting and elaborate reading of the circular and progressive models of history at work in *Riddley Walker*, concludes that both are debased, since both 'lack an adequately developed spiritual or sacral dimension' (Cowart 1989: 89). But the point is not so much the relative value of 'archaic' and 'civilised' modes of temporal consciousness, as the fact that they necessitate and lead to each other, in what Goodparley calls 'the curse roads of . . . terpitation' (39), which can be glossed as the crux, the cursed cross-roads of trepidation-causing interpretation. If understanding comes from connecting up what has been blown asunder, then connection is also the principle necessary for the rediscovery of power through scientific knowledge, in particular the rediscovery of the ingredients necessary for the manufacture of gunpowder, or 'the 1 littl 1' that is a step on the way to the '1 big 1'. The tautest irony of the narrative is contained in this recurring phrase. The '1 big 1' refers both to the principle of unity in nature, a principle which has been blasted apart in man's guilt (in splitting the 'Addom', man falls, Adam-like, in division and loss of identity), and to the culmination of scientific knowledge, 'the big one' of nuclear annihilation itself. Forward progress through the reintegration of scattered knowledge seems to have as its inevitable destination the detonation of history once more. Forward and backward, progression and recurrence come to seem interchangeable.

It is not just that integration of meaning inevitably seems to lead to its dispersal, for the novel suggests from the very beginning the complex reversibility or mutual dependence of the principles of sameness and difference, connection and disconnection. This reversibility becomes apparent when Goodparley and Orfing perform their version of the Eusa Story. At first sight, there would appear to be a close parallel between the theme of division represented in the Eusa Story and the question of how the story is interpreted. Where Orfing is satisfied to let the story just be itself, without any attempt to explain or close up its mysteries by interpretation – 'What the Littl Shyning Man is hes jus what ever cant never be put to gether. There aint no moren that to it nor you cant make it be mor' (39) – Goodparley and Riddley Walker both insist on the integrating act of interpretation. The question of whether or not the Littl Shyning Man can ever be put together again is the same question as whether the Eusa Story can ever be brought to coincide with its meaning. But in order to bring about the move towards connection, the forward movement consequent upon reintegrating knowledge, Goodparley actually has to interfere with the sacred text of the Eusa Story, inducing a split or difference within it. In the official version of the story, Eusa is himself responsible for splitting the atom and himself bears the guilt afterwards. In the version of the story that Goodparley performs, the responsibility for the Bad Time is given to the wicked Mr Clevver, a composite of the devil and Uncle Sam, leaving Eusa free of guilt. Orfing is disturbed by this change in the story, and questions Goodparley, who replies through the character of Eusa:

> Eusa says, 'Whats the diffrents if I done the acturel Bad Time things my self or if I dint?'
> Orfing says, 'Wel if you dint do it than it aint on you is it.'

> Eusa says, 'And if it aint on me then what?'
> Orfing says, 'Then youre free aint you. Nothing on you and the worl in front of you. Do what ever you like.'
>
> (Hoban 1982: 49)

The freedom to act in history, which is also a kind of freedom from the burden of history, and a freedom to inaugurate the passage of history once again, is gained here by a fracturing of the unity of the story which mimics the primal splitting of which the story tells. Eusa is healed of responsibility for the latter only by dint of the guilt incurred by the former. To begin to make connections is necessarily also to depend upon certain kinds of disconnection. Freedom from guilt can only be secured by incurring the further guilt of choice.

This has a disturbing connection with the narrative movement of *Riddley Walker* and the nature of our involvement in it. The very principle of narrative unfolding in *Riddley Walker* is shown to be queasily complicit with the principle of technological development, which looks by the end of the novel as though it is about to unleash another era of conflict and destruction. Granser, the old charcoal burner to whom Riddley yields up a precious bag of sulphur which he has previously discovered, and who is himself killed in an explosion of the gunpowder he manufactures with it, articulates the principle of this dangerous onward drive:

> What you dun to me I brung it on my self with what I done to you when I wunt let you be come your oan man, I wunt let you be come what you wer going to be nex. Thats the woal seakert of the 1 littl 1 you see . . . It wants to be its nex thing you see its a showing of the Master Chaynjis in littl.
>
> (Hoban 1982: 186)

Power and desire are thus associated not just with the discovery of knowledge but with the narrative of that discovery and our identification with it. The novel depends for its interest on the fact that there will be change, development and newness in this terrible, deteriorated world, and on the unabating forward drive of a narrative that, in Granser's words just quoted, 'wants to be its nex thing'. Against this deadly, consuming desire for the next thing and the hungry, hazardous integration it brings, Riddley attempts to withdraw into quiescence, telling himself 'Its the not sturgling for Power thats where the Power is. Its in jus letting your self be where it is' (191). But this withdrawal may prove as unsatisfactory as his identification with the frontways drive of connection and integration: certainly it will do nothing to avert the effects of the power that is now irremediably abroad once more and that Riddley is accused of having set loose (204).

The novel ends with Riddley Walker having taken Goodparley's place as the Eusa Story man, though with his repertoire enhanced by the addition of a Punch and Judy show. Riddley is left in the uneasy position of being the vehicle of a revelation that is not wholly apparent to him. The stories he performs show Punch endlessly killing his own child, accompanied by riddling formulae which seem to testify to the inescapable reversibility of good and evil, love and violence, natural and unnatural desire: '*Harm is where the hert is . . . Hart is where the wud is*' (212). These stories have their own logic and narrative impetus, which may represent the possibility of showing, if not articulating, some new, redeeming knowledge, which will allow humanity to escape from the endless cycle of power, destruction and ignorance, but whose very mutability also has something alarmingly in common with the processes (the 'Chaynjis') they seem designed to warn against:

> It aint in the natur of a show to be the same every time it aint like a story what you pas down trying not to change nothing which even then the changes will creap in. No a figger show its got its oan chemistery and fizzics. What it is its all ways trying to fynd out what it is jus now this same and very minim going thru its chaynjis. Which Ive wrote that in the old spel becaws its them same and very Chaynjis what the Littl Shyning Man tol Eusa of.
>
> (Hoban 1982: 199)

At this final point, *Riddley Walker* seems to have changed from a novel about a point distant in the future to a novel about our own predicament in the face of imminent catastrophe. Like us, Riddley must avoid the twin dangers of passivity and the precipitate desire for meaning: 'Not to lern no body nothing I cant even lern my oan self all I can do is try not to get in front of whats coming. Jus try to keap out of the way of it' (199). Riddley's desire to 'try not to get in front of whats coming' ambivalently implies not just keeping out of the way of the future, but also holding back the dangerous impulsions of the narrative imagination, and preventing himself from getting ahead of the future. Like Riddley Walker, the novel seems to say, we need neither to retreat into passive despair, nor to trust too much to our well-developed capacities for taking hold of the future, with all the disastrous consequences that has had and may have.

A number of commentators on the novel have seen it as a mirroring of our own present condition in this way. David Cowart sees Riddley Walker's world as a version of the unredeemed Waste Land that is our own time (1989: 99–105); Peter Schwenger sees Riddley Walker's search for 'the idear uv us' as parallel to our own contemporary search for a way of coming to terms with the 'unthinkable' (1986: 46) and Jeffrey Porter concludes his interesting discussion of the language of the novel with the suggestion that the world of *Riddley Walker* is 'an "isotrope" of our own, reminding us how "fissile" our nuclear culture and language are' (1990: 468). But there are dangers in claiming this simple equivalence. To do so is to suggest the possibility of integrating Riddley's world with our own, of creating a meaningful narrative continuity stretching from our world beyond our own extinction to that of Riddley Walker. Against this, I believe, must be set the suspicion of the progressive and integrative force of narrative that surfaces throughout *Riddley Walker* and results in the curious suspension of revelation or knowledge at the end of the book, along with the gap that Hoban deliberately maintains between what Riddley Walker's narratives may 'figger' and what Riddley himself may be able to figure out about them. The effect seems to be precisely to thwart the possibility of that identification between the reading present and the postnuclear future which Schwenger celebrates, when he points to the shared experience of narrative in the road that Riddley walks: 'That road is narrative as much as it is anything else: only by moving on it and being moved by it can we, despite not knowing, experience a continuous showing' (1991: 260). This reading responds aptly to the way that the novel seems to make the experience of the unthinkable available and knowable to us; but it does not register the novel's own uneasiness about this availability and its attempts not to confirm us in our dangerous sense of epistemological advantage, our sense that we know what Riddley's world does not. The problem which, in a sense because it drives the novel is unable to solve it, is how to keep open the unrepresentability of our end, how to resist the integrating allurements of narrative and to convince us of the unnarratability of annihilation without consoling us with its narration.

ENDINGS AND LIVING ON

This discussion has restricted itself principally to the work of British writers or writers such as Russell Hoban who, though American by birth, has lived and worked in Britain for most of his life. But it is worth relaxing this restriction (which, given the largeness of the theme under discussion, may seem particularly artificial) to consider the rather different solution to the problem of living and narrating beyond the ending of human life that is projected by Kurt Vonnegut's *Galàpagos* (1985). In this novel, a group of people are planning to take the 'Nature Cruise of the Century' to the Galapagos islands made famous by Darwin. Marooned by mischance on their island, they turn out to be the only human beings to survive the war and subsequent plague that exterminate the rest of humanity. They are at once the only survivors of humanity and the last of their kind, in the sense that from them evolves, over the million-year time-scale that the narrative assumes and represents, a wholly new creature, equipped with fins instead of hands, and with a much reduced brain. The narrative thus presents a hugely magnified temporal projection which is also a regression to a condition in which life, though it continues in some sort, is of so limited a kind and so unimaginatively integrated into the conditions of biological existence that no history or evolutionary 'plot' is likely ever again to emerge.

The novel chooses to highlight rather than to efface its own artifice in maintaining narrative expectations, desires and satisfactions, even though these are in principle cancelled by the end of the narrative. It does so in order to present itself as the last conceivable narrative, the narrative of an end that is also the ending of narrative. The novel has a narrator, in the figure of the ghost of Leon Trout, son of the science fiction writer Kilgore Trout who recurs in so many Vonnegut novels. Leon has lingered on this side of the afterlife for a million years to satisfy his curiosity about how the human story works out in the end. His narrative thus folds together possibility and impossibility: the figure of Leon Trout is a device to allow the events of an unimaginably remote future to be made available for narration, the discursive link that guarantees the possibility of a witness and a report following on every significant event; at the same time he is the dramatisation of the impossibility of dramatising or imaginatively inhabiting the particular experiences represented in the narrative. His is a narrative to demonstrate the impossibility of narrative: 'I have written these words in air – with the tip of the index finger of my left hand, which is also air' (Vonnegut 1987: 265). From the viewpoint supplied by Trout, it is not just the anomalous wisp of consciousness that is himself who is made ghostly by the vanishing of the human, but the whole of human history which will turn out similarly to have been haunted by vacancy:

> Does it trouble me to write so insubstantially, with air on air? Well – my words will be as enduring as anything my father wrote, or Shakespeare wrote, or Beethoven wrote, or Darwin wrote. It turns out that they all wrote with air on air.
>
> (Vonnegut 1987: 265)

The revelation that the whole of human history 'will have been' without outcome denies the rounding into significance or perfected meaning promised in the future perfect tense. In doing so, it also denies the very impulse which drives the narrative towards the imagination of absolute ending, the impulse to purloin the gathering, consummating force of death. Here, in what looks like a narrative of survival, the terminal orientation of 'being-towards-death' is deflected or diffused; to 'be absolute for death' is shown to be self-confuting in so far as absolute death dissipates the perfective force of the borrowed or vicarious death of narrative closure.

Doris Lessing's *The Memoirs of a Survivor* (1974) is an interesting example of a narrative treatment of social and cultural ending that is also an exploration of the strange effects upon narrative of such an imagination of ending. In contrast to the lurid apocalypse of such a work as Golding's *Lord of the Flies* (1954), which provides and controls a vision of social collapse by displacing it into allegory, *The Memoirs of a Survivor* deliberately sets out to represent a sort of collapse that takes place within the forms of the contemporary world. The novel is the account, given by an unnamed narrator, of her personal experience of some unspecified but generalised breakdown of social order. The narrative begins with the arrival of a small child named Emily who is left in the narrator's care by an unidentified middle-aged man. The account of Emily's growth and her developing affinities with the gangs of children who gather and come to live in the street outside is used to narrate obliquely a profound social collapse, in which urban, technological civilisation seems slowly and inexorably to be devolving into forms of nomadic, tribal organisation, or nonorganisation. No single, central event, no punctual apocalypse seems to have precipitated this process; it is rather as if late twentieth-century urban dwellers have all at a certain moment experienced a huge disillusion, a withdrawal of affect from the forms of modernity, technological culture, city life, and the centred, administered, stratifications of mass society:

> All over our city were these pockets of life reverting to the primitive, the hand-to-mouth. Part of a house ... then the whole house ... a group of houses ... a street ... an area of streets. People looking down from a high building saw how these nuclei of barbarism took hold and spread [...] people no longer in neat little families but huddled together in groups and clans whose structure evolved under the pressures of necessity.
> (Lessing 1976: 94–5. My ellipses in square brackets.)

Although we are given a certain amount of information in the novel about this collapse of social life, its causes and effects remain obscure. We know, as in more dramatic narratives of apocalypse and/or reversion, that a crucial and irreversible change has occurred and that twentieth-century life has come unmistakably and irremediably to an end, but Emily's fragmented, disconnected story narrates the immunity to narration of the 'it' that is both the precipitation and the process of social and cultural ending. The novel never makes plain what this collapse consists of, or the identity of the 'it' that has nevertheless and in such an uncertain manner been 'survived'. The narrator writes: 'I think this is the right place to say something more about "it". Though of course there is no "right" place or time, since there was no particular place marking – then or now – "its" beginning' (137). The 'it', defined a little later as 'above all a consciousness of something ending' (136), is nevertheless all-pervasive, demanding to be acknowledged and narrated, indeed, driving and determining the narrative, while yet resisting direct embodiment. If 'it' is the name for the altering force of any kind of visible crisis or disaster – 'pestilence, a war, the alteration of climate, a tyranny that twists men's minds, the savagery of a religion' (ibid.), it is also the name for a sense of the hidden, impersonal processes of history, which refuse to come to visibility or nameability:

> Perhaps I would have done better to have begun this chronicle with an attempt at a full description of 'it'. But is it possible to write an account of anything at all without 'it' – in some shape or another – being the main theme? Perhaps, indeed, 'it' is the secret theme of all literature and history, like writing in invisible ink between the lines, which springs up,

sharply black, dimming the old print we knew so well, as life, personal or public, unfolds unexpectedly and we see something where we never thought we could – we see 'it' as the ground-swell of events, experience.

(Lessing 1976: 135–6)

If the reader still feels minded to enquire, as the narrator does of herself, 'Very well then, but what *was* it?', part of the answer seems to be that the very unrepresentability or unavailability to ordinary narrative of the 'it' is part of its essence. This is not a merely metaphysical difficulty but is itself an effect of the particular mutation in social conditions that the novel has such difficulty in describing, for one of the characterising features of the social collapse that both is and is not narrated in the novel is the fragmentation or thinning of a public imaginary, or shared capacity to narrate. In fact one of the most interesting features of this novel is the way that it dematerialises its apocalypse. Thus, it is surprising to learn that the external forms of social organisation and control – government, law-courts, prisons – seem to be surviving more or less unchanged, but with less and less connection with the ordinary life that has undergone such extraordinary mutation: 'All this time, while ordinary life simply dissolved away, or found new shapes, the structure of government continued, though heavy and cumbersome and becoming all the time more ramified' (160). The fact that these institutions have been so decathected, drained of credence and imaginary investment, oddly discloses the illusion on which they had always been based:

> even at that late stage, there was a level of our society which managed to live as if nothing much was happening – nothing irreparable ... But when has it not been true? – that the section of a society which gets the most out of it maintains in itself, and for as long as it can in others, an illusion of security, permanence, order.

(Lessing 1976: 95)

This thinning of the public imaginary is an emphatically political event or effect, but is not itself easy to represent in social and political terms. It is for this reason that the narration of the book via a sequence of dreams, visions or fantasies on the part of the narrator is not a mere aesthetic device or preference for the authenticity of the private over the public. It is not exactly a matter of reading the episodes of fantasy or vision as a coded substitute for the missing social content of the novel, or as a parallel imaginative history or history of the imagination from which we can read off the 'real' history that remains unrepresented. What is most 'real' about the history that both is and is not represented is that it no longer coheres with the private world.

From early in the novel the narrator describes passing from her real surroundings into a series of imaginary rooms or scenes. Initially, these visions appear to her in the light of a task to be fulfilled, for the rooms are chilly, stale and dirty, and in need of cleaning and decoration to make them habitable. She in fact imagines herself cleaning one such room in the house, which she discovers ransacked and despoiled (39). Later on, she imagines strange, complex activities taking place in these rooms, for example in the vision of a six-sided room in which she joins a number of people in the game of matching scraps of fabric to the pattern on the carpet (72–3). But, with the arrival of Emily, these visions begin to alternate with more disturbing ones, which seem to be memories or fantasies of Emily's infancy, though transposed anachronistically to a constricting Edwardian childhood. The narrator distinguishes between these two forms of vision as between what she calls the 'impersonal' and the 'personal'. The impersonal visions are abstract and enigmatic, but characterised also by 'a lightness, a freedom, a feeling of possibility . . . the space and the knowledge of the possibility of alternative action' (40). The personal scenes are much more realistic, but also more claustrophobic:

> To enter the 'personal' was to enter a prison, where nothing could happen but what one saw happening, where the air was tight and limited, and above all where time was a strict, unalterable law and long, oh my God, it went on, and on and on, minute by decreed minute, with no escape but the slow wearing away of one after another.
>
> (Lessing 1976: 40)

The fantasy rooms represent the process whereby a public imaginary is replaced by personal vision. Gradually, the alternative world explored in these visions comes to infiltrate and even to replace the real historical world that is proceeding and collapsing round them. The novel ends with a visionary departure from and transcendence of deteriorating history. The narrator, Emily, her lover Gerald, and Hugo, a strange indeterminate creature who seems to be part human, part dog, together cross the threshold separating the imagined from the actual world. 'It all came to an end', the narrator tells us (189), but this ending cannot itself be represented in the novel other than through flight, negation and silence. We are given no indication of the nature of the transformation which has been undergone and survived in order to enable the narrator to look back in these memoirs, though it is at least plain that it involves some move beyond the linearity in which the concepts of ending and historical memory themselves have meaning. The narration that survives the end does not know it, or at least cannot encompass it, since it seems to involve the end of narrative as such, or history-as-narrative. The novel thus proposes an impossible compromise between ending as consummating eventuation and ending as unrepresentable and eventless. The promise of renewal and continuity that is proposed by the last sentences is haunted by the sense of absence and dissolution, not least the necessary dissolution of the narrative form that has framed and delivered the promise: 'Both walked quickly behind that One who went ahead showing them the way out of this collapsed little world into another order of world . . . they all followed quickly on after the others as the last walls dissolved' (190).

Another strategy for including ending in narrative without simply annulling it into narrative is practised by Julian Barnes in the inset story 'The Survivor' in his *A History of the World in 10½ Chapters* (1989). The story is really the confrontation between two competing stories. In one of these, an Australian woman, Kathleen Ferris, 38 years old and married to a brutal, beer-drinking ignoramus called Greg, becomes scared and depressed by the growing realisation of impending nuclear war. She takes a boat and heads out into the sea, taking with her only minimal provisions and a couple of cats. Getting evidence of the nuclear war only in oblique indications such as 'a shifting of the light . . . a distant rumbling noise' (Barnes 1990: 91), she sails aimlessly until she reaches an island, where she begins to have nightmares about being in some kind of institution. In these nightmares, she argues with men who explain to her that she has been rescued from a boat and is now being treated for her physical and mental breakdown.

The alternative narrative is enfolded within these nightmares. In this narrative, Kath has never reached any island but has been picked up in her boat about a hundred miles east of Darwin, going round in circles, almost dead from starvation and exposure, and been brought back to a psychiatric hospital. In this narrative, nuclear war has in fact been narrowly averted, and Kath's flight and subsequent failure to remember events properly is interpreted as a desperate disavowal, having its roots in her personal distress at the breakdown of her relationship.

Each of these two, mutually enfolding narratives includes a theory to account for and discredit the other. For Kath, the nightmares are part of the nuclear catastrophe to which male history has led inexorably, part of the brutal narrative of the actual that in fact atomises history, denying connection and continuity:

> I'm stuck with this rhyme as we head in whatever direction we're heading:
>
>> In fourteen hundred and ninety two
>> Columbus sailed the ocean blue
>
> And then what? They always make it sound so simple. Names, dates, achievements. I hate dates. Dates are bullies, dates are know-alls.
>
> (Barnes 1990: 98–9)

For Kath on her island, the challenge is to resist the story told to her by the men in the dream, and to begin telling stories differently:

> The mind got carried away, she found herself repeating. Everything was connected, the weapons and the nightmares. That's why they'd had to break the cycle. Start making things simple again. Begin at the beginning. People said you couldn't turn the clock back, but you could. The future was in the past.
>
> (Barnes 1990: 104)

For the doctors in Kath's dream, the rest of her story is accounted for as 'fabulation', a process in which, as they tell her, 'you make up a story to cover the facts you don't know or can't accept. You keep a few true facts and spin a new story round them' (109). The relations between these competing accounts become both more complex and more simple as the story moves to its conclusion. Kath uses the notion of fabulation to account for the alternative, official account of her own story, deciding that the story of her personal survival is in fact only an instance of fabulation in the interests of self-preservation, her own unconscious attempt to deny the reality of her own impending death on the island from radiation sickness.

It was all about her mind being afraid of its own death, that's what she finally decided. When her skin got bad and her hair started falling out, her mind tried to think up an alternative explanation. She even knew the technical term for it now: fabulation. Where had she picked that up from? She must have read it in a magazine somewhere. Fabulation. You keep a few true facts and spin a new story round them.

(Barnes 1990: 111)

Nevertheless, if the story seems to end with hope and a vision of survival (Kath wakes up to find that one of her cats has given birth to five kittens), this is undercut by the growing preference for the realistic, or psychiatric, reading of what comes to seem more and more Kath's tenacious delusion. This is given particular point by the sentimentality of the final vision ('She felt such happiness! Such hope!'; 111), which is in marked contrast to the more austere imaginative instructions Kath has earlier given herself about the island: 'She didn't think she was going to land on some undamaged island where you only had to throw a bean over your shoulder for a whole row of them to spring up and wave their pods at you' (92).

Read in this way, the conclusion both opens on to the future, in a guarantee of continuing consequence, and closes it off, by denying or repressing the chain of consequence that has brought Kath back into historical time. This both summons up and provides an interesting contrast with an earlier book about the question of ending, a book that is in its own way overshadowed by the prospect of the nuclear annihilation of the possibility of story altogether, William Golding's *Pincher Martin* (1956). Here, a consciousness faced with its own imminent extinction generates an entire fantasy of survival and adaptation. The final shocking revelation is that the shipwrecked Martin has never in fact found his island, that the rocky outcrop on which he has fought for survival is the precipitate of a desperate act of compensatory fabulation, in the sense of that term offered in Barnes's 'The Survivor'. Martin's island is generated simply by the feel of a tooth in his own mouth. Here, narrative is the deterrent of death, a wile employed to defer and disavow ending, even as it is produced out of the eruption of death into life, and the paradoxical and unencompassable desire to impound the unnarratable event of death within story. The narrative restores us to the propriety of historical time in one of Golding's celebrated shifts of point of view, as we are released from the grip of Martin's fictive will-to-power and provided with a narrative to account for the narrative that has occupied the whole novel. In reality, as we learn from an exchange between a Scottish islander and a naval officer, Martin has been dead almost from the outset of the narrative; Campbell's question, 'Would you say there was any – surviving?', being answered, though also partially misunderstood, by Davidson, the officer, with the emphatic declaration that 'he didn't even have time to kick off his seaboots' (Golding 1956: 208). In this way, the novel stabilises the question of ending by what we have seen as a characteristic doubling and ranking of levels, as the narrative of the end of narrative is itself enclosed within a further narrative that acts to explain it and to restore it to the continuum of articulated events.

'The Survivor' resembles and alludes to *Pincher Martin* in the idea of a consciousness taking refuge in the fantasy of an island as a fabular fold or pocket within the ordinary or actual time of extinction. But it differs from it too, in resisting the temptation to straighten things out by resolving the paradoxical time of deferral, survival and living on, into the regularity of historical time. Of course, it is always possible for the reader to make the step beyond the condition of survival into a narrative that will make sense of it, indeed it may be a weakness of Barnes's story that it gives us so much warrant to read it as a particular kind of psychopathological exception or instance. But the narrative nevertheless conspicuously holds back from supplying this explanatory step itself, forcing the reader into an odd sort of hermeneutic lurch.

Where *Pincher Martin* shows narrative as fabulation, as the tenacious clinging to continuity, connection and consequence in the face of ending, 'The Survivor' explores something like the opposite. Where Martin's narrative compensates for the fact of *not* being rescued, Kath's narrative makes up for (which is to say denies) the fact that she *has* been rescued. Her narrative is founded not on making connections but on suppressing them, to the degree that narrative connectedness is associated with the terrifying inexorability of willed annihilation. As in *Riddley Walker, Galápagos* and *The Burning Book*, (which will be discussed a litte later), the solidarity between narrative connection and the male will-to-extermination, between the history of the world and the end of the world, makes narrative itself desperately compromised:

> They say I don't understand things. They say I'm not making the right connections. Listen to them, listen to them and their connections. This happened, they say, and as a consequence

that happened. There was a battle here, a war there, a king was deposed, famous men – always famous men, I'm sick of famous men – made events happen. Maybe I've been out in the sun too long, but I can't see their connections. I look at the history of the world, which they don't seem to realize is coming to an end, and I don't see what they see.

(Barnes 1990: 97)

It is true that Kath cannot hold off entirely from narrative, since she proposes not to deny connections altogether, but rather to attend to different kinds of connectedness. Partly this means entertaining a more inclusive, a more coherent narrative than that offered by those around her who refuse to take the prospect of human self-annihilation seriously, refuse to read the story through to its end. On her island, or on her 'island', Kath reasons that it is only the excessiveness of human imagination that makes it possible to devise means for its own destruction, and tells a little story to prove to herself that 'you couldn't imagine an animal inventing its own destruction, could you' (102). The story she tells, of a bear who digs a trap in the middle of its own favourite trail into which it inevitably falls, only partially proves her point, since it shows that, no matter how unimaginable such a prospect is, it is always in fact possible for humans to imagine it and represent it in narrative. The temptation for Kath is to construct a superior story, one which will not only preserve the connections that ordinary histories suppress but also allow her a position of interpretative transcendence:

> She didn't believe in God, but now she was tempted. Not because she was afraid of dying. It wasn't that. No, she was tempted to believe in someone watching what was going on, watching the bear dig its own pit and then fall into it. It wouldn't be such a good story if there was no-one around to tell it. Look what they went and did – they blew themselves up.
>
> (Barnes 1990: 103)

But this is a dangerous stratagem, in that it falls in with the very desire for narrative that is in fact deeply implicated with the drive towards self-annihilation. If the function of the island in fiction from *Robinson Crusoe* to *Pincher Martin* has conventionally been to tell the story of an evacuation or depletion of story, which nevertheless rounds irresistibly into the resumption of all its powers and possibilities, Kath's suspicion of story leads her to repudiate this resumption. This gives her appropriation of the diagnosis of her doctors an extra point; where they see her clinging on to the fable of the island in order to avoid confronting the reality of her private pain and failure, she diagnoses the fable of the island as a veto on fabulation as such: 'We've got to look at things how they are; we can't rely on fabulation any more. It's the only way we'll survive' (111). The fact that this austere counsel is followed almost instantly by what seems like a sentimental relapse into fantasy, with the account of the birth of the kittens, should be read not as a slackening but as a tightening of this irony. For Kath to continue on her island is also to cling to the story of her inevitable death, to leave open the possibility of absolute annihilation which is closed off by the averting of the war that the doctor describes to her: 'It was very worrying. It looked as if there might well be one. But they sorted something out . . . It never happened' (108). Not for the first or last time in the fiction of absolute ending, it proves necessary to hold on to a fable in the interests of averting another fable. It proves necessary, to follow the terms of Freud's *Beyond the Pleasure Principle* (1920), to take a certain detour through life and the narrative that seems to promise its persistence in order to preserve the truth of death, or the abolition of narrative (1955: 39). But this is subject to a further convolution, in that to hold on to the possibility of death is to hold out against the narratives that seem so inexorably to lead to death; in the face of the train of historical consequences that leads to annihilation, it is necessary to insist on the completion of that story, even to the point of seemingly denying the consolations of story, in the interests of real survival. Holding on to life means 'putting a stop to the men and their temptations' (Barnes 1990: 104). So, putting it differently, it means preserving a certain loss or incompleteness, signalled in this narrative by the refusal to complete the nursery rhyme that is elsewhere in the collection of stories that makes up *A History of the World in 10½ Chapters* knitted into completion: 'In fourteen hundred and ninety two/Columbus sailed the ocean blue'. Kath can never remember the next two lines that run 'In fourteen hundred and ninety three/He sailed right back across the sea'. To hold on to connections means cleaving to the state of narrative disconnection in which Kath is left. The rhyme is completed in the story 'Parenthesis' later in the collection, though here it evokes not so much the resumption of narrative continuity as its bathetic discomposure: Barnes observes that 1493 is the year in which Columbus, on returning home, unjustly claimed the prize that should rightly have been won by an ordinary seaman on his ship who was the first to sight the New World. He thus set in train the whole series of fictions and impostures that have characterised the history of relations between the Old and New Worlds, pushing it into violently incoherent coherence.

We have seen that, faced with the dilemma I began this chapter by outlining, in which the threat of absolute ending both presses for representation and yet, precisely to the degree that it is absolute ending, resists it, most narratives of apocalypse have contented themselves with varieties of indirection, which permit them to gesture towards the horrifying fact of annihilation and to avoid the bathos or blasphemy of direct representation. Thus, the fact of annihilation is either kept in the future tense of the narration or is consigned to the past tense in the narrative of survival. In both cases, narrative avoids trying to encompass what would be as lethal to it as to the human beings whose instrument it is. Maggie Gee's *The Burning Book* is remarkable for its determination to eschew the consolations of living on, preferring to undergo or live out the consequences of annihilation in and for narrative.

And yet this novel too finds that the representation of the unrepresentable finality of nuclear ending requires a beginning in the familiar time of novelistic narration. The novel sets up an elaborate framework of narrative connections, radiating between the members of two families, the Ships and the Lambs, who are linked by the marriage of Henry Ship and Lorna Lamb. The novel moves backwards and forwards across four generations, linking and differentiating, recalling and anticipating, gradually filling out its pattern of overlapping lives, and recurrent hopes, desires and injuries. The novel is much concerned, like a number of the modernist novels it recalls, with the elaboration of time by memory and artifice into the wholeness of pattern. Henry Ship, whose delight lies in the repairing of watches, sees the world as 'a complex timepiece, immeasurably slow and vast. But you somehow had to build it yourself, and it had to be built through time' (Gee 1989: 101). The novel recalls and replicates the modernist ambition, as evidenced especially in the novels of Virginia Woolf, of remaining true to the complex unpredictability of time while yet being able to perceive the gathering design of the whole; it insists, too, on the place of the novel in reading the randomness of life into sense, and in providing the pattern for the manner in which people come to see their lives making sense. The final scene of the novel, an ecstatic afternoon spent by Henry and Lorna Ship in Kew Gardens, recalls Woolf's 1919 story of that name. Lorna and Henry drink rosé wine by an ailanthus tree at closing time, each possessed by an apprehension of completeness. Lorna looks through leaves at the sun,

> one over the other, a double exposure like Henry said she did when the photos came out wrong but she thought that it often looked better like that, a dream where everything happened at once and all of her life could be seen together, everything together in one queer garden.
> (Gee 1989: 295)

Henry looks at Lorna in the red sunset,

> a lit bright carving of living bronze with her hair spreading out in a metal river and the leaves spreading round her as far as he could see ... It seemed somehow final, this shining Lorna, as if their whole life had led to this moment.
> (Gee 1989: 296)

But all the elaboration of the narrative proves to be a huge diversion, for it is not a way of affirming the coming together of lives into completed patterns, but the demonstration of the impossibility of such completion in the radically uncertain history of the post-nuclear age. What happens in the next instant is a nuclear explosion which almost instantaneously wipes out all of the characters and the foregoing story. Gee borrows the device used in Virginia Woolf's *To the Lighthouse* (1927) of introducing the death of major characters in parenthesis. However, where in Woolf's novel the terse bracketing of the fact of death proclaims its unimportance against the power of memory and art to restore and sustain significance, the mortal parenthesis in *The Burning Book* dilates to take over the entire narrative, as the nuclear explosion recalls and mocks the conventions of narrative closure:

> (George in Germany died a little earlier, by some irony thinking of Guy: still half believing goodness would win [. . .] Angela and John in the same white second, half a mile part, in the middle of a tiff . . . Rose red and bare as in Frank's worst nightmare, drinking and weeping in her cooling bath . . . Prunella bad-tempered on a bus to see her mother . . .)
> (Gee 1989: 297; my ellipses in square brackets)

Brilliantly, the intense light of the explosion is imaged as the exposure of a family photograph, searing and sealing at once. It seems to bring to conclusion the many references to photographs through the novel and to compensate, in a metaphorical completeness, for the partialities and imperfections of these photographs, in which 'the nuclear family looks tidy, but a lot is cut off by the frame [. . .] nothing entirely fits in. There is sand at the back of the camera. Fluff as the fixative dries' (18, 20; my ellipses in square brackets). The novel presents itself at times as a proleptic memorial, holding in its temporary memory all the tiny significance that is ordinarily lost to time and narrative:

> This is the chapter of loss, where every loss is recorded. Nothing need ever be lost as long as one moment held it. Here in a dusty pile lie all the forgotten objects . . . things that slipped out of the story, things that were missed by the camera.
>
> (Gee 1989: 221)

And yet the purpose of all this is precisely to acknowledge the incapacity of memory, narrative and art in the face of the possibility of nuclear apocalypse. *The Burning Book* spins its narrative in the shape of the paradox elaborated by Derrida (see p. 202, this volume), whereby nuclear ending is both wholly other to narrative, unable to be encompassed as an event in a narrative since it is the event that ends all narratives and all events together, and yet, precisely because of this fact, wholly dependent upon narrative, representable only through its indirections and anticipations. From its very beginning, the slow, patient weave of the family history in *The Burning Book* is stretched and slit by voices and memories from the twentieth century's wholly other history of unimaginable violence, imaged at one point in the voices of the *hibakusha*, the Japanese name for the survivors of Hiroshima and Nagasaki:

> It is hardly the thing, I think, to be heard in a family play. But thousands of voices are crying. They scratch at the pane like birds [. . .] Ashamed, I must open the windows. Those syllables make no sense, but their discord shivers with grief. *Hibakusha, hibakusha.* Something broken pleading for life.
>
> (Gee 1989: 20, 21; my ellipses in square brackets)

The voices imagined here are like the ghostly voice of Catherine Linton, heard through the window crying to be let in at the beginning of *Wuthering Heights* (Brontë 1976: 23–4); though here, as elsewhere, the literary reminiscence seems designed to point to the inadequacies of the novel form, especially the kind of generational romance of which *Wuthering Heights* is an example, in registering these unrepresentable events and experiences of contemporary history. *The Burning Book* borrows both from the ramifying, accretive, organic time of the nineteenth-century novel and from the distilled, epiphanic, momentary time of modernist fiction, but sets against them a wholly alternative chronology, in which events are measured according to their distance from their inevitable destruction in what the novel repeatedly calls 'the final violence'. The time of the novel is the time of t *minus*, 'measured back from the darkness, measured back from the launch-on warning, ticking towards that edge. We are all the same age today if electric time slips forward' (253).

The novel insists on the capacity of that final violence, which so intensely provokes narrative, to revoke every discrimination and every difference upon which narrative depends. The moment of the nuclear flash is a moment of annihilating clarity, annihilating partly because in its complete transparency, or 'encyclopaedic light' (129), there are no more secrets, complexities or ambiguities: 'skies flashed white and the day cracked open   stories smashed as all became one   through the glass flaming for a split-glass second all was transparent, the last light shone' (297). *The Burning Book* borrows from the frightening power of the prospect of absolute ending to organise and unify, and yet must also resist it, since its power to unify is also its power to nullify. The novel quotes as its epigraph a Buddhist riddle which seems to refer to this struggle between the narrative that strives to maintain differences and the annihilating force of nuclear unity: 'If all is reduced to the One, to what is the One reduced?' (13).

The novel relies heavily upon linked chains of metaphor, especially the metaphors of glass, hair, blades and burning, whose purpose is to display the powerlessness of metaphor to represent a condition in which all differences are cancelled:

> They would find there was only one story, when it came to the final violence. They would find they had noticed differences where in fact all flesh is a likeness. They would die of violent shock, not the subtle wounds of the heart.

Her hair was a burning bush, but her body crackled like pork.
They would find that all hair burned, and that metaphor is a lie.

(Gee 1989: 39)

The novel multiplies images of the body reduced to the unmeaning materiality of meat – Lorna is tormented as a girl by nightmares suggested by the frozen liver her father sells in his general store. In suggesting, as it does so remorselessly, that the effect of nuclear holocaust will be to reduce the complexity and meaningfulness of human flesh to pure meat, the novel both protests against metaphor and continues to rely on it. Meat is the opposite of metaphor, but is so only as a result of a metaphorical substitution; on this side of annihilation we are still able to read the figure of nonfiguration. The novel plays conventional phrases and images to do with the skin, the medium of the body's separateness and vulnerability, against the actuality of suffering inflicted on human bodies, but it is unable any more to tolerate the shallowness of metaphor although it is also unable to escape its effects:

> Adolescents lack skin. 'You're too thin-skinned,' said her mother. Her mother also lacked skin. And this is the language of novels.
> *people lack skin   we shall all lack skin   skin will hang like gloves   skin hung like gloves   as the wounded walked in a living chain from the burning city of Nagasaki   dragging themselves in a dying chain out of burned and blasted Nagasaki   some of them blind   all of them skinned*
>
> (Gee 1989: 244)

Similarly, the novel is full of images of redness, heat and burning. All of these images derive from and anticipate the universal incineration of the final violence, but they also organise and give significance to the narrative that precedes it. All through the narrative, the power of fire to consume is converted metaphorically into the power to connect and clarify. Guy, Lorna's thwarted, unloved, violent son, thinks that 'it got easier and easier, in some ways, the more he saw life as a whole. Linked by the blaze of unfairness, his longing to burn and kill' (196); '*all things are done and undone at once, at the burning end of time*' announces one of the voices that breaks into the novel (144). Henry's first vision of Lorna looks forward to their final moment in Kew Gardens, but the redness of his vision insists on desire and miracle as well as annihilation:

> he fell for Lorna, a flame-haired child of thirteen. Magic blushed back into his plans, invading pale corridors and attics. Dimly-remembered arches and columns now bloomed with dense watercolour washes. When he saw her everything burned red: he would carry her away to red towers. The roof of the tower was incredibly precise, red hair on a cloud-white dress. They sat in elaborate gardens, stone lions, a dazzling glasshouse.
>
> (Gee 1989: 70)

The menacing flicker between figural and actual burning is there too in the title of the book itself. *The Burning Book* is a book about burning, but must acknowledge that, as a material object of paper and pages, it will be as subject to the literal consumption of fire as anything and anybody else; it will be a book that burns as well as a book about burning. The literal combustibility of *The Burning Book*, the vulnerability of its narrative action to the defacement of fire, 'blackening paper, the last leaves burning' (298), is an important part of its narrative. As elsewhere, it is hard to decide whether this is a literal or metaphorical burning. By insisting on its vulnerability to fire, the book eschews the insubstantiality of figurative language in favour of the literal fact of annihilation. But this inescapably material fact then becomes the basis for the metaphors of burning from which the novel derives its structure of meaning and which resist the possibility of annihilation. The force of the metaphor of the burning book depends in fact upon its absolute refusal of metaphor; the insistence on the absolute extermination of metaphor in nuclear holocaust provides a sustaining metaphorical principle.

The Burning Book therefore goes further than most novels in testing the resources of narrative against absolute ending and inducing discomfort about the novel itself. Like other novels of absolute ending, it suggests that it is necessary to abandon the ways of thinking that the novel as a form encourages. It is in this sense a novel against novels. Gee breaks into the narrative at various points to remind the reader of the inapplicability of novelistic expectations either for the reader or for the characters. Lorna discovers the miracle of love with Henry:

In an ordinary novel that would be the whole story, how a woman found out how to love. But Lorna was in the wrong story, the wrong century, the wrong world [...]

She did discover real love in a world which was mostly fiction. But she lived, like most of her neighbours, in a novel too late to be bought.

There wouldn't be time for this novel, there wouldn't be space for this novel.

(Gee 1989: 52; my ellipses in square brackets)

Lorna's daughter Angela is herself a writer – she has a copy of Maggie Gee's earlier novel about the arrival of nuclear holocaust, *Dying, In Other Words* (1981), on her bookshelf – and she is writing a novel as defence and defiance against the growing sense of crisis. But *The Burning Book* counsels scepticism about the consolations both of fictional narrative and of life lived according to its model. The accusation here seems to be a frightening variant on the modernist one, that plausible and regular narrative form cramps and distorts the richness of real life. Here, it seems, 'real life' is lived in all too close a conformity to the structures and expectations of realistic narrative, which, amplified by political and military forces, have brought about the possibility of a more complete and absolute ending than that envisaged in any novel. Of Angela we are told that 'she had learned a few wise rules of thumb for living [...] The shell of her fiction was coming on nicely, chapter-plan full of bright event, internal monologue showing her growing, pushing her on to the final pages' (250). But her novel, like the novel in which she features, is beginning to fall apart: 'Smoke was erasing the triumphs of the characters, all they had learned was to live in a novel [...] These gentle lessons would not survive [...] Survival was a matter of other things entirely. Another narrative' (250). *The Burning Book* is perhaps an example of that required 'other narrative', in its use of the novel to warn against the novel's temptations.

There is a much-remarked tendency in discussions of the contemporary novel to revert to the question of the death and survival of the form, in unconscious verification perhaps of Walter Benjamin's insight, in his essay, 'The Storyteller' (1970), that the meaning of narrative is bound up with death. I have suggested throughout this book that during the postwar period the novel itself is variously, but continuously, concerned with the possibility of its own death and the conditions of its own survival. Maggie Gee's novel, like those other terminal narratives that I have been considering, shows that the real significance of the survival of narrative lies in the question of the relation between narrative and survival as such. In its development of a deterrent narrative, whose force resides simultaneously in its grasp of the paradoxes wrought upon the human inhabitation of time, history and narrative, and in its determination to hold out, as its final chapter has it, 'against ending', *The Burning Book* may be representative of the particular kind of resourcefulness that the novel displays in postwar history, in turning the conditions of its very death into the various possibilities of its renewal and survival.

REFERENCES

Ackroyd, Peter (1983) *The Last Testament of Oscar Wilde*, London: Hamish Hamilton.
—— (1987) *Chatterton*, London: Hamish Hamilton.
—— (1988) *Hawksmoor*, London: Abacus. First published in 1985.
Aldiss, Brian (1973) 'The origin of the species', *Extrapolation* 14: 167–91.
—— (1991) *Frankenstein Unbound*, London: Hodder and Stoughton. First published in 1973.
—— (1992) *Dracula Unbound*, London: Grafton.
Alexander, Marguerite (1990) *Flights From Realism: Themes and Strategies in Postmodernist British and American Fiction*, London: Edward Arnold.
Amis, Kingsley (1953) *Lucky Jim*, London: Gollancz.
Amis, Martin (1984) *Money: A Suicide Note*, London: Jonathan Cape.
—— (1989) *London Fields*, London: Jonathan Cape.
Anderson, Benedict (1983) *Imagined Communities: Reflections on the Origin and Spread of Nationalism*, London: Verso.
Annan, Gabriele (1989) 'On the high wire: review of Ishiguro, *A Pale View of Hills*, *An Artist of the Floating World* and *The Remains of the Day*', *New York Review of Books* 36 (19): 3–4.
Auster, Paul (1987) *The New York Trilogy (City of Glass, Ghosts, The Locked Room)*, London: Faber and Faber. First published in 1986.
Ball, Michael, Gray, Fred and McDowell, Linda (1989) *The Transformation of Britain: Contemporary Social and Economic Change*, London: Fontana.
Banville, John (1993) *Ghosts*, London: Secker and Warburg.
Barnes, Julian (1990) *A History of the World in 10½ Chapters*, London: Picador. First published in 1989.
Barth, John (1974) *Chimera*, London: André Deutsch.
—— (1988) *The Tidewater Tales*, London: Methuen.
Barthes, Roland (1968) *Writing Degree Zero*, trans. Annette Lavers and Colin Smith, New York: Hill and Wang.
Baudrillard, Jean (1988) *The Ecstasy of Communication*, trans. Bernard and Caroline Schutze, New York: Semiotext(e).
Beckett, Samuel (1959) *The Trilogy: Molloy, Malone Dies, The Unnamable*, London: Calder and Boyars.
—— (1965) *Proust and Three Dialogues With Georges Duthuit*, London: John Calder.

REFERENCES

Beer, Gillian (1989) 'Origins and oblivion in Victorian narrative', in Beer, *Arguing With the Past: Essays in Narrative From Woolf to Sidney*, London and New York: Routledge, 12–33.

Benjamin, Walter (1970) 'The storyteller: reflections on the work of Nikolai Leskov', in Benjamin, *Illuminations*, trans. Harry Zohn, London: Jonathan Cape, 83–109.

Bergonzi, Bernard (1979a) 'Fictions of history', in Malcolm Bradbury and David Palmer (eds) *The Contemporary English Novel*, London: Edward Arnold, 42–65.

—— (1979b) *The Situation of the Novel*, 2nd edn, London: Macmillan.

Bergson, Henri (1971) *Time and Free Will: An Essay on the Immediate Data of Consciousness*, London: Allen and Unwin.

Bhabha, Homi K. (1990a) 'DissemiNation: time, narrative, and the margins of the modern nation', in Homi K. Bhabha (ed.) *Nation and Narration*, London and New York: Routledge, 291–322

—— (ed.) (1990b) *Nation and Narration*, London and New York: Routledge.

Blanchot, Maurice (1978) *Death Sentence*, trans. Lydia Davis, Barrytown, NY: Station Hill Press. First published in 1948.

Bourdieu, Pierre (1984) *Distinction: A Social Critique of the Judgement of Taste*, trans. Richard Nice, London and New York: Routledge and Kegan Paul.

Bowlby, Rachel (1993) 'But she should have been reading Lady Chatterley: the obscene side of the canon', in Bowlby, *Shopping With Freud*, London: Routledge, 25–45.

Bradbury, Malcolm (1975) *The History Man*, London: Secker and Warburg.

—— (1983) *Rates of Exchange*, London: Secker and Warburg.

Braine, John (1957) *Room at the Top*, London: Eyre and Spottiswoode.

—— (1962) *Life at the Top*, London: Eyre and Spottiswoode.

Brennan, Timothy (1990) 'The national longing for form', in Homi K. Bhabha (ed.) *Nation and Narration*, London and New York: Routledge, 44–70.

Brontë, Charlotte (1985) *Shirley*, Harmondsworth: Penguin. First published in 1849.

Brontë, Emily (1976) *Wuthering Heights*, ed. Ian Jack, Oxford and New York: Oxford University Press. First published in 1847.

Brooke-Rose, Christine (1968) *Between*, London: Michael Joseph.

—— (1984) *Amalgamemnon*, Manchester: Carcanet.

—— (1986) *Xorandor*, Manchester: Carcanet.

—— (1990) *Verbivore*, Manchester: Carcanet.

—— (1991) *Textermination*, Manchester, Carcanet.

Brooks, Peter (1984) *Reading for the Plot: Design and Intention in Narrative*, Oxford: Clarendon Press.

Browning, Robert (1970) *Poetical Works 1833–1864*, ed. Ian Jack, London: Oxford University Press.

Burgess, Anthony (1983) *The End of the World News: An Entertainment*, Harmondsworth: Penguin. First published in 1982.

Byatt, A. S. (1991) *Possession: A Romance*, London: Vintage. First published in 1990.

Carey, Peter (1991) *Oscar and Lucinda*, London: Faber and Faber. First published in 1988.

REFERENCES

Carroll, Lewis (1970) *The Annotated Alice: Alice's Adventures in Wonderland and Through the Looking Glass*, ed. Martin Gardner, Harmondsworth: Penguin.
Carter, Angela (1979) *The Bloody Chamber, and Other Stories*, London: Gollancz.
—— (1982) *The Passion of New Eve*, London: Virago. First published in 1977.
—— (1984) *Nights at the Circus*, London: Chatto and Windus.
—— (1991) *Wise Children*, London: Chatto and Windus.
Celan, Paul (1990) *Selected Poems*, trans. Michael Hamburger, Harmondsworth: Penguin.
Coetzee, J. M. (1987) *Foe*, Harmondsworth: Penguin. First published in 1986.
Connor, Steven (1988) *Samuel Beckett: Repetition, Theory and Text*, Oxford: Basil Blackwell.
—— (1992) *Theory and Cultural Value*, Oxford: Basil Blackwell.
—— (1994) 'Rewriting wrong: on the ethics of literary reversion', in Theo d'Haen and Hans Bertens (eds) *Liminal Postmodernisms: The Postmodern, the (Post-)Colonial, and the (Post-)Feminist*, Amsterdam and Atlanta, GA: Rodopi, 79–97.
—— (1996, forthcoming) 'Reading: The contretemps', in Nicola Bradbury (ed.) *The Year's Work in English Studies*, Oxford: Basil Blackwell.
Conrad, Joseph (1967) *The Nigger of the 'Narcissus': A Tale of the Forecastle*, London: Heinemann. First published in 1897.
—— (1902) *Heart of Darkness*, Edinburgh: Blackwood.
Coover, Robert (1970) 'The magic poker', in Coover, *Pricksongs and Descants*, New York and Scarborough, Ont: New American Library, 20–45.
—— (1991) *A Night at the Movies: Or, You Must Remember This*, London: Heinemann. First published in 1987.
—— (1991) *Pinocchio in Venice*, London: Heinemann.
Cosby, Christina (1991) *The Ends of History: Victorians and 'The Woman Question'*, New York and London: Routledge.
Cowart, David (1989) *History and the Contemporary Novel*, Carbondale and Edwardsville, Ill: Southern Illinois University Press.
Crompton, Don (1985) *A View From 'The Spire': William Golding's Later Novels*, Oxford: Blackwell.
Darwin, John (1988) *Britain and Decolonisation: The Retreat From Empire in the Postwar World*, Basingstoke: Macmillan.
De Certeau, Michel (1986) *Heterologies: Discourse on the Other*, trans. Brian Massumi, Manchester: Manchester University Press.
Defoe, Daniel (1985) *The Life and Adventures of Robinson Crusoe*, Harmondsworth: Penguin. First published in 1719.
Debord, Guy (1990) *Comments on the Society of the Spectacle*, trans. Malcolm Imrie, London: Verso. First published in 1967.
DeLillo, Don (1985) *White Noise*, New York: Viking.
Derrida, Jacques (1980) 'Living on: borderlines', in Harold Bloom, Paul de Man, Jacques Derrida, Geoffrey Hartman and J. Hillis Miller, *Deconstruction and Criticism*, London: Routledge and Kegan Paul, 75–176.
—— (1984) 'No Apocalypse, Not Now (full speed ahead, seven missiles, seven missives)', trans. Catherine Porter and Philip Lewis, *Diacritics* 14: 20–31.

REFERENCES

Dickens, Charles (1969) *Hard Times, for These Times*, Harmondsworth: Penguin. First published in 1854.
—— (1985) *Our Mutual Friend*, Harmondsworth: Penguin. First published in 1865.
Dijkstra, Bram (1986) *Idols of Perversity: Fantasies of Feminine Evil in Fin-de-Siècle Culture*, New York and Oxford: Oxford University Press.
Doyle, Brian (1989) *English and Englishness*, London: Routledge.
Drabble, Margaret (1969) *Jerusalem the Golden*, Harmondsworth: Penguin. First published in 1967.
—— (1978) *The Ice Age*, Harmondsworth: Penguin. First published in 1977.
—— (1978) 'The art of fiction: interview with Barbara Milton', *Paris Review* 74.
—— (1980) *The Middle Ground*, London: Weidenfeld and Nicolson.
—— (1988) *The Radiant Way*, Harmondsworth: Penguin. First published in 1987.
—— (1991) *The Gates of Ivory*, London: Viking.
Eagleton, Terry (1988) 'The silences of David Lodge', *New Left Review* 172: 93–102.
Eco, Umberto (1983) *The Name of the Rose*, trans. William Weaver, London: Secker and Warburg. First published in 1980.
Fabian, Johannes (1983) *Time and the Other: How Anthropology Makes Its Object*, New York: Columbia University Press.
Farrell, J. G. (1973) *The Siege of Krishnapur*, London: Weidenfeld and Nicolson.
Faulkner, Peter (ed.) (1992) *A Modernist Reader: Modernism in England 1910–1930*, London: Batsford.
Fish, Stanley (1980) *Is There A Text In This Class? The Authority of Interpretive Communities*, Cambridge, Mass: Harvard University Press.
Fleishman, Avrom (1971) *The English Historical Novel*, Baltimore, Md: Johns Hopkins University Press.
Forster, E. M. (1910) *Howard's End*, London: Edward Arnold.
—— (1924) *A Passage to India*, London: Edward Arnold.
Foucault, Michel (1972) *The Archaeology of Knowledge*, trans. A. M. Sheridan Smith, London and New York: Tavistock Press.
Fowles, John (1966) *The Magus*, London: Jonathan Cape.
—— (1969) *The French Lieutenant's Woman*, London: Jonathan Cape.
—— (1977) *The Magus*, rev. edn, London: Jonathan Cape.
—— (1991) *A Maggot*, London: Picador. First published in 1985.
Friedman, Ellen G. and Fuchs, Miriam (1989) 'A conversation with Christine Brooke-Rose', *Review of Contemporary Fiction* 9: 81–90.
Freud, Sigmund (1955) *Beyond the Pleasure Principle*, in *The Standard Edition of the Psychological Works of Sigmund Freud*, trans. James Strachey, vol. 18, London: Hogarth Press, 1–64.
Gaskell, Elizabeth (1986) *North and South*, Harmondsworth: Penguin. First published in 1855.
Gee, Maggie (1981) *Dying, In Other Words*, Sussex: Harvester.
—— (1989) *The Burning Book*, London: Faber and Faber. First published in 1983.
Gibson, William (1984) *Neuromancer*, London: Gollancz.

REFERENCES

Glinga, Werner (1986) *Legacy of Empire: A Journey Through British Society*, trans. Stephan Paul Jost, Manchester: Manchester University Press.
Golding, William (1954) *Lord of the Flies*, London: Faber and Faber.
—— (1955) *The Inheritors*, London: Faber and Faber.
—— (1956) *Pincher Martin*, London: Faber and Faber.
—— (1964) *The Spire*, London: Faber and Faber.
—— (1980) *Rites of Passage*, London: Faber and Faber.
—— (1987) *Close Quarters*, London: Faber and Faber.
—— (1989) *Fire Down Below*, London: Faber and Faber.
Gorra, Michael (1986) 'Review of Timothy Mo's *Sour Sweet*', *Hudson Review* 38: 671–2.
Gould, Tony (1983) *Inside Outsider: The Life and Times of Colin MacInnes*, London: Chatto and Windus.
Gray, Alasdair (1992) *Poor Things*, London: Bloomsbury.
Habib, Claude (1991) 'Nagasaki et après: sur les romans de Kazuo Ishiguro', *Esprit* 2: 114–20.
Hall, Stuart and Jefferson, Tony (eds) (1975) *Resistance Through Rituals: Youth Subcultures in Post-War Britain*, Birmingham: Centre for Contemporary Cultural Studies, University of Birmingham.
Harvey, David (1989) *The Condition of Postmodernity: An Enquiry into the Origins of Social Change*, Oxford: Blackwell.
Hashmi, Alamgir (1992) 'Hanif Kureishi and the tradition of the novel', *International Fiction Review* 19: 88–95.
Hawkins, Susan E. (1991) 'Innovation/history/politics: reading Christine Brooke-Rose's *Amalgamemnon*', *Contemporary Literature* 32: 58–74.
Hill, Susan (1992) *The Mist in the Mirror*, London: Sinclair–Stevenson.
Hiro, Dilip (1991) *Black British White British: A History of Race Relations in Britain*, London: Grafton.
Hoban, Russell (1982) *Riddley Walker*, London: Picador. First published in 1980.
—— (1987) *The Medusa Frequency*, London: Jonathan Cape.
Hodges, Devon (1983) '*Frankenstein* and the feminine subversion of the novel', *Tulsa Studies in Women's Literature* 2: 155–64.
Hoffman, Gert (1988) *The Parable of the Blind*, trans. Christopher Middleton, London: Secker and Warburg. First published in 1985.
Hoggart, Richard (1957) *The Uses of Literacy: Aspects of Working-Class Life With Special References to Publications and Entertainments*, London: Chatto and Windus.
Hutcheon, Linda (1988) *A Poetics of Postmodernism: History, Theory, Fiction*, London: Routledge.
Iser, Wolfgang (1974) *The Implied Reader: Patterns of Communication in Prose Fiction from Bunyan to Beckett*, Baltimore, Md: Johns Hopkins University Press.
Ishiguro, Kazuo (1982) *A Pale View of Hills*, London: Faber and Faber.
—— (1986) *An Artist of the Floating World*, London: Faber and Faber.
—— (1989) *The Remains of the Day*, London: Faber and Faber.
Iyer, Pico (1991) 'Review of *The Remains of the Day*', *Partisan Review* 58: 585–9.
Jameson, Fredric (1981) *The Political Unconscious: Narrative as a Socially Symbolic Act*, London: Verso.

REFERENCES

Johnson, Barbara (1982) 'My monster/my self', *Diacritics* 12: 2–10.
Joyce, James (1916) *A Portrait of the Artist as a Young Man*, New York: Huebsch.
—— (1971) *Finnegans Wake*, London: Faber and Faber. First published in 1939.
—— (1986) *Ulysses: The Corrected Text*, ed. Hans Walter Gabler, Harmondsworth: Penguin. First published in 1922.
Kingsley, Charles (1983) *Alton Locke, Tailor and Poet: An Autobiography*, Oxford and New York: Oxford University Press.
Kolbert, Elizabeth (1986) 'Wandering through history: interview with Peter Ackroyd', *New York Times Book Review*, 19 January: 3.
Kureishi, Hanif (1990) *The Buddha of Suburbia*, London: Faber and Faber.
Lawrence, D. H. (1915) *The Rainbow*, London: Methuen.
—— (1921) *Women in Love*, London: Martin Secker.
—— (1990) *Lady Chatterley's Lover*, Harmondsworth: Penguin. First published in 1928.
—— (1992) 'Why the novel matters' in Peter Faulkner (ed.) *A Modernist Reader: Modernism in England 1910–1930*, London: Batsford, 143–8.
Leavis, F. R. (1948) *The Great Tradition: George Eliot, Henry James, Joseph Conrad*, London: Chatto and Windus.
Leavis, Q. D. (1932) *Fiction and the Reading Public*, London: Chatto and Windus.
—— (1983) 'The Englishness of the English novel: in *Collected Essays: Vol. 1, The Englishness of the English Novel*, ed. G. Singh, Cambridge: Cambridge University Press, 303–27.
Lee, Alison (1990) *Realism and Power: Postmodern British Fiction*, London and New York: Routledge.
Lessing, Doris (1969) *The Four-Gated City*, London: MacGibbon and Kee.
—— (1976) *The Memoirs of a Survivor*, London: Picador. First published in 1974.
Levinas, Emmanuel (1991) *Totality and Infinity: An Essay on Exteriority*, trans. Alphonso Lingis, Dordrecht: Kluwer.
Lodge, David (1975) *Changing Places: A Tale of Two Campuses*, London: Secker and Warburg.
—— (1977) *The Modes of Modern Writing: Metaphor, Metonymy and the Typology of Modern Literature*, London: Edward Arnold.
—— (1984) *Small World: An Academic Romance*, London: Secker and Warburg.
—— (1989) *Nice Work*, Harmondsworth: Penguin. First published in 1988.
Lukács, Georg (1962) *The Historical Novel*, trans. Hannah and Stanley Mitchell, London: Merlin.
Lyotard, Jean-François (1984) *The Postmodern Condition: A Report on Knowledge*, trans. Geoff Bennington and Brian Massumi, Manchester: Manchester University Press.
—— (1988) *The Differend: Phrases in Dispute*, trans. Georges van den Abbeele, Manchester: Manchester University Press.
MacCabe, Colin (1993) *On the Eloquence of the Vulgar: A Justification of the Study of Film and Television*, London: British Film Institute Publications.
McEwan, Neil (1987) *Perspective in British Historical Fiction Today*, London: Macmillan.

REFERENCES

MacInnes, Colin (1961) *England, Half English*, London: MacGibbon and Kee.
—— (1980a) *Absolute Beginners*, London: Allison and Busby. First published in 1959.
—— (1980b) *Mr Love and Justice*, London: Allison and Busby. First published in 1960.
—— (1993) *City of Spades*, London: Allison and Busby. First published in 1957.
McLuhan, Marshall (1967) *Understanding Media*, London: Sphere Books.
Malamud, Bernard (1982) *God's Grace*, London: Chatto and Windus.
Martin, Richard (1988) '"Stepping stones into the dark": redundancy and generation in Christine Brooke-Rose's *Amalgamemnon*', in Ellen G. Friedman and Miriam Fuchs (eds) *Breaking the Sequence: Women's Experimental Fiction*, Princeton, NJ: Princeton University Press, 177–87.
Mason, Gregory (1989) 'An interview with Kazuo Ishiguro', *Contemporary Literature* 30: 335–47.
Melville, Herman (1962) *Billy Budd, Sailor (An Inside Narrative)*, Chicago and London: University of Chicago Press. First published in 1924.
Miller, D. A. (1988) *The Novel and the Police*, Berkeley, Los Angeles and London: University of California Press.
Milton, John (1959) *Areopagitica*, in *Complete Prose Works, Vol. 2, 1643–1648*, ed. Ernest Sirluck, New Haven, Conn: Yale University Press and London: Oxford University Press, 480–570.
Mo, Timothy (1986) *An Insular Possession*, London: Chatto and Windus.
—— (1990) *Sour Sweet*, London: Abacus. First published in 1982.
—— (1991) *The Redundancy of Courage*, London: Chatto and Windus.
Moers, Ellen (1979) 'Female gothic', in George Levine and U. C. Knoepflmacher (eds) *The Endurance of Frankenstein*, Berkeley, Los Angeles and London: University of California Press, 77–87.
Moretti, Franco (1987) *The Way of the World: The Bildungsroman in European Culture*, London: Verso.
Murdoch, Iris (1965) *The Red and the Green*, London: Chatto and Windus.
—— (1978) *The Sea, The Sea*, London: Chatto and Windus.
Newell, Stephanie (1992) 'The other god: Salman Rushdie's new aesthetic', *Literature and History*, Third Series, 1, 67–87.
Orwell, George (1933) *Down and Out in Paris and London*, London: Gollancz.
—— (1935) *A Clergyman's Daughter*, London: Gollancz.
—— (1936) *Keep the Aspidistra Flying*, London: Gollancz.
—— (1937) *The Road to Wigan Pier*, London: Gollancz.
—— (1981) *Nineteen Eighty-Four*, Harmondsworth: Penguin. First published in 1949.
Pavel, Thomas (1986) *Fictional Worlds*, Cambridge, Mass: Harvard University Press.
Poovey, Mary (1980) 'My hideous progeny: Mary Shelley and the feminization of romanticism', *PMLA* 95: 332–46.
Porter, Jeffrey (1990) '"Three quarks for Muster Mark": quantum wordplay and nuclear discourse in Russell Hoban's *Riddley Walker*', *Contemporary Literature* 31: 448–69.

REFERENCES

Potter, Dennis (1984) *Waiting for the Boat: Dennis Potter on Television*, London: Faber and Faber.
Pykett, Lyn (1995) *Engendering Fictions: The English Novel in the Early Twentieth Century*, London: Edward Arnold.
Radway, Janice (1987) *Reading the Romance: Women, Patriarchy and Popular Literature*, London: Verso.
Rimmon-Kenan, Shlomith (1989) *Narrative Fiction: Contemporary Poetics*, London: Routledge.
Riffaterre, Michael (1990) *Fictional Truth*, Baltimore, Md: Johns Hopkins University Press.
Robbe-Grillet, Alain (1966) *The Erasers*, trans. Richard Howard, London: Calder and Boyars.
Roe, Sue (1982) *Estella: Her Expectations*, Sussex: Harvester Press.
Rolph, C. H. (ed.) (1961) *The Trial of Lady Chatterley: Regina vs. Penguin Books Ltd*, Harmondsworth: Penguin.
Rothfork, John (1989) 'Confucianism in Timothy Mo's *Sour Sweet*', *Journal of Commonwealth Literature* 24: 49–64.
Rushdie, Salman (1982) *Midnight's Children*, London: Picador. First published in 1981.
—— (1983) *Shame*, London: Jonathan Cape.
—— (1988) *The Satanic Verses*, London: Viking.
—— (1991) '"Commonwealth literature" does not exist', in Rushdie, *Imaginary Homelands: Essays and Criticism 1981–1991*, London: Granta Books, 61–70.
Sage, Lorna (1983) *Doris Lessing*, London and New York: Methuen.
Said, Edward (1993) *Culture and Imperialism*, London: Chatto and Windus.
Sayers, Dorothy L. (1935) *Gaudy Night*, London: Gollancz.
Scanlan, Margaret (1990) *Traces of Another Time: History and Politics in Postwar British Fiction*, Princeton, NJ: Princeton University Press.
Schwenger, Peter (1986) 'Writing the unthinkable', *Critical Inquiry* 13: 33–48
—— (1991) 'Circling ground zero', *PMLA* 106: 251–61.
Shakespeare, William (1987) *The Tempest*, ed. Stephen Orgel, Oxford: Clarendon.
Sharpe, Tom (1973) *Porterhouse Blue*, London: Secker and Warburg.
Shelley, Mary (1985) *Frankenstein: Or, The Modern Prometheus*, Harmondsworth: Penguin. First published in 1818.
Sinfield, Alan (1989) *Literature, Politics and Culture in Postwar Britain*, Oxford: Blackwell.
Sterne, Laurence (1985) *The Life and Opinions of Tristram Shandy, Gentleman*, Harmondsworth: Penguin. First published in 1760–7.
Stevenson, Robert Louis (1979) *The Strange Case of Dr Jekyll and Mr Hyde*, Harmondsworth: Penguin. First published in 1886.
Stratton, Jon (1990) *Writing Sites: A Genealogy of the Postmodern World*, London: Harvester/Wheatsheaf.
Sutherland, John (1978) *Fiction and the Fiction Industry*, London: Athlone.
Swinden, Patrick (1984) *The English Novel of History and Society, 1940–80: Richard Hughes, Henry Green, Anthony Powell, Angus Wilson, Kingsley Amis, V. S. Naipul*, London: Macmillan.

REFERENCES

Tennant, Emma (1989) *Two Women of London: The Strange Case of Ms Jekyll and Mrs Hyde*, London: Faber and Faber.
—— (1992) *Faustine*, London: Faber and Faber.
—— (1993) *Tess*, London: Harper Collins.
—— (1993) *Pemberley: A Sequence to Pride and Prejudice*, London: Hodder and Stoughton.
Thomas, D. M. (1981) *The White Hotel*, London: Gollancz.
Thomas, Sue (1991) *Correspondence*, London: Women's Press.
Ulmer, Gregory L. (1989) *Teletheory: Grammatology in the Age of Video*, London and New York: Routledge.
Voloshinov, V. N. (1986) *Marxism and the Philosophy of Language*, trans. Ladislav Matejka and I. R. Titunik, Cambridge, Mass: Harvard University Press.
Vonnegut, Kurt (1987) *Galàpagos*, London: Grafton. First published in 1985.
Warner, Marina (1993) *Indigo: Or, Mapping the Waters*, London: Vintage. First published in 1992.
Watt, Ian (1957) *The Rise of the Novel: Studies in Defoe, Richardson and Fielding*, London: Chatto and Windus.
Westlake, Michael (1989) *Imaginary Women*, London: Paladin. First published in 1987.
White, Hayden (1973) *Metahistory: The Historical Imagination in Nineteenth-Century Europe*, Baltimore, Md: Johns Hopkins University Press.
—— (1987) *The Content of the Form: Narrative Discourse and Historical Representation*, Baltimore, Md and London: Johns Hopkins University Press.
—— (1989) '"Figuring the nature of the times deceased": literary theory and historical writing', in Ralph Cohen (ed.) *The Future of Literary Theory*, London: Routledge, 19–43.
Wiggins, Marianne (1989) *John Dollar*, London: Secker and Warburg.
Williams, Raymond (1970) *The English Novel From Dickens to Lawrence*, London: Chatto and Windus.
Wilson, Angus (1992) *Anglo-Saxon Attitudes*, Harmondsworth: Penguin. First published in 1956.
—— (1961) *The Old Men at the Zoo*, London: Secker and Warburg.
Winterson, Jeanette (1985) *Boating for Beginners*, London: Methuen.
Woolf, Virginia (1925) *Mrs Dalloway*, London: Hogarth Press.
—— (1927) *To the Lighthouse*, London: Hogarth Press.
—— (1931) *The Waves*, London: Hogarth Press.
—— (1937) *The Years*, London: Hogarth Press.
—— (1944) 'Kew Gardens', in *A Haunted House and Other Stories*, London: Hogarth Press, 32–9.
Worpole, Ken (1984) *Reading By Numbers: Contemporary Publishing and Popular Fiction*, London: Comedia.
Yelin, Louise (1992) 'Cultural cartography: A. S. Byatt's *Possession* and the politics of Victorian studies', *Victorian Newsletter* 81: 38–41.

INDEX

Ackroyd, Peter: *Chatterton* 167; *Hawksmoor*, 142, 143–6; *The Last Testament of Oscar Wilde* 167
address 42–3, 62, 73–4, 80, 81, 90–3, 102–4, 112, 158–9, 164–5, 210; and addressivity 8–13
Aldiss, Brian: *Dracula Unbound* 177–8; *Frankenstein Unbound* 167, 168, 169–77, 178, 182, 185
Alexander, Marguerite 186–7
Amis, Kingsley 70; *Lucky Jim* 70, 71
Amis, Martin 94; *London Fields* 92; *Money* 92
Anderson, Benedict 30, 83
Annan, Gabriele 107
apocalypse 200–6
Arts Council 46
Austen, Jane: *Pride and Prejudice* 178
Auster, Paul: *New York Trilogy* 166

Bakhtin, Mikhail 9
Ballantyne, R. M.: *Coral Island* 166
Balzac, Honoré de: *La Comédie Humaine* 138
Banville, John: *Ghosts* 187
Barnes, Julian: *A History of the World in 10½ Chapters* 167, 232–8
Barth, John: *Chimera* 166; *The Tidewater Tales* 166
Baudrillard, Jean 5
BBC 46, 60
Beckett, Samuel 8, 84, 85, 129, 166; *Malone Dies* 203; *Molloy* 203; *The Trilogy* 138, 166

Beer, Gillian 201
Bennett, Louise 85
Bergson, Henri 129
Bhabha, Homi 44, 86, 120–1
Bildungsroman 6–7, 84, 94
Blanchot, Maurice: *Death Sentence* 203
Booker Prize 25
Bourdieu, Pierre 15
Bowlby, Rachel 14
Bradbury, Malcolm: *The History Man* 73; *Rates of Exchange* 73
Braine, John 95; *Life at the Top* 136; *Room at the Top* 136
Brennan, Timothy 44
Brontë, Charlotte: *Jane Eyre* 167; *Shirley* 74
Brontë, Emily: *Wuthering Heights* 241
Brooke-Rose, Christine 42; *Amalgamemnon* 39–41; 'between' 42; *Textermination* 39; *Verbivore* 39; *Xorandor* 39
Brooks, Peter 8
Browning, Robert 148–9
Burgess, Anthony: *The End of the World News* 213–18
Byatt, A. S.: *Possession* 147–51

campus novel 69–74
Carey, Peter: *Oscar and Lucinda* 141
Carlyle, Thomas 77
Carroll, Lewis: *Alice Through the Looking Glass* 49
Carter, Angela 33–8, 39, 42; *The*

INDEX

Bloody Chamber 167; *Nights at the Circus* 36; *The Passion of New Eve* 33–5; *Wise Children* 36–8, 167
Celan, Paul 193
Cervantes, Don Miguel de: *Don Quixote*, 166
citation 126–7
Coetzee, J. M.: *Foe* 168, 169, 193
Coleridge, Samuel Taylor: *The Rime of the Ancient Mariner* 173
'colonisation in reverse' 85–6, 120
Commonwealth Immigrants Act 87, 88
commonwealth literature 107–8
Connor, Steven 22
Conrad, Joseph: *Heart of Darkness* 84, 159
Conservative Government 64, 163
consumption 26, 27
Coover, Robert: 'The Magic Poker' 187; *A Night at the Movies* 39, 166; *Pinocchio in Venice* 166
Cosby, Christina 142
Cowart, David 222, 226
Crompton, Don 159
'Cross, Amanda' 69
cultural difference 89
cultural identity 96–8, 104
culture 36–7; common culture 29; mass culture 5, 24, 25, 28, 74; *see also* cultural difference, cultural identity, culture industry
culture industry 24–5, 27

Darwin, Charles 120
Debord, Guy 25
de Certeau, Michel 130
decolonisation 86–7, 118
Defoe, Daniel 11; *Robinson Crusoe* 168, 169, 182–4, 198, 237
DeLillo, Don: *White Noise* 41
Derrida, Jacques 202–3, 204, 241
Dexter, Colin 69
Dickens, Charles 44, 77; *Bleak House* 57, 61, 77, 123; *Great Expectations* 167, *Hard Times* 74, 76; *Little Dorrit* 57–8; *Our Mutual Friend* 124–6

digestion, as metaphor 99–100
Dijkstra, Bram 180
Disraeli, Benjamin, 44
Doyle, Brian 72, 83
Drabble, Margaret 45, 95; *The Gates of Ivory* 136; *The Ice Age* 59–64, 77; *Jerusalem the Golden* 47–8, 49; *The Middle Ground* 64; *A Natural Curiosity* 136; *The Radiant Way* 29, 64–9, 136
Durrell, Lawrence: *Alexandria Quartet* 138

education 24, 46, 70–4
Eagleton, Terry 70
Eliot, George 44, 56; *Middlemarch* 50
Empire 2, 3, 86–7, 134
ending 199–245; and power 214–15
Englishness 3, 44–127, 72–3
Eco, Umberto 69
exile 84–6, 93, 115, 190
existentialism 55

Fabian, Johannes: *Time and the Other* 116
Falklands campaign 88, 119, 163
Fanon, Frantz 118
Farrell, J. G.: *The Siege of Krishnapur* 134–5, 141
Fielding, Joseph 11
film 27–8, 29–30, 35–6, 38–9, 126–7
Fish, Stanley 20
formula fiction 15, 17, 18
Forster, E. M. 84; *Howard's End* 84; *A Passage to India* 84
Foucault, Michel 3 4, 162, 164
Fowles, John 85; *The French Lieutenant's Woman* 141–2, 167; *A Maggot* 141–2, 146–7; *The Magus* 187
Freud, Sigmund: *Beyond the Pleasure Principle* 237
future 40, 135–6, 203, 209; narrative and 228, 234–5

Galsworthy, John: *The Forsyte*

INDEX

Saga 138
Gaskell, Elizabeth 44; *North and South* 74, 75, 76
Gee, Maggie: *The Burning Book* 205, 238–45; *Dying, In Other Words* 244
generation, idea of 95
Gibson, William: *Neuromancer* 41
Glinga, Werner 85
Golding, William: *The Inheritors* 153; *Lord of the Flies* 15, 69, 153, 166, 229; *Pincher Martin* 234–5, 236; *Rites of Passage* 150–62; *The Spire* 150, 151, 152, 153; *To the Ends of the Earth* 161, 166
Gorra, Michael 103
Gray, Alisdair: *Poor Things* 167
Greenaway, Peter: *Prospero's Books* 187
Greene, Graham 85
Gulf War 163

Habib, Claude 107
Hall, Stuart 23
Hardy, Thomas: *Tess of the D'Urbervilles* 178
Harvey, David 26, 125
Hashmi, Alamgir 97
Hawkins, Susan E. 42
Henry V (film) 49
Hill, Susan: *The Mist in the Mirror* 167
historical novel 140–65; 'historical' vs. 'historicised' novel 142–3, 146–7, 149, 162; language of 141–6, 151, 152
history 1–3, 128–65; assertion of 187, 194–7, 216–18; continuous 162–4; denial of 115–17, 119; fixated 50–1; forgetfulness of 216; freedom and 224; linear and recurrent 144, 155; paradoxical 203, 204–6, 235–6; pluralised 163; public 129–30, 231; relativsed 143; translation 140–2, 155–6; universal 133–4; 'virtual' 150;
Hoban, Russell: *The Medusa Frequency* 39; *Riddley Walker* 204,
217–27, 236
Hoffman, Gert: *The Parable of the Blind* 166
Hoggart, Richard 23
Holocaust 202, 206
Homer: *The Odyssey* 166
Hutcheon, Linda 8, 130–1. 143, 144, 147
hybridity 120, 125

immigration 87–90, 102, 115, 123
Iser, Wolfgang 10
Ishiguro, Kazuo 86; *An Artist of the Floating World* 104; *A Pale View of Hills* 104; *The Remains of the Day* 104–12
Islam 113, 114–19
islands, and narrative 237
Iyer, Pico 107, 108

Jakobson, Roman 70
James, Henry 28
Jameson, Fredric 8
Jefferson, Tony 23
Johnson, B. S. 8
Jonathan Cape 17
Joyce, James 12, 16, 84, 85; *Finnegans Wake* 113–14; *A Portrait of the Artist as a Young Man* 84; *Ulysses* 44

Kelman, James 94
Kingsley, Charles: *Alton Locke* 74
Khomeini, Ayatollah 112, 116
Kureishi, Hanif: *The Buddha of Suburbia* 94–8

Labour Government 67, 68
Lamarck, J. B. de Monet 120
landscape 105–6
Lane, Allen 14
Lawrence, D. H. 14, 16, 19, 28, 84; *Lady Chatterley's Lover* 77–8; *The Rainbow* 44; *Women in Love* 44
Leavis, F. R. 19, 28, 55–6, 71–2, 74; *The Great Tradition* 55
Leavis, Q. D. 18, 56, 89
Lee, Alison 8, 132, 143, 144
leisure 80–2

INDEX

Lessing, Doris: *The Four-Gated City* 138–9; *Martha Quest* 138; *The Memoirs of a Survivor* 228–32
Levinas, Emmanuel 9
Lodge, David: *Changing Places* 73, 136; *Nice Work* 73, 74–82, 136; *Small World* 73, 136
London 89, 103, 117–18, 121–5
Lucretius 119–20
Lukàcs, Georg 130, 134
Lyotard, Jean-François 7, 119, 133

McEwan, Neil 140, 153
MacInnes, Colin 91; *Absolute Beginners* 89–94, 95; *City of Spades* 89; *Mr Love and Justice* 89
McLuhan, Marshall 13
Mailer, Norman 14
Maitland, Sara 66
Malamud, Bernard 204
Manning, Olivia: *Balkan Trilogy* 138
Martin, Richard 40
metaphor 79, 242–4
metonymy 79
Miller, D. A. 5
Mills and Boon 20
Milton, John: *Areopagitica* 62; *Paradise Lost* 174
mimicry 96–7, 100, 114, 120–1, 167; see also performance
Mo, Tomothy 86, 104; *An Insular Possession* 100, 102, 141; *The Redundancy of Courage* 100; *Sour Sweet* 98–104
modernism 12, 22, 44, 69, 84–5, 145, 239, 241
Moretti, Franco 6
Murdoch, Iris: *The Red and the Green* 141; *The Sea, The Sea* 187

narrative 93–4: as action 4; and addressivity 8–13; collapse of 211–12; definition of 3–4; and ending 199–245; ethics of 184–5; and futurity 228; narrative effects 4–8, 133; and nation 83, 86, 89, 112; struggle over 7, 208–9, 233–5; suspicion of 226–7, 244–5

nation 44, 56, 62, 64, 67, 83–6
Nazism 49, 51–2, 54, 104, 199
Newell, Stephanie 113
novel-sequence 136–9

Oedipus 166
Olivier, Laurence 49
origins 169, 173–5, 182–6, 188–90, 192, 194, 197–8, 201, 218–19
Orwell, George: *A Clergyman's Daughter* 212; *Down and Out in Paris and London* 84; *Keep the Aspidistra Flying* 68; *Nineteen Eighty-Four* 206–13; *The Road to Wigan Pier* 84
Ovid 119–20
Oxford University Press 16

Pavarotti, Luciano 25
Pavel, Thomas 8
Penguin Books 14–15
performance 95, 96–7, 108–9, 111–12; see also mimicry
perspective 53–5, 58–9, 61–2, 78, 82, 90–1; female 66
Pevsner, Niklaus 91–2
Porter, Jeffrey 219, 226
post-Fordism 26–7
postmodernism 23, 69, 145
Potter, Dennis 139
Powell, Anthony: *A Dance to the Music of Time* 137, 138, 139
publishing 13–27
Pykett, Lyn 180

radio 30–1
Radway, Janice 17, 20–1
reader: homogenised 20–3; ideal 12; implied 10; plural 24–7
reading 79–82
redundancy 40
reversion 169, 179, 182, 185, 186, 198
revolution 125
rewriting 166–98; and control 171, 173–4, 176–7; and history 167; and gender 169, 171–6, 178–84, 192–3; as 'prewriting' 169, 182

258

INDEX

Rhys, Jean 85; *Wide Sargasso Sea* 167
Richardson, Dorothy 129
Riffaterre, Michael 8
Rimmon-Kenan, Shlomith 8
Robbe-Grillet, Alain: *The Erasers* 166
Roe, Sue: *Estella: Her Expectations* 167
romance 20–1
Rothfork, John 98
Rushdie, Salman 22, 39, 42, 86, 104, 107–8; *Midnight's Children* 30–33, 36; *The Satanic Verses* 112–27

Sage, Lorna 139
Said, Edward 85
Sayers, Dorothy L. 69
Scanlan, Margaret 134, 216
Scheherezade 166
Schwenger, Peter 204–5, 226, 227
Scott, Paul: *Raj Quartet* 138
Scrutiny 71
Secker and Warburg 17
Shakespeare, William: *The Tempest* 168, 169, 186–98, 198
Sharpe, Tom: *Porterhouse Blue* 71
Shelley, Mary: *Frankenstein* 167, 168, 169–77, 198
Sillitoe, Alan 95
Sinfield, Alan 7, 46–7, 87, 91, 153
Snow, C. P.: *Strangers and Brothers* 137, 138
'society of the spectacle' (Debord) 25
space 105, 110, 124–5, 152
Spark, Muriel 85
Sterne, Laurence 11: *Tristram Shandy* 32, 158
Stevenson, Robert Louis: *The Strange Case of Dr Jekyll and Mr Hyde* 168, 178–82, 198
Stratton, Jon 5
'subject of history' (Foucault) 3–4, 133, 162, 164
Suez Crisis 87, 110
Sutherland, John 14, 15, 16, 19, 85
'symbolic capital' (Bourdieu) 15

symbolism (in *The Ice Age*) 63
television 18, 28–9, 67, 68, 92–3, 100–1
Tennant, Emma: *Faustine* 178, *Pemberley* 178; *Tess* 178; *Two Women of London* 167–8, 169, 178–82, 185
Thatcher, Margaret 163
Thomas, D. M.: *The White Hotel* 166
Thomas, Sue: *Correspondence* 39
time 3–4, 30, 34–6; calendrical and subjective 128–9; modernist 241; and the nation 83; in nineteenth-century novel 241; paradoxical 235–6; recurrent and progressive 143–5, 191–2, 220–3; syncopated 155; turnover 16; *see also* history
transmission 159–61, 164
travel writing 5
Trollope, Anthony 137, 138
Turner Prize 25

Ulmer, Gregory L. 13
university 69–71, 75; *see also* campus novel
unrepresentability 64

voice 184–6, 193, 197
Voloshinov, Valentin 9
Vonnegut, Kurt: *Galàpagos* 227–8, 236

Warner, Marina 141; *Indigo* 168, 169, 186–97
Watt, Ian 6
Waugh, Evelyn: *The Sword of Honour* 138
Welfare State 2, 46, 47, 65, 88
Westlake, Michael 41, 42; *Imaginary Women* 38–9
White, Hayden 130
Wiggins, Marianne: *John Dollar* 166–7
Williams, Raymond 19
Williamson, Henry: *A Chronicle of Ancient Sunlight* 137

INDEX

Wilson, Angus 85: *Anglo-Saxon Attitudes* 49–55; *The Old Men at the Zoo* 213
Winterson, Jeanette: *Boating for Beginners* 167
Wittgenstein, Ludwig 109
Woolf, Virginia 16, 66, 238–9; *Mrs Dalloway* 67; 'Kew Gardens' 239; *To the Lighthouse* 239; *The Waves* 44, 129; *The Years* 67
work 79–82
Worpole, Ken 13, 15

Zola, Emile 137